THE
EXECUTIVE'S
GUIDE TO
CONSULTANTS

THE

EXECUTIVE'S
GUIDE TO
CONSULTANTS

How to
FIND, HIRE, *and* GET
GREAT RESULTS
from OUTSIDE EXPERTS

DAVID A. FIELDS

NEW YORK   CHICAGO   SAN FRANCISCO
LISBON   LONDON   MADRID   MEXICO CITY   MILAN
NEW DELHI   SAN JUAN   SEOUL   SINGAPORE
SYDNEY   TORONTO

Copyright © 2013 by David A. Fields. All rights reserved. Printed in the United States of America. Except as permitted under the United States Copyright Act of 1976, no part of this publication may be reproduced or distributed in any form or by any means, or stored in a database or retrieval system, without the prior written permission of the publisher.

1 2 3 4 5 6 7 8 9 10   QFR/QFR   1 8 7 6 5 4 3 2

ISBN 978-0-07-180192-8
MHID 0-07-180192-8

e-ISBN 978-0-07-180193-5
e-MHID 0-07-180193-6

Library of Congress Cataloging-in-Publication Data

Fields, David.
   The executive's guide to consultants: how to find, hire, and get great results from outside experts / by David Fields.—1st ed.
       p. cm.
     ISBN-13: 978-0-07-180192-8 (alk. paper)
     ISBN-10: 0-07-180192-8 (alk. paper)
  1. Business consultants. I. Title.
     HD69.C6F54 2013
     658.4'6—dc23   2012026525

McGraw-Hill books are available at special quantity discounts to use as premiums and sales promotions or for use in corporate training programs. To contact a representative, please e-mail us at bulksales@mcgraw-hill.com.

This book is printed on acid-free paper.

For my parents, whose counsel and guidance have always been worth seeking. They are the epitome of high-value, outside experts.

Contents

Foreword   X

Acknowledgments   XII

Introduction   XIV

PART I

Choosing High-Value Projects

CHAPTER 1

Why Bother?
Estimating the Value of Doing Any Project   3

CHAPTER 2

Can We? Should We?
When to Use Employees and When to
Use Third-Party Help   25

CHAPTER 3

What's the Context?
Become the Perfect Client Before
You Call the Consultant   45

PART II

Finding and Choosing
the Right Consultant

CHAPTER **4**

Who's Our Partner?
Finding and Selecting Great Consultants — 69

CHAPTER **5**

Big or Small?
The Surprising Value of Independent Consultants — 96

PART III

Risk, Fees, and Contracts

CHAPTER **6**

What Could Go Wrong?
Reducing Risk — 119

CHAPTER **7**

What Are Our Options?
Value Wizardry and Sophisticated Contract Negotiation — 144

CHAPTER **8**

What's the Deal?
Fees and Contracts for Consultants — 167

PART IV

Successful Implementation

CHAPTER 9
How Do We Prep for Success?
Readying Your Company Before the Project Starts 193

CHAPTER 10
How Do We Run a Great Project?
Deriving Outstanding Value from Your Consultant 216

CHAPTER 11
How Do We Lock in Value?
Making Change Stick After the Consultant Leaves 235

Easy Reference Guide 253
Notes 260
Index 262

Foreword

Since I am an outside expert who, for nearly 30 years, has provided executive coaching for a living, this book by David Fields is highly interesting to me. It is an examination of the other side of consulting work: what organizations should seek from consulting work and how to hire the best external expert so that a win-win is achieved for the organization and the consultant.

Interestingly enough, David's intention is to help executives get great results from outside experts like me and, as one of those outside experts, I find our outlook on how to work together is very similar. One thing that I would emphasize from this book is that when hiring an external consultant, do not describe the needs of the organization and then ask the consultant if he or she is qualified to handle this type of challenge. Rather, begin by asking the consultant to describe his or her area of specialty. For example, my own area of expertise involves helping successful leaders achieve positive, lasting change in leadership behavior.

My credentials are fairly well known. I was recently recognized as the Most Influential Leadership Thinker in the world at the Thinkers 50 Conference (sponsored by *Harvard Business Review*), and I am one of a select few executive advisors who have been asked to work with more than 120 major CEOs and their management teams. I don't do strategic, functional, technical, how-to-give speeches, or how-to-get-organized coaching. There is nothing wrong with these; they are just not what I do, and I know that. What do your potential external consultants do? Do they know exactly what they do, and is it what you need?

Personally, I have had requests that border on the insane. A pharmaceutical company recently asked me to coach a potential head of R&D. When I asked about the major challenge faced by the person, I was told, "He is not updated on medical technology!" I replied, "Neither am I!"

I cannot help a bad scientist become a good one. If your organization needs help in marketing or finance, the consultant who is hired should be an expert in providing advice in that field. And, be careful from whom you ask advice, especially in areas of strategy. Far too many "experts" pretend to be knowledgeable about strategic coaching when their backgrounds show that they are not qualified to give advice on strategy. While I am not an expert on strategy, at least I know enough to know that I am not an expert!

In *The Executive's Guide to Consultants*, David offers practical, proven lessons that, when applied, will meld clients and consultants into a single team, with unified objectives and a shared passion for winning. Practice what you learn here and you'll reap outstanding results, spare yourself and your organization hours upon hours of misspent time and money, and find true success for yourself, your organization, and your team.

Life is good.

—Marshall Goldsmith,
million-selling author of the
New York Times bestsellers, *MOJO* and
What Got You Here Won't Get You There

Acknowledgments

This book would never have come to fruition without the generous support of dozens of individuals, all of whom have my deepest gratitude. My family, of course, has provided stalwart support throughout the project. Robin Epstein, my partner, bolstered my resolve countless times over the years to publish a book. My siblings, Ruth and Derek, and my parents believed in my talent as an author even when the words weren't flowing and the concepts were maddeningly out of reach. My sons, Mitchel and Jeremy, provided ongoing inspiration even if they didn't know it.

I have the good fortune to be part of a community of elite consultants who have provided insights and support in many forms over the course of this project. Alan Weiss, the architect of the community and one of the most brilliant consultants I have ever met, deserves credit for attracting the best of the best. Many of his ideas served as a springboard for the thinking in these pages and are sprinkled throughout the book. Alex Goldfayn, Roberta Matuson, and Donna Brighton all are members of that community and deserve special mention for their help. Outstanding consultants outside of Alan's community also helped, including Michael Clingan, Bob Endres, Jeff Hill, John Lindeman, and Jamie Barrickman, without whom I never would have learned critical lessons about consulting.

Many, many executives also contributed to this book. Mike Ferry, Neil Heller, Clark Day, Gino Iasella, Sandy Katz, Paul Fonteyne, Carl Marchetto, Marty Graen, Brian McCue, Robert Reiss, Don Dumoulin, and Brad Casper all read advance versions and contributed their excellent ideas throughout. Many other executives gave their time and insights during the writing process and earlier, when I was conducting preliminary research. These include Tony Hsieh, Chris Combe, Mark Horak, Wilson Farmerie, Bob Baird, Barry Cohen, Steve Jegier, Paul Sagan, Tom Rogers, De Lyle Bloomquist, George Quesnelle, Dick Snell, Jim Reisenbach, Torrence Boone, Chuck Smith, Steve Michaelson, Zan Guerry, Bob Riordan, John Ulizio, David Rich, Joe Messner, Colleen Barrett, Marc Eskridge, Herb Kelleher, Patrick Taylor, Mike Eskridge, Michael Kehoe, David Novak, Dave Thompson, Mark Shapiro, Dawn Lapore, Roland Smith, Scott Cotherman, Bill Pollard, Brian Walker, Ken Blanchard, Matt Mannelly, Lee White, Ralph Scozzafava, Drew Madsen, Doug Gernert, Martin Madaus, Mark Sherwin, Dick Hogan, Mike Boyce, Larry Futterman, John Andrews, Pete Vatulli, Jim DeCicco, Roger Byford, Pat Galliger, Tom Noonan, Michael Wilson, Roger Scarlett Smith, Ted Leonsis, David Riberi, Ray Moncini, Chris Connor, Garry Ridge, Kurt Brykman, and Matt Rubell. The list of helpful clients exceeds my faltering memory, and I offer my apologies to anyone whom I inadvertently left out.

An unpublished book is nothing more than a lovingly crafted paperweight; therefore, I am deeply indebted to my agent, Joelle Delbourgo, for masterfully placing the project in no time at all, to Stephanie Frerich at McGraw-Hill, for passionately supporting the project from the very first glance, and to Janice Race at McGraw-Hill for coaxing an excellent publication out of a rough manuscript. Wendy Cohen has my profound appreciation for being my first line of defense against befuddling sentences, puzzling visuals, and malapropisms. Finally, the entire process would have sputtered and ground to an ignominious halt on many occasions were it not for the ceaseless, tireless support of my writing partner, Jamie Broughton of Footprint Leadership.

Countless others are also responsible for turning this dream into a reality. Thank you all!

Introduction

That knot in the pit of your stomach as you seal the deal on some vital task with a consultant is a familiar feeling.* Persistent questions pester you like a swarm of gnats on a sweaty summer day: Will the project work? Will this expert live up to his promises? Will you actually get a great return on the hard-earned dollars flowing from your coffers toward his Armani suits, shiny Lexus, and bold, confident smile? Probably not.

Common wisdom has it that 90 percent of consulting projects fail to deliver the value they should, and research suggests only one-third of projects are successful.[1] If you enjoyed spectacular results from 8 of the last 10 projects on which you engaged an outside expert, you're at the top of the class—and you still wasted one dollar in five. Needlessly wasted, because you can lower your risk and increase your returns on virtually every project, and that's what *The Executive's Guide to Consultants* will guide you to do.

In these pages, you'll learn tips and techniques to flip those statistics on their head, so that 90 percent of the time you bring in third-party experts, they'll exceed your expectations. Why don't the consultants you hire use these approaches? Because their expertise is in leadership, strategy, operations, cost reduction, or some other business specialty, not

---

*Throughout the book I use the term *consultant* to describe a broad group of outside experts, including trainers, coaches, designers, agencies, and all manner of advisors. Similarly, consulting projects and initiatives can be thought of as any instances in which you pay outsiders for their expertise.

in constructing consulting contracts and projects. Why certain projects work and others don't has surprisingly little to do with how smart or seasoned the consultant is. The thinking in this book, however, is based on my study of what differentiates successful projects, regardless of the subject matter.

You're not alone when you experience gnawing angst each time you engage a consultant. Executives at every level in every size company, from home-based businesses to multibillion-dollar conglomerates, worry about whether the project will work, whether their money will be wasted, whether this was the best use of their resources, and whether they chose the right person or company. Are your fears well founded?

Unfortunately, yes. In the United States, we spend more than $800 billion every year on outside experts ($100 billion on management consultants alone),[2] and my surveys find a staggering proportion of that sum is unproductive. There are, of course, the projects that are total failures—the $35 million disaster that plunged FoxMeyer Drugs into bankruptcy or, perhaps, the marketing wizards you hired who somehow managed to produce no new business beyond what you already had in the pipeline. More insidious are the projects I liken to the emperor's new clothes. These projects return mediocre results and have been purchased at such expense that no one at the top wants to publicly admit that the return on investment is tepid at best. For instance, large companies commonly convene annual sales meetings, part of which consists of a self-proclaimed guru upgrading all the sales reps' skills via a training session or workshop. The guru is usually a fabulous presenter, and everyone struts out of the session brimming with confidence. Three months later, is there any noticeable change in behaviors? Are the new skills used widely? No. I view that as a failure, and yet companies repeat this cycle year after year after year.

Equally troubling are the projects that didn't have precisely defined enough objectives for anyone to know at the end whether they failed or succeeded. These are the business equivalent of running a weekend tag sale. Early Sunday evening you survey your garage and see that the ugly water pitcher from Aunt Tilly didn't sell; nor did stacks of books, racks of used clothes, old kitchen appliances, and a dismaying amount of other flotsam. But you've got $250 cash in your pocket, so you scratch your head and wonder whether it was worth a full weekend's effort. Did you set a cash target up front? Was there a minimum volume of storage space you hoped to recover? Was it imperative to find Aunt Tilly's vase a loving new home? Unfortunately, you had only vague, high-level goals, and that makes the tag sale frighteningly similar to many consulting projects. There are targets, expectations, and intentions, but at the end of the project the forward progress is unclear, and you judge success based on your gut feeling that the results met your expectations or were disappointing.

Should you even bother with consultants? The fact is, you need help to move your business forward. As Marshall Goldsmith's best-selling book accurately proclaims, "What got you here won't get you there." On this much, the best business executives agree, though there is plenty of disagreement over when and where you need outside expertise. Should you engage an expert at lead development, or is drumming up new business a core competency you should keep in-house? Does hiring a costly website design agency make sense when inexpensive, off-the-shelf packages are widely available? After you tackle those questions, you're still left wondering how to make your investment pay off. Most consulting projects fail to deliver the value they should, but whose fault is it? You know you're doing everything you can. When you choose an outside expert, you are putting your trust in her that she will deliver on her promises. So, are consultants purposely underperforming?

No. I talk with hundreds of consultants every year who are applying to be part of my consortium, are in my mentor program, or work for clients on projects I've been asked to review. Every one of them admits to having participated in projects that underdelivered. Yet, overwhelmingly, their goal is to provide so much value within the scope of a project that clients will love them and hire them for more work. Despite their reputation, consultants want to make a real, lasting difference for their clients by bringing something to the table that the client didn't have. Consultants dream of being hailed as heroes and showered with accolades thanks to their unquestionable role in saving your company while your competition falters. They want credit for conceiving your industry's version of the iPod and inspiring your employees to be happy, motivated, and productive forevermore.

Something is not making sense. On the one side are clients hoping to get tremendous value; on the other side are consultants striving to provide more value. Yet most consulting projects fail to deliver the promised results. Ironic, isn't it? Considering the staggering sums spent every year on outside experts, both the size and the cost of the disconnect between intention and actual results are mind-boggling. How is it that companies squander hundreds of billions of dollars every year, projects fail constantly, and corporate executives often approach consultants with skepticism, apprehension, and distaste despite the fact that clients and consultants both want the same thing?

The Roots of *The Executive's Guide to Consultants*

I wrestled with this question for the better part of a decade. In 1997, after only a short time working for one of the most successful boutique consulting firms in the country, I could sense that something was terribly wrong with the traditional consulting model. Our clients were a veritable Who's Who of consumer products manufacturers. Companies such as Nabisco, Kodak, Valvoline, Kimberly Clark, and dozens of others came to us for solutions, and for a fee worthy of any big-time consultancy, we gave them what they wanted. However, in my opinion there were too many cranberries and buckets of popcorn—results that initially tasted sweet but then delivered a bitter flavor, or were filling for a little while but left the client hungry.

It took me eight years to figure out what the problems were and how to successfully address them. While exploring this conundrum, I rose to the partner level at the boutique firm, cofounded a new consulting firm, and, eventually, created the Ascendant Consortium based on the new models for client-consultant relationships I had developed.

Of course, I also built upon the decade I spent hiring and interacting with consultants while I occupied senior positions in the retail sector and at GlaxoSmithKline. GSK, like most large companies in that era, constantly engaged all manner of consultants: big-name firms to help with strategy, global experts to create cross-country processes, cost-cutting gurus who had written a book. Those years and the three corporate mergers they encompassed brought an abundance of good, bad, and frequently ugly consulting projects. What you hold in your hands (or have on your screen) now is the result of my inquiry into the fundamental irony in consulting: clients and consultants seem to be on the same team and shooting for the same goal, and yet they still manage not to win the game. *The Executive's Guide to Consultants* is my answer to the quest for consistently outstanding results and contains specific directions to prevent you from misspending time and money on outside experts.

The new models you'll read about in *The Executive's Guide to Consultants* have been tested and refined in the marketplace via the Ascendant Consortium and the many clients who have been willing to explore new ways of working with temporary talent. Together we have found that results can be obtained faster, working with outside experts can be less painful, and the return on consulting investments can take a quantum leap upward.

Two attorneys can claim credit for setting me on the path to understanding. Neither one knew of his eventual contribution to the field of consulting, which is a good thing or they might have considered charging me more! The first attorney inadvertently taught me an important lesson while the only movement during ongoing litigation was the steady march of funds from my bank account to his. What I learned—and you need to hang on to with a vise grip—is that when the client's goal and the hired gun's goal are not perfectly aligned, sometimes it's the client who gets shot. The same thing happens with trainers, coaches, consultants, and other outside experts. It's not uncommon to have misaligned goals, and the result, unfortunately, is not very different from litigation: a lot of time, pain, and expense going toward efforts that don't increase your chance of winning the case. That's simply unacceptable.

The second revelation arrived while I was chatting over breakfast with a seasoned labor attorney in New York City. As he was explaining the nuances of labor law, he offhandedly offered something profound: "Companies get the unions they deserve." I immediately realized that this philosophy didn't just apply to unions. It applies to most relationships and, without a doubt, to consultants, trainers, coaches, and other experts. You get what you deserve. That's the philosophy underpinning this book. If you want an outstanding consultant, then become an outstanding client. To enjoy extraordinary results, you must (1) choose high-value opportunities, (2) scope the project exactly right, (3) find an outstanding consultant, (4) optimally allocate the real-world risks, and (5) effectively reap the benefits of the consultant's work. This book is designed to help you succeed on all five fronts far more than you ever have before.

There's no magic to getting a great consulting project every time. You may find 90 percent of it is commonsense thinking, just applied in a different way, and 10 percent is breakthrough ideas you haven't encountered before. One hundred percent is easy to grasp and apply and can be implemented immediately. By the end of this book, you'll be able to geometrically increase your returns on investments in outside experts.

Who Will Benefit from *The Executive's Guide to Consultants*?

The primary audience is senior executives in midsize to large companies, particularly those who hire consultants. However, the lessons here can be applied successfully by anyone who engages any type of outside help—no matter how big your company is and no matter what kind of expert advice you are seeking. This includes, for instance, the following:

- Part-timers who operate a business out of their home
- Full-time "solopreneurs"
- Owners and managers of small businesses
- Doctors, accountants, and similar professionals who run offices
- Leaders of churches, synagogues, and other religious institutions
- Principals in venture capital companies

If you're a consultant, you'll also find the answer to your worries within these pages. You will learn how to build better projects, align better with your clients' needs, negotiate better contracts, and deliver more value.

How This Book Is Structured

I've divided the process of finding, using, and benefiting from outside experts into four parts that roughly follow the path from the time you first conceive of a project until the time the results are pouring in. In reality, the process from concept to cash is not linear, and some of what you will learn in later chapters about the different types of projects will help you with the earlier task of finding the best outside expert. Therefore, my recommendation is that you skim the introductions to each chapter and then dive back in at the beginning.

If you are actually in the midst of negotiations with a consultant right now, put that discussion on hold and jump into Parts III and IV. Though they do build on the earlier parts of the book, you'll get the key information you need to boost the value of the project you are embarking upon.

Part I. Choosing High-Value Projects

Most projects that fail are doomed from the start. The chapters in Part I are intended to help you eliminate low-value projects before they happen and to identify the projects with the highest return. When I started in consulting, the common wisdom said that companies bring in consultants for one of two reasons: capability or capacity. The company either didn't have the expertise to accomplish its objective or didn't have the personnel. The common wisdom is only partially right. Executives typically miss many opportunities where bringing outside expertise to bear would have provided huge value. Paradoxically, it is also very common to overestimate the value of the projects that do receive an investment of resources. Therefore, Part I contains a simple model for more accurately assessing the value of potential projects. I give additional guidance for evaluating when you should stick with your employees and when it makes the most sense to bring in an outside expert.

Executives invariably appreciate a consultant who can frame the situation for them, and most senior managers will admit they've often turned to outsiders before fully thinking through the issues. The downside to this approach is that you are letting the fox design the henhouse. Consultants will naturally depict your world in a way that plays to their own strengths, and their take on the best course of action for you invariably also benefits them. Therefore, Part I covers the project context. Having these pieces in place positions you to hire the best expert—one who will take the best actions at the best time to achieve your desired outcome.

Part II. Finding and Choosing the Right Consultant

Last time I checked the statistics, there were a zillion consulting, training, and coaching firms and agencies of all sizes employing two bazillion self-proclaimed experts. That's a lot to choose from. The typical bell curve applies to their capabilities: about 15 percent of consultants are very good, 15 percent are downright lousy, and the vast majority of consultants perform satisfactory, uninspiring work. Part II is about helping you find the 1 percent of consultants on the very tail of the curve who will produce the most outstanding results for your situation. If you are operating a small business out of your home, that 1 percent may look very different from the 1 percent available to GE, Microsoft, or McDonald's; nevertheless, a range of talent is available to you. One proven way to leave the competition in the dust is to insist on employing extraordinary talent (full-time or contracted) while your rivals settle for good enough. I'll show you how to locate the very best of the best.

Part III. Risk, Fees, and Contracts

Typically, by this stage in the process, both sides are focused on details of what the outside expert will do and how much that service will cost. The intent in these chapters is to steer you away from the standard view of cost to a more sophisticated approach that will build significantly higher value. The two building blocks of that approach are using the right contract structure and addressing risk. Since most consultants bill on a time-and-materials basis, most clients assume that is the best (or only) way a contract can be structured. Not so. You'll learn about a number of contract structures and when each is used to the greatest advantage. Risk, interestingly, is one of the least-considered aspects of consulting contracts and is, therefore, one of your greatest opportunities to build in value. To capture this opportunity, cutting-edge work being done in the field of contracting has been ported over to consulting projects. The results from these techniques consistently produce significant increases in the value of your end results.

Part IV. Successful Implementation

One of the most consistent complaints about outside experts—consultants in particular—is that they cost a lot of money but don't produce lasting results. Six months after the project or training is completed, the only difference from before is that a few pretty new binders are collecting dust on the office bookshelf. The promised value mysteriously dissipates until, a year later, the consultant is available to "refresh" the project. Another common complaint is that consultants are arrogant know-it-alls who, even if they eventually do produce a lasting end result, cause disruption, ill will, and months of painful hiccoughs along the way. Therefore, the final part of *The Executive's Guide to Consultants* endeavors to help you make your experience with outside experts a more enjoyable, painless, productive experience that produces lasting benefits. Again, much of the onus rests on you. You'll read about how to prepare your company to accept outside help, how to keep important initiatives running smoothly, and, importantly, how to ensure that the results of the project stick around after the consultant departs.

Hiring an outside expert can be one of the best decisions you ever make, catapulting your business faster and farther than you could achieve on your own. On the flip side of the equation, providing expert services to clients in need can be a noble, highly rewarding calling. Historically, too few client-consultant marriages have produced healthy, happy outcomes, but that doesn't need to be the case going forward. Regardless of which side of the table you're on, you never need to settle for a disappointing consulting project again. If you apply the tips in this book, you can create an extraordinary relationship and a project that produces extraordinary results. You'll feel optimistic and confident each time you sign on a new expert, knowing the odds are now firmly in your favor.

THE
EXECUTIVE'S
GUIDE TO
CONSULTANTS

Choosing High-Value Projects

Why Bother?

Estimating the Value of Doing Any Project

In This Chapter

In this chapter you step back and ask whether your project is even worth doing and, if so, what value you can reasonably expect from it. You will walk through a real-life example that illustrates how to get a better handle on your initiatives. After all, why bring in a super guru if the project will generate low return? Conversely, if an initiative is enormously valuable for your company, isn't it worth bringing in the best resources available to make sure it goes well? As you go through the chapter, you will encounter suggestions that increase your valuation of a project as well as some that decrease the estimate. The point is to help you to help develop an accurate picture that can guide your decisions on consultants.

Key concepts in Chapter 1 include the following:
- "Why bother?"
- Contribution, scale, duration, and frequency
- Underestimation error
- Egocentricity error
- Multiplier effect

"Why Bother?"

On September 15, 2004, a division administrator in the Federal Highway Administration approved a project to build a bridge. This particular span, which would stand taller than the Brooklyn Bridge and stretch nearly as far as the Golden Gate Bridge, would improve access to an international airport. It's hard to argue against the Golden Gate and the Brooklyn Bridges as valuable additions to our national landscape, and improving access to an international airport seems like a worthwhile endeavor, right?

Wrong. The new bridge was a pet project of a powerful person with parochial interests, the airport serves fewer passengers in an entire year than fly through JFK International Airport in a single day, and the home of this airport has a total of 50 residents. In February 2005 a small, non-profit organization based in our nation's capital issued a scathing report on the project titled, "$315 Million Bridge to Nowhere," and eventually the project was scrapped.

As an executive thinking about hiring an outside expert, your first task is to make sure you're not building a Bridge to Nowhere! Everything else in this book will be for naught if you shouldn't be doing the project in the first place. The question that, if it had been answered correctly, would have stopped the Bridge to Nowhere before the first contractor showed up on the snowy shores of Ketchikan, Alaska, is "Why bother?"

"Why bother?" is the first question the very best consultants ask. They (and the very best clients) always begin the discussion of a project by taking a serious, second look at the value.

In fact, the answer to "Why bother?" is critical whether or not you turn to outside resources. A lot of the initiatives that companies hire consultants to take on are not worth doing, period; not with a world-class expert, not with the unemployed bloke down the street, and certainly not with your own people. They are Bridges to Nowhere—simply not a good use of time and money.

Before you skip this section under the assumption that you already know that your reasons for pursuing your project are sound, remember that the Bridge to Nowhere had advocates and that the document approving the project was a dry, 38-page report chock full of supporting statistics and compelling rationale.

In my examination of hundreds of potential consulting projects, I have found that over 95 percent of the conversations start without a rigorously developed response to "Why bother?" Precious few executives could say that the risk-adjusted value they expect from their project is $725,000 based on seven assumptions, or some similar statement. This is as true of multimillion-dollar projects for blue-chip companies as it is of ten-thousand dollar projects for the local liquor store owner.

"Why Bother?" in Action—A Real-Life Example[1]

Take a look at this conversation between a consultant and a senior officer of a global manufacturing firm. Other than editing it slightly to make it shorter and to cut out identifying information, this is exactly how the discussion went. At the point we pick this conversation up, the client has related just a bit of background about why he called.

Consultant: *So, if I'm hearing you right, you are hiring a well-known consultant to help you develop a global digital platform and roll it out across your organization. Is that right?*

Client: Yes. That's essentially what we're doing.

Consultant: *And since this is looking like it will be an expensive proposition which will affect a lot of people in your company, you would like me to work my magic so that the resulting value is higher and the risk is lower. Yes?*

Client: Yes, if you think you can do that.

Consultant: *Well, let me ask you a question first. Why bother?*

Client: What?

Consultant: *Why bother to do this? Why bother to bring me in, and if you don't mind my asking, why are you even bothering to do this digital platform project?*

Client: Well, we have no standard process for our digital efforts, and every country is doing it differently, so it's haphazard and inefficient.

Consultant: *Okay, so what real difference will it make if you are standardized globally rather than how it works now? What measurable, beneficial impact will it have on your customers, your business, or your employees?*

Client: Uhmm, right now we don't have a consistent way to get our message out. There's a lot of inefficiency. This project should reduce our inefficiency.

Consultant: So you're a bit inefficient? What does that matter? Will it make a material impact on your customers, your business, or your employees if you're more efficient in this area?

Client: Yes. If we're more efficient and more consistent, we believe it will materially improve our digital efforts worldwide. They will be more effective.

Consultant: Why bother being more effective? Seriously, how much of a difference will it make being more effective at your digital efforts?

Client: Uhmm … well … we don't have that totally modeled out, but we have some estimates of how much incremental business we can capture if we improve our digital efforts.

Consultant: Fine. Let's start there. How much business do you think you can gain?

Client: Probably around $65 million worldwide if we do this right and execute it well. This is a significant effort, which is why we're bringing in a big consulting firm.

Let's break down what has happened so far. Probably very few consultants have pushed back on your projects that hard, which is why you need to do it yourself. While the consultant may not realize it, you are both better off if you are working on a project that creates the most possible value for you. A Bridge to Nowhere may be fun and lucrative while you are building it, but it definitely won't serve anyone's best interests in the long run.

You should use two questions to start establishing value:

1. Why bother?
2. What is the real, measurable impact on your customers, your business, or your employees?

When I ask these questions, clients will often launch into exhaustive, eloquent explanations of why the project is so important and what the strategic thinking is behind it. That's well and good, but it dances around the point. What is the *measurable* difference versus what you are doing now? Soft benefits are fine; however, the projects you pursue should add measurable value. (See Figure 1-1.)

Virtually anything can be quantified. You don't need to go overboard with this; for our purposes you can probably suffice with some deep thinking, a pencil, and a calculator. (Yes, I know that's archaic.)

Figure 1-1 Your Project Must Create Meaningful, Sustained Value

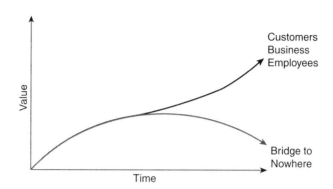

You do this by asking the two "Why bother?" questions until you run into meaningful numbers. If you are familiar with the Six Sigma "five whys" process, the "Why bother?" approach will sound familiar:

1. "Why bother running leadership training?"

   "Because it boosts morale and our employee survey shows morale is crushingly low."

2. "So? Why bother boosting morale?"

   "Because we think low morale is contributing to higher attrition rates than we'd like."

3. "So? Why bother lowering attrition rates?"

   "Because each time we have to hire a new employee, it costs us $50,000 in hiring and related expenses plus we lose at least three months of productivity."

4. "So? Why bother capturing that three months of productivity?"

   "Because three months of productivity for an average employee is equivalent to about $200,000 in operating margin."

Great. Now you've hit some meaningful numbers. If you have a thousand employees and you can successfully lower your attrition rate from 6 percent to 4 percent per year, that's a difference of $4 million on the bottom line, which may very well be worth pursuing.

Figure 1-2   The Answer to "Why Bother?" May Be the Gap
Between Previous and Current Performance

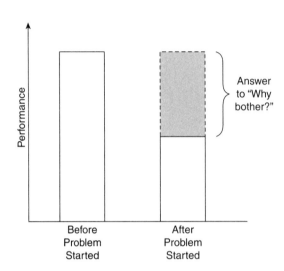

You may only have to ask "Why bother?" once or twice, or you may have to doggedly drill down five or six times to arrive at meaningful numbers. Sometimes the "Why bother?" questions are easy to answer and quantify, particularly if the project is intended to resolve a problem that has arisen. You just look at the difference between what you were achieving before the problem occurred versus what you're achieving now (see Figure 1-2). If attrition was 4 percent and has risen to 6 percent, then you know exactly why you are doing the project. If a time-log study shows your sales team is spending 20 percent more of its time doing administrative work *and* you have seen a commensurate drop in sales versus target, then the quantification is pretty easy.

Is profit the only meaningful number? No. If you are measured on attrition, then, for you, lowering your attrition rate from 6 percent to 4 percent is a 33 percent reduction, and that may be the only meaningful number you need to go forward with the project.

Contribution, Scale, Duration, and Frequency

Let's pick up the earlier conversation where we left off.

Consultant: Fine. Let's start there. How much business do you think you can gain?

Client: Probably around $65 million worldwide if we do this right and execute it well. This is a significant effort, which is why we're bringing in a big consulting firm.

Consultant: So over the course of three years that's a hair under $200 million of incremental business. How much of that $200 million do you think you could capture if you scrapped the whole global standardization thing and just sent out some general best practices and direction to each country—a minor effort to get everyone focused in the right way?

Client: Uhmm … we didn't really look at that. I'd guess maybe $50 million. We really do need standardization.

Consultant: Okay, standardization will bring in an incremental $150 million over three years, if everything is executed well. It sounds like there are a lot of pieces to this, one of which is this project. You also need to build some infrastructure, nego- tiate with some new partners, get everyone on board with the plan, and ensure excellence in execution. So, what portion of that $150 million is attributable to this project rather than those other critical elements?

Client: Well, this standardization project is critical. Without it we won't succeed. So I think the entire $150 million is a benefit of this project.

Consultant: No doubt you're right that the project is critical. What I've heard from you, though, is that there are many critical ele- ments necessary to capture the business. Let's say that this project was the only thing that mattered. You could spend $50 million on it and still come out $100 million ahead. But if there are five critical elements, and you used the same logic for each one, then you could justify $50 million on each element and lose your shirt. So, let's factor this down a bit. May I suggest that, given all the other critical pieces to this puzzle, the standardization project contributes around 40 percent? We can always change that num- ber later.

Client: Sure.

Consultant: According to your annual report, your operating margin is around 20 percent. Is that a fair number to use to estimate the incremental margin from this project?

Client: Yes. That's the number we use internally.

> *Consultant: So, we have $150 million times 40 percent for the project's contribution times 20 percent for the incremental margin. That's $12 million over three years. That's a good starting point. Let me ask you a few more questions and we can get an even better idea of the project's value.*
> Client: This is really helpful. Why didn't the other consulting firm ask these questions?

Do you use that level of rigor before starting your projects? Too many executives make a strategic decision about what is needed, which leads to a decision to hire a consultant, and everyone is off to the races. The consultant says, "Sure, we can do that. Here's why we're best, and this is how much it will cost." Rein that horse in a bit by asking three more questions to get at the true value of doing the project.

Question 1. How Much Does This Project Contribute to the Overall Goal We Are Trying to Achieve?

Rarely is a project done in a vacuum. It is part of a bigger picture. A cascade of priorities. A range of efforts that, in combination, will carry you to a better place. In the example above, the client gave an important clue when he said that the digital initiative could lead to an incremental $65 million "if we do this right and execute it well." This shows that simply coming up with the plan would not, in itself, deliver the benefit. At a minimum, some additional pieces were tied to execution of the plan that would also make a difference.

Your goal is to guesstimate what percentage of the overall benefit will be delivered by this particular project. Draw two lines down the center of a blank page to create a simple Bigger Picture form, like the one in Table 1-1, with three columns: the first specifies the project

Table 1-1

Bigger Picture Form		
Project	Larger Context	Other Tasks

you have in mind, the middle column contains the larger context that emerges when you go through the "Why bother?" questions, and the last column captures a short list of other major elements that contribute to the larger context. While the exercise may seem simplistic, it will help a great deal when you try to eliminate the egocentricity bias, which I cover a bit later. This will be clearer with a few other examples.

In the first example, a discount retailer asked for help improving its buying department's performance. These types of retailers make their money by scouring the market for closeouts, overruns, near-expiry products, and other situations in which a manufacturer is willing to offload its products for fire-sale prices. It didn't take much probing to find out that management felt the buying department was holding back profit growth by not identifying enough great acquisition opportunities.

After a bit of discussion we also agreed that it would take more than the identification of a specific skill set to get the buyers up to snuff. We would have to develop a plan to build that skill set and also execute the plan. Plus, those big opportunities could only be captured if we improved the group's ability to negotiate the deals after the buyers spotted the opportunities. There were a few other pieces that would have to fall into place too. Table 1-2 shows how I captured them in the Bigger Picture form.

Here's another example: a different client had determined that focusing on the biggest customers was the path to improved profit, and

Table 1-2

Bigger Picture Form		
Project	**Larger Context**	**Other Tasks**
Determine what we should focus on to help our buyers identify more discount opportunities	We believe we could be more profitable if our buying department performed better	❏ Develop plan ❏ Execute plan ❏ Build negotiation skills ❏ Reorganize department ❏ Upgrade staff ❏ Improve communication between buyers and merchandisers

Table 1-3

Bigger Picture Form		
Project	**Larger Context**	**Other Tasks**
Implement a strategic account management program	We want to capture and retain more than our fair share of strategic partnerships with our largest customers	❑ Choose personnel to participate in the program ❑ Develop offerings attractive to strategic partners ❑ Put systems in place that will support the program ❑ Reorganize operations group to support initiative ❑ Develop legal agreements appropriate for partnerships

as part of the plan to increase its business with the largest customers, the company needed to put a strategic account management program in place. Table 1-3 shows the Bigger Picture form with the notes I jotted down during the initial conversation.

One more example: in this one, the client company wanted to reorganize one of its divisions that wasn't performing up to expectations. Reorganization projects done in a vacuum are never the answer to a company's problems, and this case was no exception. In addition to building and staffing the right roles, the way the division called on its customers needed to be improved, many people were not prepared for their roles in the new organization, and the mechanics of how products were produced in that division were not in line with the company's best practices. The Bigger Picture form for this project is provided in Table 1-4.

There are times, of course, when a project will deliver 100 percent of the value you are seeking. This may be the case, for instance, when a project is designed to fix something that has gone wrong and was working previously. For instance, if you suddenly have climbing attrition in one department, a project to identify and address the source of the problem (probably a manager who needs coaching) may bring everything back to the happy days when you practically had to pry employees away.

Table 1-4

Bigger Picture Form		
Project	**Larger Context**	**Other Tasks**
Reorganize the Carlisle division	The Carlisle division is our least profitable division, and we need to bring it in line with our other divisions	❑ Redesign the operational flow to match that of other divisions ❑ Upgrade personnel's capabilities through training ❑ Hire new staff as appropriate ❑ Review customer list and coverage

Question 2. Is There a Way to Put the Value of the Project on the Same Scale as the Cost of the Project or the Value of Other Projects?

It will be easier to understand whether or not to bother with a project if you can compare the cost and benefits on the same scale. For instance, if the meaningful benefit of a "leadership improvement" initiative is a significant increase in morale as measured on your annual survey, how will you know whether that project is worth doing compared with the "innovation efficiency" project that slashes the time to market for new offers? And how will you know whether either project is worth doing for $20,000 or $200,000 or $2 million?

One way you can address this question is by matching the scale you use for evaluating the costs and values of projects. For example, if the benefit of the project is measured in time, then look at the cost in terms of time. A 2-year effort to cut your sales cycle time in half probably won't make sense. On the other hand, a 2-year-long project that carves 12 months off all your future product development efforts may very well be worthwhile.

There's no form for answering this question. Just keep in mind that when you are focused on soft benefits such as morale, stress, confidence, or cooperation between departments, all of which could be quantified (by using surveys, for instance), look for ways to match those benefits with the cost of the project. Is it possible the project will lower team morale in the short term or increase interdepartmental stress? If so, you are in a much better position to judge the value.

Question 3. How Often, or for How Long, Will the Impact Be Enjoyed?

In the example conversation, the client *said* that the project would probably deliver an incremental $65 million if it was done right and executed well. Does that mean the value of the project is $65 million? Not unless the entire benefit of getting his digital initiative in place dissipated after one year.

On the other hand, it's unlikely his company will still be getting benefit from that project 25 years from now—who knows what the technology and competition will be like then. The company might not even exist in its current form in 25 years. You need to figure out a reasonable length of time to consider the impact of a project.

The easiest projects to figure out are the ones that change the time horizon on a unique event—for instance, adding a few months of production before a machine needs to be replaced or shaking loose a product launch that is stalled by unusual circumstances. Let's say you are involved in a merger and you have determined that the efficiencies you will gain from the merger are worth $300,000 per year. A consultant who can shave three months off the time it takes to consummate the merger is delivering three months' worth of benefit, or $75,000. It's a one-time gain, and calculating it is easy (see Figure 1-3).

Most projects aren't simply accelerating the benefit or delaying the cost of a single event. For instance, if a product launch is moved up by

Figure 1-3   Changing the Timing of a Unique Event
Delivers a One-Time Gain

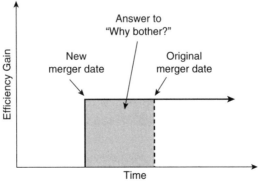

Figure 1-4 Improving Performance Delivers Sustainable Benefits

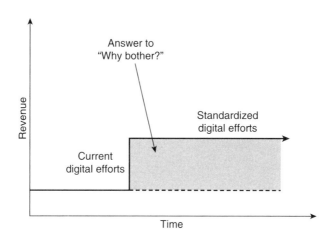

three months, the same processes can be used in the future on other product launches. In the example of the client with the digital initiative, if standardizing his digital efforts across the globe would deliver $65 million the first year, there was every reason to believe it would deliver similar benefits the next year. Maybe some of the value would evaporate as people started to get sloppy. Or maybe the value would actually increase as personnel around the world bought into the value of global standards and the digital project turned into a springboard for more cross-country efforts (see Figure 1-4).

When you remedy a problem, it's the same type of scenario. The only difference is that you are bringing your expected value back up to where it used to be. For instance, let's say attrition has suddenly spiked in one division. Once you bring attrition back down to acceptable levels, you will gain the benefit of that return to normality for the foreseeable future (see Figure 1-5).

Great projects increase in value over time. For instance, for the client mentioned earlier who wanted to institute a strategic account management program, it was reasonable to assume that the benefits would be pretty small the first year and then would build over time as improved focus on the top customers resulted in better programs, increasing cooperation, and continuously improved sales. In addition,

Figure 1-5   Resolving a Problem Results in Ongoing Value

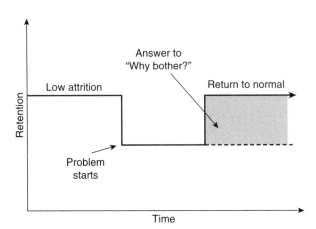

the best practices we installed for the top accounts would trickle down to the next tier of accounts too over the next couple of years (see Figure 1-6). These are the types of projects that can change the trajectory of a corporation.

What, though, is the foreseeable future? If you're lucky, you'll know the answer to that with some precision. Perhaps you know that your

Figure 1-6   The Value of Great Projects May Expand over Time

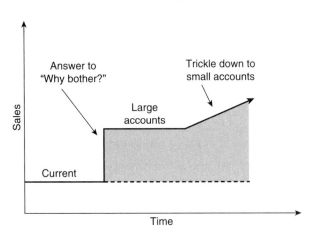

competition is going to introduce a new product in two years, or that new regulations are scheduled to go into effect in five years and very little will change until then. In cases like those, you may have a solid rationale for estimating how far out you should take the benefit.

More often, there's no clear rationale for 2 years, 5 years, or 10 years. One or 2 years doesn't capture the real benefit, and more than 5 years is too unpredictable. In those cases, my suggestion is that you use a 3-year time horizon.

That is why, when the digital project delivered $65 million incremental per year, I suggested a $195 million total gain. A project that fixes an attrition problem that was costing a company $250,000 per year is worth $750,000. If you are running a pizza shop in a community that eats $1 million worth of pizza every year and you think bringing in a marketing expert will allow you to gain an extra share point per year going forward, then your benefit is $10,000 the first year, $20,000 the second year, and $30,000 the third year. Total value is $60,000.

We jumped right into how long the project value would be enjoyed; however, if you look back, you'll see the question actually started with the words *how often*. Many times you hire an outside expert to help you with a problem or opportunity you run into over and over. For instance, you hire the consultant to show you how to address flagging sales in one division and then apply those lessons to other divisions, or the consultant leads you through one new product development effort and you use the same process in other, similar efforts around the company. Another example is when experts are brought in to train the trainer, which is an effective way to apply the multiplier effect to one person's knowledge. The question "How often?" uncovers the multiplier effect, which occurs when you look for the consultant to transfer skills that you will then use in a much broader arena (see Figure 1-7).

In these cases, if you want to value the project correctly, you need to ascribe the multiplier effect, at least somewhat, to the other instances where the new expertise will be used. It's perfectly fair to discount the effect, however. The multiplier effect extends the range of your consultant's power, but it's like using a series of mirrors to direct a flashlight's beam around corners: the farther away you are from the source, the less light is shed.

Figure 1-7   The Multiplier Effect

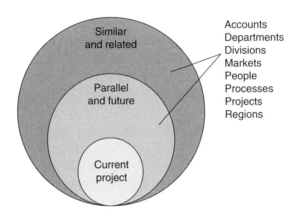

Accounts
Departments
Divisions
Markets
People
Processes
Projects
Regions

Improving Your Valuations: "Is That All?" "What If You Didn't?" and "What's the Risk?"

You have a solid starting point for estimating the value of your project, and at this point in the process I have some good news and some bad news. The good news is that by correcting a common error, the estimate of your project's value will increase. The bad news is that by correcting a second common error, your valuation will probably decrease. Do these two errors cancel each other out? Alas, no. Though it's really all good news because a better estimate of your project's value—whether it's higher or lower—will help you hire the right consultant for the right project and negotiate the right contract.

Fixing the Underestimation Error: "Is That All?"

How many countries can you name? A lot of people respond to this question by first jotting down the countries they can think of quickly (United States, China, Japan, England, France ...), and once they have exhausted that list, they go continent by continent. North America, South America, Europe, Africa, Australia, Asia. Oh, and Antarctica, but there aren't any countries dividing all those penguins.

When I speak in front of large groups, I will often go through this exercise and ask people to raise their hand if they remembered the

United States. Every hand goes up. Then I ask them to keep their hands up if they remembered Indonesia. What about Nigeria? Bangladesh? Jordan? Malta? Seychelles? Djibouti? The hands drop as I mention each country until there are no hands up at all. Most groups are done by Nigeria, rarely does a group make it to Malta, and no one so far has remembered Djibouti. Yet if you skip Nigeria and Bangladesh, you miss a population roughly equivalent to that of the United States.

Identifying the sources of project value is a similar exercise, except it's as if the world's population flits from country to country, usually congregating in China and India but sometimes flocking to Nigeria or Jordan or even tiny Djibouti. Different projects are valuable for different reasons; however, regardless of the source, it's critical to capture most of the value in order to decide whether or not you should bother with the project. Just like forgetting Nigeria and Bangladesh robs you of populations equal to that of the United States, forgetting some important value drivers can unfairly diminish your estimate of project value.

Most projects create value in an obvious place. For instance, in the digital standardization example, the client quickly identified standardization, which reduced inefficiencies and increased sales. Later in the conversation—after my "What about" response—they continued answering the questions "Is that all? Are there any other ways this project adds value?" and they went on a hunt similar to the hunt to remember the countries of the world. Their hunt was replete with "Oh yeah" and "I've never thought of that" responses. After the exercise, the project didn't create more value; however, the estimate of the value created was more complete.

You approach "Is that all?" the same way you approached the countries problem: start with the obvious and then go area by area. Just like the world has seven continents, consulting projects have four common drivers of value that can be quantified:

- Increasing
- Reducing
- Improving
- Creating

Virtually every project is designed to deliver in one or more of those four "value continents," and if you go through them one by one, you are more likely to uncover the value your project can create for your company. Tables 1-5 to 1-8 present four checklists you can use a springboard for answering "Is that all?" What you will likely see is that the project you have in mind can have an effect in more areas than you originally anticipated.

In addition to the four continents of quantifiable value, continue to ask "Is that all?" to uncover softer benefits of a project, which often

Table 1-5

Projects often create value by *increasing* one of the following:	
❏ Revenue	❏ Return on assets
❏ Profit	❏ Efficiency
❏ Growth	❏ Visibility
❏ Value of offerings	❏ Equity
❏ Retention	❏ Net preference
❏ Return on investment	❏ Other _____

Table 1-6

Create value by *reducing* one of the following:	
❏ Costs	❏ Risk
❏ Time	❏ Conflict
❏ Effort	❏ Administrative burden
❏ Complaints	❏ Infrastructure
❏ Attrition	❏ Other _____

Table 1-7

Raising the bar will help you leave the competition behind. Add value by *improving* one or more of the following:	
❏ Productivity	❏ Information
❏ Processes	❏ Reputation
❏ Motivation	❏ Loyalty
❏ Capabilities	❏ Quality
❏ Service	❏ Other _____

Table 1-8

Creation is often the biggest source of value in a project. Add value by *creating* one of the following:	
❑ Strategy	❑ Products
❑ Alignment	❑ Inspiration
❑ Systems	❑ Transformation
❑ Processes	❑ Other _____
❑ Business	

accrue to you personally as the project owner, sponsor, or leader. Soft benefits are often as important as or more important than the quantifiable benefits, and the old adage that people act on emotion and then justify their actions with logic certainly applies to many consulting projects. By making good use of "Is that all?" you will ensure that both logic and emotion are considered in the equation before deciding to hire an outsider to help you. Table 1-9 provides a checklist of the most common *soft benefits* of consulting projects.

Correcting the Egocentricity Error: "What If We Didn't?"

The March 1979 *Journal of Personality and Social Psychology* contained a powerful study by Michael Ross and Fiore Sicoly that explains an error you encounter every day. The study, which possessed the singularly unsexy name, "Egocentric Biases in Availability and Attribution," showed that the members on a team think they individually add more to the team's results than is logically possible.

Table 1-9

Common *soft* benefits of projects:	
❑ Recognition	❑ Stress reduction
❑ Personal awards and rewards	❑ Job satisfaction
❑ Pride	❑ Discretionary time
❑ Authority	❑ Personal growth
❑ Stature	❑ Other _____
❑ Budget	

Let's say you and four buddies take on another fivesome in a game of pickup basketball. After you win the game and you're all collapsing from exhaustion, you privately ask the individual members of your team how much they contributed to the win. When you add up the numbers, you'll come up with a total much higher than 100 percent.

The exact same thinking bias happens with consulting projects because, as we discussed when introducing the Bigger Picture form, a project is virtually always just one part of achieving a larger goal. When executives individually consider every element that contributes to their goal, they will invariably add up to far more than 100 percent. This is partially because more than one item is critical, and it's partially due to the egocentricity biases.

In the digital standardization project example, the consultant used his experience to factor the client's original estimate that his project contributed 100 percent of the value down to 40 percent. Use your experience or turn to the Bigger Picture form and start asking, "What if you didn't?" about each element. This question is a way of refining, quantifying, and correcting the answers to "How much does this project contribute to the overall goal we are trying to achieve?"

Answering "What if we didn't?" is not always as easy as it first appears. What if your project was to build a wheel for a car? A car, as we all know, has four wheels as well as about 30,000 other parts. What is the value of one wheel in a car? We know we can't simply look at the cost of a wheel on the open market, because if you try to build a $20,000 car from parts, it will cost you over $125,000 (see Figure 1-8). Talk about egocentricity bias!

A knee-jerk answer might be, "The car is not worth anything if you take away one wheel, because a car can't go anywhere with only three wheels." But, of course, that's not true. A car can scrape along the road, screeching and sending sparks flying for quite a few miles. If you bust out your creative MacGyver skills and a few cases of duct tape, you could create a functional, silvery, squishy wheel replacement. A pallet of duct tape isn't the most cost-efficient way to replace a wheel, but it's a small fraction of the cost of an entire car.

You can do much better than duct tape, however. Your bigger picture was a car, but what is a car? It's a transportation vehicle, and transportation vehicles with two wheels are quite popular. Therefore, even though it first appears that the answer to "What if you didn't have a wheel?" is that the car would be useless, you can actually recapture the

Figure 1-8   What Value Does It Really Contribute?:
The Parts of a $20,000 Car Cost $125,000

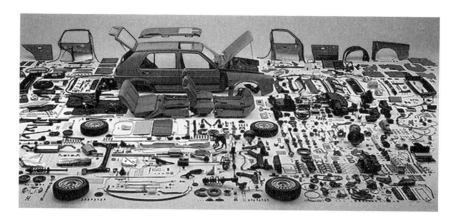

vast majority of the car's value by creatively achieving your goal without the missing part.

Almost nothing is irreplaceable, and that includes your project. If the company's life was riding on achieving your overall goal and you did not do your project, is there any other way you could succeed? In most cases, the answer is yes. Even a project that is critical to achieving your ultimate goal may be contributing only 10 percent to the total value when nine other factors are also critical to success. A reasonable rule of thumb is to factor down your estimate by about 35 percent. Recently, a pharmaceutical firm asked me to improve the return and lower the risk on a $3.5 million project it was engaged in with a consulting megafirm. Since the firm had not estimated that project's contribution to its overall goal, I walked the executives through the same exercise you see above and then factored the whole thing down by 40 percent. For the purposes of knowing whether or not to pursue the project, this was a perfectly fine estimate.

"What's the Risk?"

Every project is replete with risks. The project may not succeed, it may not produce the value you expected, it may cost more than you anticipated, and so forth. If you do not take into account the risks associated with a project, you are, at best, guessing at the value of the project, and you are robbing yourself of huge amounts of value. Answering "What is the risk-adjusted value?" is so important, that Part III of this book is, essentially, entirely devoted to that question.

Summary

You can probably improve your valuations of the projects you are considering, whether those projects will be completed by internal personnel or are destined for an outside expert's attention. No one really wants to build a Bridge to Nowhere, and political considerations aside, the most common reason those doomed ventures get their start is because the value and cost of the project were not thoroughly considered.

The new product design effort that obviously needs an outside touch may, in fact, not be worth doing at all and certainly not with a hired gun. On the other hand, that off-site meeting for which you were going to hire a cheap facilitator may warrant paying extra to find the best maestro available. It depends on what those projects are truly worth. With the questions and checklists above, you can get a much better estimate of which roads will take you to success and which are actually leading into the barren wilderness.

From here you still need to decide whether it's worth bringing in an outsider. "We can do that ourselves" is the mantra intoned by many an executive whose company performs far short of potential. In the next chapter we'll take a look at when to bring in temporary, expert resources.

Can We? Should We?

When to Use Employees and When to Use Third-Party Help

In This Chapter

Now that you have a high-value initiative on your hands, should you use a consultant, or your own internal staff, or some combination? This chapter gives you a straightforward framework and a number of questions that will help you make this determination.

Key concepts in Chapter 2 include the following:
- "Can we?" versus "Should we?"
- Capability and capacity
- Sufficiency, criticality, competitive advantage, and efficiency
- Keep, prioritize, learn, or partner

A Tale of Two Outside Experts

Just after World War II, Isadore Klein decided to sell products that would address the simple business needs of people around the world. Something to write with, something to write on, something to keep papers together—not sexy products, but used universally. Over the next 30 years, Izzy's company grew steadily; and in the late 1970s, IBM suggested that automation would take the burgeoning company to the next level of success.

These were the halcyon days for IBM, when computers were first supplanting humans on routine, numbers-oriented jobs. All kinds of benefits were promised in areas such as inventory control, manufacturing efficiency, accounts payable and receivable, and payroll management. The convincing computer experts were hired, and within days a team of blue-suited young men were tearing into Izzy's home-grown systems, most of which were developed by Richard and Lilly, two employees who had been with Izzy since the start. Two months and tens of thousands of dollars later, the lead engineer from IBM sheepishly approached Izzy to report that his team could not develop a system that provided better results than Richard and Lilly did.

Izzy's story warmingly harks back to the legend of John Henry versus the machine; however, tall tales aside, if Izzy had realized the outside experts had little to offer, he could have saved his company a bushel of money and a family-size bottle of headache medicine.

Similarly, a few months ago I heard from Roger, a Wharton graduate who traveled through Deloitte and a boutique consulting firm before landing as a partner in a private equity firm. Roger often calls when one of his portfolio companies needs an injection of resources or new thinking, and on this particular occasion, he was looking for help improving the internal communications at a West Coast tech company. Roger's firm had installed new management, and the tech company was slipping into disarray as employees became more and more confused over the strategic direction.

I listened to Roger for about 15 minutes and then asked him the last question you'd expect to hear from a consultant: "Why don't you just do this yourself?" Roger did, indeed, have reasons. However, with a few key questions and a bit of back-of-the-napkin analysis, we both concluded this was a project that would be best tackled in-house.

Why would a Wharton grad, a successful investor, and a former consultant turn to the outside when he was better off completing the project internally? How could Izzy Klein have avoided the expensive and, ultimately, fruitless encounter with IT consultants? What were the key questions they hadn't thought through? That's what we'll look at next.

Start by creating a list of 5 to 10 projects you are working on or are thinking about launching. Make sure the list contains projects in each of the following categories:

1. Definitely won't use outside help
2. Probably won't use outside help
3. Probably use outside help
4. Definitely use outside help

Your list of projects can span the range of corporate activities. For instance, Table 2-1 offers a few examples of typical projects and shows how one executive might group them and why (the rationale).

Every company's list of projects is unique, of course, and yours may look similar to or totally different from the list of projects in the table.

Table 2-1

Project	Rationale
Definitely won't use outside help	
Coaching a key employee to smooth some "rough edges"	The employee's manager should do this and should have this skill set
Getting the senior team aligned around a single objective	We can do this ourselves simply by getting the senior team in a room together and hashing it out
Segmenting our customers	Our marketing and sales teams are perfectly capable of doing this, and they should be able to find the time

(continues)

Table 2-1 (*continued*)

Project	Rationale
Probably won't use outside help	
Building a plan to enter a new market	Our marketing team has the skills to tackle this; however, we might bring in some outside expert who knows the new market and can give some guidance. It depends on the cost.
Improving the operational efficiency of a plant	We have plenty of great ideas on how to do this already. Maybe an "expert" could help, but experts are too expensive to warrant the assistance
Probably will use outside help	
Improving the skill set of our sales force	Our sales training team simply doesn't have the capacity. Besides, hiring sales training companies is relatively inexpensive
Installing a customer relationship management system	We could probably build our own system that would be perfect for our situation. However, our IT resources are already stretched, and off-the-shelf systems may be good enough, depending on how much they cost.
Definitely will use outside help	
Converting our tangled mess of data systems into one, coordinated system across the company	We simply do not have the capability inside to clean up this mess. It is going to take an expert who has done this many times before
Creating a stronger digital presence among target customers	Our marketing team could probably do this, but it is already stretched pretty thin. Besides, this is important enough to warrant bringing in outside experts

"Can We?" and "Should We?"

Most executives think about whether or not to hire consultants by asking themselves this question: "Can we achieve our desired outcome ourselves?" If you skim through the sample projects, you will see most of the rationales are based on whether or not internal resources are able to achieve the desired outcome without external assistance.

The classic thinking is that there are only two reasons a company should turn to outside experts: capability and capacity. In other words, when the company either doesn't have the skill set to achieve its desired outcome or has the skill set but doesn't have enough qualified people to get the job done in the time frame required.

Capability and capacity answer "Can we achieve our desired outcome ourselves?" However, just because you can doesn't mean you should. Therefore, you have to introduce another question into the mix: "Should we achieve our desired outcome ourselves?" Again, whether or not you should be able to succeed on your own, you still may lack the wherewithal to do it. We'll take each question in turn.

The Capability Questions: Competency, Experience, and Perspective

While many executives consider the capability question by simply asking, "Can we achieve our desired outcome ourselves?" capability actually breaks down into three pieces: competency, experience, and perspective.

1. Do We Have the Competency Inside to Achieve Our Desired Outcome Using Only Inside Resources?

This is about skills and talents and capabilities. The five prompts below will help answer this question:

- **Do we have proven success achieving our desired outcome?** It's one thing to say, "Sure, no problem. I know how to do that" and quite another to have proved it on the field of battle. Any golfer knows that as easy as the pros make it look to bang a ball down the middle of the fairway, when you step up to the tee yourself, the story is quite different. Do you have proven ability or just self-confidence?

- **Do we have the required skill sets?** A fair retort to the previous question is, "We haven't proved we can solve this problem, but only because we haven't encountered it. We certainly have the *ability* to get the job done." Jot down a quick list of the skill sets you believe are required to succeed with your project, and you will be able to confirm that you do or don't actually house those skills in your organization.

For instance, if you are considering coaching a key employee to smooth some "rough edges," you might determine that some of the skill sets are active listening, effective observation, and the ability to sustain forward progress when the coachee's motivation flags. With that list in hand, you can look at the manager you would call upon to polish the employee and realistically assess whether or not he has demonstrated those skill sets previously. If so, you're in business. If not, then perhaps your competency to tackle the coaching assignment is not as strong as you originally thought.

- **Is our in-house talent strong enough to tackle this particular initiative?** Professional football teams don't put their standard offensive lineup on the field for a kickoff. Situations like that are why they have special teams. Certain projects and initiatives demand the nuanced competency found in a special team, which is beyond the standard level needed to successfully execute most plays. Is the project you are considering an everyday sort of play or a special teams situation?

- **Is our in-house talent strong enough to achieve success quickly enough?** The old saw is that if you put enough monkeys in a room of typewriters for enough time, they will eventually churn out Shakespeare's plays. That may or may not be the case, but I certainly wouldn't want to wait around for *Hamlet* to emerge from the simian brain trust. You are not dealing with a room full of chittering employees swaying from the ceiling by their tails. Nevertheless, you may be in a situation where time is of the essence.

- **Is the knowledge or skill needed to take on this initiative transferable? If we don't have it, is it easy to take on?** Sometimes capability is very easy to acquire, and in those cases even if you do not have the skills or knowledge in-house right now, you could bring the needed talent in so quickly or inexpensively that it does not make sense to hire an outside expert.

For example, if you run a small company and have never written a marketing plan, you could start by buying one of the many, many business plan "kits" that are available online, or you could go to the library, or you could consult with a mentor at your local SCORE office. All these steps would help you quickly transfer expert capability from the outside and let you tackle the project yourself.

2. Is Our Experience Helping Us or Hurting Us on This Particular Initiative?

Often experience is a good thing, and then again, occasionally it actually detracts from our ability to achieve our goals. The following four prompts will help determine whether your experience will help or a hinder your efforts:

- **Do we have a lot of familiarity with this issue or with achieving this goal?** Clearly if we *don't* have much familiarity with the project we're tackling, it is less likely our in-house abilities will be sufficient. For instance, if we want to segment our customers and we've never actually gone through that process ourselves, then do we really know how to sort our customers into the right buckets? Is it likely we know the best practices, such as looking at each customer's service preferences, or would we resort to more simplistic approaches, such as segmenting purely based on size or geography?

- **Are we aware of the limitations of our knowledge?** When we think we know something that, in fact, we don't, it's never a good thing. The model in Figure 2-1 is an adaptation of the Johari window developed in 1955 by Joseph Luft and Harry Ingham. The gray areas show two possibilities that arise when we know less than we think we know.

  The dupe believes her company's experience makes her as good as an expert. Unfortunately, when this is not the case, she often looks foolish. Think about how an executive appears when it would have been so easy to call in an expert and, instead, she forges ahead herself and creates a mess.

  Equally dangerous is the rasha, who confidently presents the path forward when, in fact, neither he nor outside experts have experience nailing the problem. This is the overconfident mariner who claims he knows the channel just before shipwrecking his vessel on the shoals. Might he have foundered his ship even with an expert on board? Possibly; however, when no one has experience in a problem, it's usually worth having many points of view to consider before moving forward.

Figure 2-1   The Consequence of Knowing Less Than
We Think We Do

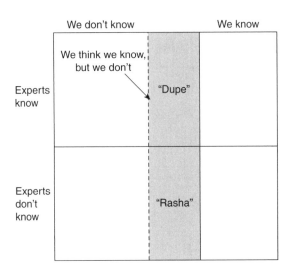

The way to avoid being a dupe or a rasha is simple: call an expert to get an outside perspective on your experience. If you call a couple of good consultants, you will learn quickly whether you know what you don't know.

· **Are we suffering from the curse of knowledge?** In other words, is it possible we are viewing an unfamiliar situation as a familiar one or believing a familiar solution will work when an unfamiliar one is called for? Sometimes when you have experience, it leads you astray because you only see the situation in one way.

Again, a simple prophylactic is to get the perspective of an outside expert, which any good consultant will offer for free. I always let my clients know whether they are on track and whether their experience is insufficient or leading them astray.

3. Is Our Perspective Helping Us or Hurting Us on This Initiative?

In addition to experience and capabilities, or perhaps because of them, we have perspectives on the situation, and those perspectives may be a boon or may be a serious impediment to success. In this case, the perspective you need to consider tends to reside at the individual level, since that's where it can affect success.

- **Are any internal personnel threatened by the initiative and trying to protect their turf?** Any time a project may shift resources, people, or management's attention, there are inside forces doing their best to fight the change.

  A nutrition company in Ohio put its director of planning in charge of a project to improve the company's planning process. Unfortunately, the director was so tied to the process he had instilled previously that every change the consultant suggested was viewed as a threat. Since the other employees on the team knew they would have to work with the director long after the project wrapped up, they didn't want to anger him by defying his views. Can you imagine what would have happened if there was no independent, external consultant? I can: modest adjustments with little impact and, at worst, a valuable, knowledgeable director getting fired.

- **Do any internal personnel see this as an opportunity to acquire more power or prestige?** On the flip side of the coin are those who see the project as a vehicle to further their own ambitions. A large chemical company on the East Coast brought in a small consultancy to build the launch plan for its foray into the telecommunications market. After some analysis in the field, the consultants told the client they wouldn't build a plan because the company shouldn't be entering the market at all. Would the executive in charge of the launch have canceled the whole shebang? Probably not since his next step up in the company was to manage the telecommunications team, which he had already envisioned as extensive.

- **Are internal resources resistant to taking on work outside their normal course of duty?** It's fairly common for employees' reaction to temporary assignments to be, "That's not my job!" Virtually every project requires some help from inside personnel; however, if vital aspects of the project rest in the hands of personnel who view the extra work as an unwelcome intrusion on their routine, the results will not be optimal.

- **Are any internal personnel fearful of a possible outcome of the initiative?** This is similar to the turf issues discussed above. In an engagement my group is working on now, the client has a manager who would, were it left solely to her, point her company in the wrong direction because she does not want to fire or reassign two people she has spent time nurturing.

- **Will people's need to "save face" influence them to take on the project when they shouldn't or avoid the project when they should take it on?** Sometimes executives do not want to admit that they or their department needs outside help in order to complete a project with excellence. Newly promoted senior personnel, for instance, often feel they need to prove their intellectual prowess, which hardly means they should instantly call in the cavalry.

The capability questions are captured in the checklist in Table 2-2.

Table 2-2

Can We Achieve Results on Our Own? Part I
Capability Checklist

❏ Competency
  ❏ Do we have proven success achieving our desired outcome?
  ❏ Do we have the required skill sets?
  ❏ Do we have strong enough talent to tackle this particular initiative?
  ❏ Do we have strong enough talent to achieve success quickly enough?
  ❏ Is the knowledge or skill needed to take on this initiative quickly transferable?
❏ Experience
  ❏ Do we have a lot of familiarity with this issue or with achieving this goal?
  ❏ Are we are aware of the limitations of our knowledge?
  ❏ Are we suffering from the curse of knowledge?
❏ Perspective
  ❏ Are any personnel threatened and trying to protect their turf?
  ❏ Are any personnel trying to acquire more power or prestige?
  ❏ Are internal resources resistant to additional work?
  ❏ Are any personnel fearful of a possible outcome of the initiative?
  ❏ Is the need to "save face" driving this project?

The Capacity Questions: Long Term and Short Term

Assuming you have the capability as an organization to successfully tackle a project, there is still the matter of whether or not you have enough resources available. This issue should be considered through both short-term and long-term questions.

1. Short-Term Capacity

The focus on short-term capacity revolves around this question:

- **Do we have the necessary resources available right now to succeed with this project?** In other words, are the right people (those with the capabilities) currently working below full capacity? If so, could they be diverted to your project in a timely fashion without putting whatever they are currently working on at risk?

2. Long-Term Capacity

Do we need or have the necessary resources after the immediate need has passed? Here we're making a judgment about whether we could handle the same project next time.

- **Is this a frequent or recurring need?** In other words, do we encounter variations on this initiative fairly often? If you need the same capacity over and over and you are constantly juggling people and responsibilities to create it, then you really don't have the capacity in-house.
- **How often is peak capacity needed?** At my office, Fridays are always deluged with client calls, project changes, deliverable deadlines, and all manner of other tasks. There's no room to add a task to Friday's schedule that could be handled on a different weekday. We have a "peak-capacity" problem because on Fridays we are already running at 110 percent. If you are constantly at peak capacity, then you need to address your systemic issues, or you will be pushed into using consultants every time rather than at the right times.

Table 2-3 is a checklist that sums up the capacity questions.

Table 2-3

Can We Achieve Results on Our Own? Part II
Capacity Checklist

❑ Short term
  ❑ Do we have capacity right now to accomplish this initiative?
❑ Long term
  ❑ Is this a frequent or recurring need?
  ❑ Is peak capacity consistently needed?

The "Should We?" Questions: Sufficiency, Focus, Intellectual Property, and Efficiency

In the case of Roger, the private equity executive from the beginning of this chapter whom I talked out of hiring a consultant, the rationale for changing his mind was not only that the members of his group *could* complete the work in house, but that they *should* do the project themselves. There are times when your expertise may be not quite up to the level of an expert's, and yet you should be completing the project with in-house talent anyway.

1. Can We Get a Sufficient Result on Our Own?

If you can get 90 percent or more of the risk-adjusted value you expect from a project by using your own resources, it may not be worth bringing in outside experts to achieve the remaining 5 to 10 percent. As Alan Weiss, Ph.D., the best selling author of books on consulting such as *Million Dollar Consulting*, puts it: "You're after success, not perfection."

- **If the consultant will be doing something we can't do, will that make a meaningful difference to the result?** An outside firm may be able to promise 60 customer interviews versus the 10 you are likely to get using internal staff, but will the extra 50 actually make a difference in the knowledge that results from the survey? You need to reflect on your capability and capacity and ask whether you can get close enough to achieve success, rather than whether you can do the project as well as an expert.

- **Do we want familiar results, or are we trying to raise the bar?** Internal resources are most likely to deliver familiar results, which may be appropriate when trying to fix a problem; in comparison, external resources are more likely to deliver unfamiliar results, which is more appropriate when trying to achieve an aspiration.

2. How Core Is This Initiative to Our Ongoing Success, and Is the Project Focused on Performance Improvement?

When an activity is critical to our success, two factors are at play: we should make sure we are as good at it as we can possibly be, and, separately, we should maintain control over the activity. Therefore, bring in outside experts to improve core activities if the outside experts can raise the bar significantly. Conversely, routine performance of core activities should remain in-house. (See Figure 2-2.)

In western Pennsylvania there is a small innovation development firm that helps its clients leapfrog their competitors with outstanding new products. Should the firm outsource its ongoing design work? Absolutely not! That is the beating heart of the company, and routinely putting design in the hands of outsiders would increase the risk of failure.

Figure 2-2   What Activities to Outsource and What to Tackle In-House

	Noncore activity	Core activity
Routine performance	Outsource	Keep in-house
Improve performance	In-house or consultant	Use best in class

As you move farther away from core activities, outsourcing for routine performance becomes a more viable option. To achieve improvements on noncore activities you can use either internal resources or external experts based on your answers to the other questions in this chapter. Thus, the innovation company should not outsource the training of its designers since that is directly connected to the core activity of designing. However, the human resources task of identifying new designers to interview is definitely far enough away from the core that the firm could outsource without introducing risk.

3. Does the Project Involve Unique Intellectual Property?

For many companies, their intellectual property is a key source of competitive advantage. Patents, copyrighted materials, and all kinds of trade secrets arm them to win in the marketplace. The very notion of having a trade secret may obviate the use of outside experts, since outsiders put those secrets at risk.

4. Is It More Efficient to Use Internal Resources or Outside Experts?

In other words, will we get a better return on investment by running the project in-house or with hired hands? The whole question of fees and return on investment (ROI) is addressed in more depth in Chapter 8. For now, three efficiency questions will start you in the right direction:

- **If we do have capacity right now, is this project the best use of it, or are our resources more productive elsewhere?** This may seem obvious, but if we do have internal personnel with the right capabilities and extra time on their hands, is this the project that they should be doing?

- **Is it worth bringing temporary capacity in-house?** This option is very different from bringing in a consulting firm or outsourcing. Temporary staffing means you retain control and the work is done in-house; however, the people doing the work are not on your permanent payroll. Typically this is done with more tactical projects.

- **Is it more efficient to have peak capacity in-house or to arrange for external coverage?** To make the best use of outside expertise on recurring projects, you need to compare the ROI of periodically bringing external resources into play versus hiring full-time employees to provide peak capacity.

See Table 2-4 for a checklist of the "Should we?" questions.

One other set of factors that falls under the heading of "Should we?" is not included on the checklist in Table 2-4: factors unrelated to project results such as the desire to protect underutilized employees from being laid off rather than direct money to outsiders. It's very possible that you can and should use an outside expert; yet you decide not to because you have someone idle in Iowa whom you want to keep busy. Whether this is good for you or the idle employee is debatable; therefore, this type of strategic, stakeholder decision is not part of the best practice of when to use consultants.

Table 2-4

Should We Achieve Results on Our Own?
Checklist

❑ Sufficiency
  ❑ Will the consultant's unique addition make a meaningful difference to the result?
  ❑ Do we want familiar results, or are we trying to raise the bar?
❑ Focus
  ❑ How core to our ongoing success is this initiative?
  ❑ Is the project focused on performance improvement, or is it routine performance?
❑ Intellectual property
  ❑ Does the project involve unique intellectual property that we do not want to put at risk?
❑ Efficiency
  ❑ Is this project the best use of our internal resources?
  ❑ Could we use temporary capacity?
  ❑ Is it more efficient to have peak capacity in-house or to arrange for external coverage?

Your Next Actions: Keep, Prioritize, Learn, or Partner

As you went through the various "Can we?" and "Should we?" questions for each of your projects, you probably came to a few unexpected conclusions. You also were left with four different combinations of answers, each of which has an appropriate action (see Table 2-5):

Keep

If you determine that you can accomplish the initiative using internal resources and that you are best off keeping it in-house, then forgo the consultant. In the example of Roger, the private equity manager, he had assumed he didn't have the capability in-house to tackle the communication questions. What he eventually realized was that his managers could get close enough (sufficiency) with very little drain on employees' time; and, in fact, the ancillary benefits of having employees complete the project actually made the value higher than if an outside expert were brought in.

Prioritize

One of the toughest situations to handle correctly is when you *can* take on a task internally but you know you *shouldn't*. Current personnel who fear for their jobs may insist on doing the work themselves rather than bringing in an outside expert. Or a flawed assessment of ROI may sway a company to continue insourcing when outsourcing would be more efficient. If you can do a project but shouldn't, then you need to prioritize how you allocate your resources. Could your personnel generate more value by working on tasks other than this project?

To take an extreme example, most corporate executives are perfectly capable of making their own travel arrangements, and yet doing

Table 2-5

"Can We?"	"Should We?"	→	Action
We can	We should	→	Keep
We can	We shouldn't	→	Prioritize
We can't	We should	→	Learn
We can't	We shouldn't	→	Partner

so is generally not a good use of their time. Whether they decide to sort through flights themselves or to avail themselves of an executive assistant is based on an assessment of whether or not they could add more value to the company by using their time to focus on higher-level issues.

Learn

When you *can't* accomplish a project but *should* be able to, your long-term goal is to bring the capability or capacity—whichever you are missing—in-house. You could do that by creating more capacity, e.g., by redirecting your resources. Or you could acquire more capacity by hiring more people or buying other resources. Similarly, if necessary, you could acquire the capability by hiring or acquiring the right skill sets. If you do bring in an outside expert on a "We can't but we should" initiative, then your charge is to structure the project so that you transfer capabilities inside as quickly and comprehensively as possible.

Partner

Finally, if you do not have the capacity or capability to take on a project in-house and you determine you *shouldn't* find a way to bring it inside, then you partner with an outside expert. These are the perfect situations for bringing in consultants or other outside resources. The rest of the book will help you bring in the right outside experts and get the best possible results from their work.

Now go back to your list of projects. Table 2-6 illustrates how the example projects I listed at the beginning of the chapter might be recategorized after going through the "Can we?" and "Should we?" questions.

Table 2-6

	"Can We?"	"Should We?"	Action and Rationale
Coaching a key employee to smooth some "rough edges"	No	Yes	**Learn.** Since the manager is not currently a good coach, we will bring in a coach for a few months who will help the employee *and* train the manager on how to continue coaching.

(continues)

Table 2-6   (*continued*)

	"Can We?"	"Should We?"	Action and Rationale
Getting the senior team aligned around a single objective	No	Yes	**Learn.** The perspective issues preclude us from doing this well ourselves. Ideally we would find a way to bring this frequent task in-house; therefore, we will look for an expert who can equip us to get past our perspective problems while leading us through the process once or twice.
Segmenting our customers	Yes	No	**Prioritize.** While our marketing and sales teams are perfectly capable of doing this and we feel they should be able to find the time, having them run the segmentation exercise is not the most efficient use of our resources. We will hire a cost-effective expert for this project.
Building a plan to enter a new market	Yes	Yes	**Keep.** While we considered bringing in some outside expertise, our team has a good enough skill set to get us 95% of the value a consultant would provide, and this project is so critical that we should be keeping it inside.
Improving the operational efficiency of a plant	Yes	No	**Prioritize.** Initially we thought an outside expert was too expensive; however, when we analyzed the true ROI, taking into account lost productivity from people we would have to dedicate to the project, it turns out hiring a consultant is a good spend.

Table 2-6   *(continued)*

	"Can We?"	"Should We?"	Action and Rationale
Improving the skill set of our sales force	No	No	**Partner.** Our sales training team simply doesn't have the capacity. Besides, hiring sales training companies is relatively inexpensive.
Installing a customer relationship management system	Yes	No	**Prioritize.** We could probably build our own system that would be perfect for our situation. However, our IT resources are already stretched, and the off-the-shelf systems an expert can provide are good enough and far more efficient.
Converting our tangled mess of data systems into one, coordinated system across the company	No	No	**Partner.** We simply do not have the capability inside to clean up this mess. It is going to take an expert who has done this many times before. There is also no reason we should be keeping this in-house.
Creating a stronger digital presence among target customers	Yes	No	**Prioritize.** Our marketing team could probably do this, but it is already stretched pretty thin. Besides, this is an important project where the value created by outside experts will be a lot higher than what our group would produce.

Summary

Knowing when to bring in consultants can win you lasting competitive advantage. The WD-40 Company has tripled in size over the past decade, and vital to its success, according to CEO Garry Ridge, is focusing on the company's core competencies while making extensive use of third-party experts to handle the rest. Knowing when to rely on your internal team can head off heartache and wasted resources. Izzy Klein's company survived the futile attempt by IBM to upgrade the company's systems, but he and his employees would have been a lot happier had they simply stuck with Lilly and Richard's systems all along.

By conscientiously working your way through "Can we?" and "Should we?" you will know when to partner and when to keep your work inside; when to build competencies for the long term and when to let someone else take over tasks that you could perform quite competently.

You may be ready to jump right into finding a consultant for those projects where an outside expert is the best path forward. Before you do that, a bit of preparation work is in order so that you can find the best consultant for your project and have the greatest chance of success. That's what the next chapter is all about.

What's the Context?

Become the Perfect Client Before You Call the Consultant

In This Chapter

You know you have a project worth doing, and you know the type of consultant you need. Before you pick up the phone and start calling experts, create a Context Document, which will thoroughly brief prospective consultants.

Key concepts in Chapter 3 include the following:
- The six sections of the Context Document
- Objectives versus activities
- The indicators of success CRAVE checklist
- Time, people, and money parameters
- What is not in the Context Document—leave the approach to the expert

Top Speed of the 2009 Toyota Camry Hybrid?

The Camry question was the title of a post on an online forum dedicated to cars and frequented by car fanatics. The person with the question explained that he had been called by a hospital to deliver an emergency supply of blood platelets for a patient bleeding out in surgery. He had driven the 80-mile stretch of dry, flat, Colorado highway in the blood bank's Ford Expedition, topping out at 103 miles per hour, while the hospital waited and the patient's condition worsened.

The original post didn't comment on the patient's condition when the platelets finally arrived. Rather, the poster worried that he might have been able to scream down the highway faster in his hybrid Camry. What did the car community think? After pages of posts on different engine packages, wind resistance, the speed rating of tires, and the question of whether driving at that speed is even safe, a new entrant to the conversation asked, "Why didn't you just take the helicopter? You chose the wrong vehicle for the job in the first place." Oops.

While virtually everyone responded to the original question, only one person stepped back, looked at the overall context, and gave a better solution to the underlying need. A lot of executives jump into the search for a consultant as if they're on the car forum—asking for the consultants' top speeds, torque, and rpm and requesting a few reference pictures of them winning races on the track. Or they issue a detailed request for proposal (RFP) with all sorts of specifications about capabilities. As a result, when they ask for a Camry hybrid, they get one, and no consultant suggests or provides a helicopter.

When you only specify that you want to be 80 miles yonder as fast as possible, but you don't have a watch and you have no idea what the weather conditions are or how many people you need to take along, what's the likelihood that you're going to get the best solution? In this chapter, I will introduce a very simple tool that dramatically boosts the likelihood that your project produces a Comanche helicopter, not a Camry hybrid.

The Context Document

At the heart of a project that delivers great results—one that delivers the value it should by delivering the desired outcome when and how you want it—is a thorough project brief, which I call the Context Document. Abraham Lincoln purportedly said that if he were given six hours to chop down a tree, he would spend the first four sharpening his axe. Think of the consultant's approach as the chopping and the Context Document as the sharpening. For every project you take on with an outside consultant, you should be drafting a Context Document as a first step.

Note that this isn't an RFP per se, which has become an often misused, abused, and poorly developed weapon wielded primarily by corporate purchasing departments to bludgeon vendors. RFPs in most companies tend to be squarely focused on prices or costs, whereas your focus should be on value.

Your Context Document will contain the answer to six questions, some of which are addressed in detail in other chapters:

1. What is the situation that is leading us to bring in an outside expert?
2. What are our desired outcomes?
3. What are our indicators of success?
4. What are the risks in this project?
5. What is the value of taking on this project?
6. What parameters will limit or affect the project?

Section 1. Situation

The first section of your Context Document answers the question "What situation is leading us to bring in an outside expert?" It explains, as concisely and precisely as possible, what has led you to the point of bringing in an outside expert. Generally you do not need to go into a long, detailed narrative about the history of your company and every outside factor that has or might have an influence on your success. Stick to the relevant details while giving an outsider (who has signed a nondisclosure agreement, of course) a clear picture.

Here's an example of an excellent situation description, taken from a recent project (with certain information redacted or changed to protect the confidentiality of the client).

Situation

Our hospital wants to increase the number of (fully paying) patients from outside the United States. The driving forces for pursuing this strategy are the changing payer dynamics in the domestic market, which are putting downward pressure on our gross revenue and margins. As a result, it is increasingly important to the hospital as a worldwide leader to create a strong revenue stream from international patients.

Currently we do have some revenue from international patients—roughly $X million, and we anticipate that this amount can double or triple based on the revenue brought in from these types of patients by other, best-in-class hospitals around the country.

However, at this point we do not have internal agreement on the best markets to focus on and, importantly, what marketing tactics will be most effective in increasing the revenue from international patients. Further, the information (and ability to gather the information) needed to determine which markets are best is not available in-house.

A well-constructed situation statement, like the example, displays five elements:

1. **Strategy.** It shows how the project fits in strategically with what the company is doing. The strategy behind the international expansion is clear.

2. **Conciseness.** It is very short. A consultant or anyone in the company can read it in a few minutes and understand exactly why the project is being undertaken.

3. **Catalyst.** It explains what change is driving the project, i.e., the events that have led to needing this project to succeed. The catalytic change always results in:

   a. A decrease in performance now versus historically. This is a problem.

   b. A need or desire for performance to be higher now versus historically. This is an aspiration.

4. **Decision.** It explains what decisions have been made already, based on either evidence or strategy, and what is to be tackled now.

5. **Need.** It articulates why the project is being directed to outside resources rather than being handled by current employees.

Section 2. Objectives

The Objectives section of your Context Document answers the questions "What are our desired outcomes from this project?" and "How will we be better off when it is completed?" These questions are worth more than a passing thought. Early in 2011, the vice president of sales for ERQuip set out to find an expert who could train his salespeople in strategic selling. However, he was hunting for the wrong expert. Strategic selling skills were not the best solution for ERQuip's woes, and hiring a training company, no matter how talented, would have turned out to be a colossal waste. The game-changing, high-ROI solution in this case was a wholesale shift in communication between headquarters and the sales team combined with new sales processes.

The problem with heading into a search for consultants with the wrong objective in mind is that most consultants will reassure you, "Yes, we do that, and here's how . . ." Only a few will honestly admit, "No, I don't do that, exactly, but I can help you when you get to the next stage." Neither of those answers will put you on the path to outstanding results.

The first step toward getting the right expert is pausing to reflect on whether you have the right objectives. More executives skip this step than any other; however, there is good reason to make it part of your regular, consultant-hunting routine: the curse of knowledge is leading you astray. In short, your experience makes you think you know the problem or issue you are tackling even when it's a different problem altogether. There is a fantastic explanation of this phenomenon in the book *Made to Stick* and also in a white paper on my website: http://www.davidafields.com/curseofknowledge.

The curse of knowledge hits you when you are formulating a project—before you make your first call to an outside expert. The more often you've faced a similar situation, the more confident you are in your objectives. In fact, you *are* more likely to have the right objectives in situations you have faced many times. Alas, the curse of knowledge makes it far less likely that you will recognize when you're wrong.

The following series of questions will help you past the curse of knowledge:

- **Why are we undertaking this project?** Asking a series of "why" questions forces you to think at least one level higher in the chain of decisions that led you to this project. You are not asking why you need a consultant, which we addressed in the previous chapter, nor are you asking whether it's a project worth doing; rather, you are asking why you are doing the project at all. What is the higher-level goal this project serves? The Bigger Purpose form you filled out in Chapter 1 may help in this exercise. In ERQuip's case, the answers to why it was conducting sales training were that their salespeople's skills were no longer effective and that sales were flagging.

- **What is required to achieve our higher-level goal?** As discussed in Chapter 1, your project is usually one of a number of pieces that must be in place for the overall goal to be met. What else is required? Keep to elements that *must* be in place, not those that are helpful or enablers. For the ERQuip salespeople's skills to be effective, the following had to be in place: they had to have the right skills, and they had to be motivated to use them.

- **What is our evidence that this is the best area of focus, or is it a strategic decision?** Assumptions are not the best basis for marshaling your resources to attack a problem. What observable evidence do you have that, of all the pieces that must be in place for you to achieve your goal, the focus of this project is the best one? In ERQuip's case, the need for improved negotiation skills was based on the vice president's sense that the marketplace was changing and his salespeople were too reliant on relationships. That's not evidence; it's assertions. Upon further inspection, it turned out that motivation was also a problem and that it hinged on poor collaboration between marketing and sales. There are also times when strategic choices rather than evidence will dictate the focus of your project.

- **Is this the best way to proceed?** Even if you have solid evidence supporting the focus of your project, you should still question your approach. For instance, ERQuip called some outside experts, explained the situation, and posed the question "Is this *the best way* to move forward?" A top-notch consultant will tell you quickly and free of charge whether you were already on the right track or will present you with compelling evidence that you should reexamine your alternatives.

The next step in formulating your objectives is based on a little-known fact—that there are only three types of outcomes from a consulting project that add value: a recommended decision, a recommended plan for implementing that decision, and the implementation of a plan (see Figure 3-1). Every consulting project in the world should deliver a recommended decision, a plan, implementation, or some combination of the three. If you have the wrong outcome in mind, you will seek the wrong type of consultant.

Decisions and plans are the outcomes of diagnostic projects. Consultants use their expertise to diagnose what is wrong with morale, or how you should enter China, or whether you should close the plant in Lexington. They may recommend a decision such as focusing on leadership or closing the plant, or they may give you a market-entry plan. Execution projects, on the other hand, are focused on implementing a plan you have already developed.

To be fair, every project involves a bit of diagnosis and a bit of execution. When you hire a consultant to implement a detailed plan, the consultant will still have to make decisions en route, and, similarly a diagnostician still needs to execute his diagnostic process. However, that theoretical rabbit hole leads nowhere fast. Ultimately, the distinction revolves around this question: are you looking for advice, or are you looking to delegate a task?

Figure 3-1 The Three Valuable Project Outcomes

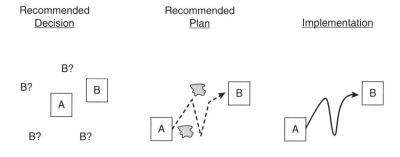

Once you have confirmed the focus of your project and you know whether the project is oriented toward diagnosis or execution, you can outline the Objectives section of the Context Document. Below is an example of the Objectives section.

Objectives

The overall objective is to have a more diversified revenue stream that lowers our dependence (and risk) on our current, single market. The objective of this specific initiative is to identify the best market segments for expansion. Criteria for identifying high-opportunity market segments include:

- Which market segments are likely to experience substantial growth due to either governmental or private commercial interest
- To what extent the surge in interest is likely to translate into viable commercial opportunities for our company
- What likely solutions would we offer in those segments
- Whether any new market opportunities would require truly incremental programs
- Which of our company's capabilities would be leveraged to meet the new business opportunities

---

There are three criteria for a great Objectives section:

1. **Precise outcome statements.** It is clear whether your desired outcome is a decision, a plan, or implementation. In the example above, there is no doubt the client was looking for a recommended decision on which market segments to enter. The bullet points clarify what would allow the team to home in on one or another segment as a great opportunity.

2. **Overall goal.** If there is a bigger goal that this project fits into, it should be captured in the Objectives section. The bigger purpose identified in the example was to lower the company's risk and dependency on its current market.

3. **Result.** Every objective statement should be a result, not an activity. Notice in the example above that the Objectives section didn't contain a long list of activities the consultant was expected

Table 3-1

Activity	Objective (Result)
Develop a market appraisal	Know whether or not to enter the market
Coach the director of operations in teamwork and leadership skills	Improve morale and productivity among operations staff
Implement a strategic account management program	Enroll the top 10 accounts in a fully functioning strategic account management program
Reorganize the Carlisle division	Have a detailed rollout plan in place for a new organizational structure at the Carlisle division, which we believe will increase profitability
Analyze the rail-yard statistics and determine where the bottleneck is in car storage	Increase rail-yard capacity at least 8%

to take on. You are trying to describe how you will be better off when the project is done, not how you will get there. In other words, in the story about the Toyota Camry, the objective is to have the platelets to the hospital 80 miles away as soon as possible, not to *drive* to the hospital at the car's top speed.

Distinguishing between activities and objectives can be tricky for a lot of people, and it is vitally important. On diagnostic projects you should be hiring a consultant to achieve a certain result, not to conduct a certain activity. The examples in Table 3-1 demonstrate the difference between activities and objectives.

Section 3. Indicators of Success

The third section of your Context Document answers the question "How will we know whether our project is on the right track and whether we have achieved the objective?" This particular section is eerily absent from most consulting agreements. As I have asked executives whether a project was successful or not, I have witnessed a lot of equivocating and fuzzy answers. "It was pretty successful." "We achieved most of what we had hoped." "I think it could have gone a bit better." Those are all signs that the indicators of success were not concrete and were not clearly identified before the project commenced.

For each of the objectives you have identified, simply ask yourself how you will know if you met the objective. For instance, if your objective is that every operations manager can competently calculate five key quality metrics, then your indicator of success would be 100 percent of operations managers passing a test on the five metrics. The excellence of this section in your Context Document may be jumping out at you now. Whereas most consultants would claim they are successful if all your operations managers went through their training session, by setting the indicator of success as passing the test you very clearly show the consultants that they are responsible for the outcome, not just the activity.

Table 3-2 presents a few examples of indicators of success.

Since most executives have less experience articulating their indicators of success than their situation or objectives, I'll explain how to write them in more detail than appears in the prior two sections.

There are seven guidelines that will help you make this section outstanding:

1. **Include quantitative and/or qualitative indicators of success.** As a quant-geek with a couple of degrees from Carnegie Mellon, I naturally want everything to boil down to numbers. It turns out that isn't necessary. Sometimes it isn't even best! Success can be a team's perception, a level of confidence, or unanimity in a decision. It could be agreement on an area of focus or the existence of a plan that is sufficiently comprehensive and detailed.

2. **Establish at least one indicator of success for each of your objectives.** It's certainly cleanest and easiest to know when the race is over if there is a single red tape at the finish line; however, understanding success is often more complex than that. It's like determining whether or not the weather is right to take a dip in the pool. Maybe there's a single metric, like temperature. Or before you'll don your trunks and frolic with the kids, you may want the sun to be shining, the skies to hold no threat of lightning, the pool temperature to approximate bathwater, and nearby glasses of refreshments to be sweating enticingly.

Table 3-2

Objective	Indicators of Success
Know whether or not to enter the market	Management team is confident it has the information necessary to make a well-supported decision on whether or not to enter the market
Improve morale and productivity among operations staff	Operations managers report improved morale: ❏ On the three internal survey questions related to morale, the average score increases from a 2.1 to at least a 3.0 ❏ Monthly absenteeism drops from 6% to below 4%
Enroll the top 10 accounts in a fully functioning strategic account management program	All 10 accounts have participated in at least one strategic planning session The strategic account management group is fully staffed; comprehensive process manuals for strategic account management have been rolled out
Have a detailed rollout plan in place for a new organizational structure at the Carlisle division, which we believe will increase profitability	Senior management has approved the organizational structure and rollout plan
Increase rail-yard capacity at least 8%	At least 3,000 cars are in the yard on peak days; blocking time is less than 2 hours per day

3. **Choose indicators that don't bias the result.** In particular, if your project is designed to give you a message, don't make a possible outcome that the messenger can get shot! For instance, if your project is focused on validating the healthcare industry as a new market, then your metric of success should not be the

achievement of some level of sales in healthcare. If you chose that metric, then the consultant can only succeed by pointing out how to achieve sales, not by showing you that your resources would be better invested in a different market.

4. **Incorporate short-term indicators to assess progress.** The point of the indicators of success is to have a mechanism that keeps you on track while the project is in progress and that tells you whether you hit the bull's-eye when the project concludes. Therefore, three-year compound annual growth of 11 percent is not an ideal indicator of success for a three-month project. Instead, you may need to set one-year growth or quarterly growth versus the prior year as a short-term indicator.

   Similarly, on a project designed to drive down attrition, the turnover rate during three months may be your short-term indicator of success, after which you will keep an eye on how many employees you lose for a couple of years.

5. **If necessary, find proxy indicators.** Sometimes you can't measure what you're trying to achieve reliably or in advance. Consider a project where we were trying to raise morale in a certain division of a global company. Senior management wanted to look at scores on the annual company survey; however, those surveys have veracity issues. Some managers may cajole their employees to "think positively" on the survey so that their departments' ratings look good. Conversely, some employees may give low marks that don't reflect their true opinions in order to send a message to management or draw attention.

   Therefore, we suggested a number of proxy indicators that would give us a window into the division's mood. These included absenteeism, participation at meetings, and negative posts on an intranet site. Were these perfect indicators of morale? No; however, they were good proxies.

6. **Use leading indicators rather than lagging indicators.** You want metrics that will give you early warning signals if something is going astray in your project. For instance, while both profit and purchase intent are indicators of success, profit is less useful since it is a lagging indicator; it is a calculation of revenue and costs that have already occurred. Purchase intent is, in most cases, a

Figure 3-2 Leading and Lagging Indicators of Success

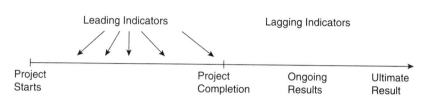

leading indicator. Throughput is generally a lagging indicator on a production line, whereas waiting time at a manufacturing station, immediately before the bottleneck, may be a great leading indicator of the line's improvement. In most cases you can find indicators that will give you an early read on the direction in which the project is headed (see Figure 3-2). As you may have noticed from the examples, leading indicators are often proxies.

The caveat on proxies and leading indicators is that you must make sure you truly understand when they will point you in the right direction and when they could lead you astray. Automobile enthusiasts gauge performance based on how long it takes for a car to go from a standstill to 60 miles per hour. A Porsche 911 takes around 4.5 seconds, whereas the old VW buses took a couple of decades. Is the time it takes to get to 15 miles per hour or 30 miles per hour a good short-term indicator of zero to 60? As it turns out, not really. A car accelerating out of the gate like a gunshot may not continue accelerating strongly. Early indicators on consulting projects can be similarly misleading if you don't understand them well.

7. **Vet your indicators using the CRAVE checklist.** *CRAVE* stands for *concrete, reliable, available, valid,* and *engaging.*

Concrete means it is something you can actually measure rather than something amorphous. Look at these three indicators of success for a website redesign:

- It looks great.
- Most visitors rate it highly.
- Eighty percent of visitors click through to the sales page.

All three are indicators of success, but which one is most help-ful? The third indicator is most helpful because it is more concrete.

Reliable means you would get the same score on the indi-cator from the same project results every time. More subjec-tive indicators of success tend to be less reliable simply because humans are fickle. That doesn't make subjective indicators bad, of course, just trickier. If you are redesigning your web-site, the number of people who click on the "Solutions" tab is a more reliable indicator than a visitor's rating of the site as good or bad, which might vary from day to day.

Available means you can actually get the data. If you decided to judge your outside expert's website designs based on the visits to the sales page but you have no way of track-ing that, then you don't really have an indicator of success. Availability is sometimes the toughest part of developing excel-lent indicators of success because the obvious data are not always available. It's not unusual for us to create simple sur-veys or ask for data that were not previously captured so that we can have a working indicator of success. Just because the information is not available now doesn't mean you can't make it available!

Valid means the indicator of success actually points you in the right direction. An executive whose project objective is decreased attrition might look to the competitiveness of sal-aries as a leading indicator of success. Unfortunately, this is probably not a valid indicator because attrition is rarely due to compensation. Satisfaction with employees' direct manager would be a better metric.

Engaging means your indicators of success inspire action. There is no point in holding up a bar if no one is going to try to leap over it. Compare "80 percent of salespeople meet their sales targets" with "80 percent of salespeople achieve bonus payout levels." The sales may be the same, but the activity and engagement will be different.

Finally, stick to a few indicators of success that are relevant and tightly focused on what you are trying to achieve, and don't provoke conflicting responses.

Section 4. Perceived Risks and Concerns

This section answers the question: "What are the primary risks associated with this project?" By including this section in your Context Document, you enable consultants to develop proposals that meet more of your needs and create astronomically higher (in some cases) risk-adjusted returns. Surprisingly, very little attention has been paid to risk in consulting projects; therefore, Part III of this book is dedicated to the subject of risk. However, to get you started, jot down your answers to two questions:

1. When you think of engaging consultants for projects like this, what are your biggest concerns?

2. When you think about this specific project, what are your biggest concerns?

Your responses might reference what the project's outcomes are, how the project affects your organization, how the consultant works or doesn't work, what the cost is, or quite a few other areas. Below are examples of this section from two recent projects.

Perceived Risks and Concerns

For this initiative, we are most concerned with two different types of outcome risk:

1. Will the learning session provide significant, tangible gains for us? For instance, are the sales executives able to conduct higher-level discussions with their accounts, and as mentioned in the Objectives section, will the ROI on the contracts improve?

2. Will the participants walk away with the sense that the learning session delivered big "Ahas" and "Wows" rather than just a couple of interesting nuggets?

Perceived Risks and Concerns

The primary perceived risks are:

1. A less than optimal outcome if the people designing the organizational structure do not have a deep understanding of our industry

2. Attrition of important personnel if the initiative takes too long

3. Distraction or defocusing of personnel

4. Creation of friction between the division and the parent company if the latter is seen as mandating poor ideas or exhibiting hubris

---

The first thing you might notice about these examples is how different they are from each other. Another observation that might pop out is how common it is to have personnel-related risks. The great thing about this section is that there are no wrong or invalid answers.

Section 5. Value

This section answers the question "What is the value of taking on this project?" In Chapter 1 we spent a long time answering "Why bother?" and thinking through the value of your projects. The Context Document is where you spell out, clearly and concisely, the result of all your hard work refining your valuations. I recommend explicitly articulating all the refinements and adjustments you made. Chances are that if you needed to correct an assumption in your thinking, then other people looking at the project's value are going to make similar assumptions and need similar corrections. Table 3-3 provides an example of an excellent Value section.

Two best practices for your Value section are:

1. **Conservatism.** If you take a very conservative approach to valuation and the project is still clearly worth doing and still provides a fabulous return, then your chances of being thrilled with the outcome are high. Chapter 6 covers the topic of risk-adjusted value, and the example in Table 3-3 demonstrates some risk adjustments.

2. **Concreteness.** The assumptions are spelled out and the math is worked all the way through so that anyone looking at the project (or reconsidering it) knows exactly what value is expected and how that value was derived.

Some executives balk at sharing the value of their project with consultants—especially with prospective consultants who have not yet bid on the project. The most common objection is that if you show the consultant what the project is worth, the consultant will charge more. As

Table 3-3

Project Value

Our estimate of the value of this project is roughly $1.1 million based on the following assumptions:

a. We have set $50 million in annual revenue as the goal for 2015 based on the performance of our competitors. To be conservative, we are assuming this project will close the gap between current revenue and the goal over time, with more of the gap closed in 2014 and 2015 than in the next two years.

b. A goal adjustment of 50%. Since it's possible our competitor-based goal is unrealistic, we are cutting the value of the incremental revenue in half.

c. Project contribution factor of 10%. Many elements must be successfully executed in order to enjoy the incremental revenue from [this project]. Marketing plans must be put in place, partnerships must be consummated, operational issues must be addressed, top-notch services and customer experiences must be provided, and so forth. Consequently, we have assumed this initiative only contributes 10% of the potential gain from [the overall goal].

d. Consultant's contribution factor of 50%. Although we don't believe we have the internal capability or capacity to successfully complete this project, if push came to shove, our people could make headway on their own. Therefore, we are assuming that bringing in a consultant only contributes 50% of the total potential gain.

e. Risk factor of 65%. Based on the risks we outlined in the previous section, we are including a 35% chance that the project does not create any value at all.

In addition to the quantitative benefit, successfully completing this project also builds the credibility of our team and solidifies [our group] as an important partner for many other areas of the company.

the owner of a busy enterprise with few employees, I constantly bring in outside experts to help in my own business, and I empathize with that concern; it crosses my mind every time I search for a new consultant. Nevertheless, as you will learn in Chapter 8, sharing the value of your project is more likely to get you the best approach from the best consultant than is holding that information close to the vest. That is why, despite my reservations, I always share the value of my projects with the consultants I am considering.

You want consultants who are going to put everything they can into helping you meet or exceed your risk-adjusted value while delivering an outstanding return on their fees. Showing the value to prospective consultants puts the whole project in context for them and, if you structure your contract correctly, inspires them to develop an approach that will give you the absolute highest risk-adjusted return on the fees you pay them.

Section 6. Parameters

This section answers the question "Are there any parameters that will affect or limit the project?" The real world often intrudes on projects in unfortunate ways. For instance, if the project team expects 4 weeks of assessment time and senior management is expecting the results in 10 days, that's a problem. Or, if the consultant's recommendations on your marketing campaign must all be approved by your legal and regulatory departments, that may result in significant extra work and time.

Ask yourself, "Are there any issues that could affect how our objectives are achieved?" Here are two examples of answers to that question.

Parameters

- Kickoff should occur the week of January 23, when senior staff will be in one location for annual planning meetings.

- Rollout of the first incarnation of the [project results] will be at the June 2011 national sales meeting.

- Work on this project should be coordinated with [another consulting firm] since its work on territory optimization is likely to affect the results of this project.

Parameters

The detailed [project outcome] must be available by March 31. In addition, the fees for this project must be kept under $100,000, or else signing authority for this project will be exceeded and we would lose at least four weeks getting approval (assuming it can be obtained) from the executive vice president of global finance.

Typically, parameters come in three flavors: time, people, and money. As well, other factors could affect the success of your project, such as geography (work must be conducted in certain locations) or language (it can be pretty tough to run that project in Montreal if no one on the team speaks French).

- **Time.** Time limitations are the most common parameters, though not all the time constraints are thoroughly thought through, which can expose the project to a sudden, unfortunate rush to meet a deadline. The timing parameters I see most often are:
  - Internal meeting dates such as board meetings, sales meetings, and internal launch meetings
  - External meeting dates such as investors meetings, regulatory agency meetings, or presentations to a customer
  - Launch dates for new products, services, or programs
  - Fiscal calendar dates such as close of the quarter or close of the year
  - Vacations, holidays, and other events that will make key personnel unavailable
  - Timing of other tasks in the overall project such as information that is not available until a certain time or another project that is waiting for the output from this initiative. For example, perhaps your software upgrade project can't start until everyone in the finance department has been issued a new computer, or suppose that the labeling project that is critical to a June 15 product launch is waiting for the output of your linguistic analysis project.

- **People.** People limitations are less common, though they do happen; and if there is any way to wrestle them down in advance, your odds of successfully achieving your objectives go up. The most frequently encountered people parameters are:
  - People who should be kept informed, such as senior management, other departments, peers, and regulatory bodies.
  - People who should not be informed, such as personnel who may be affected by reorganization. (Generally I do not recommend opaqueness or secrecy as a part of any project, since it compromises trust and jeopardizes the long-term success of the initiative.)

- People who should be consulted for input during the course of the project, though including these people is not mandatory.
- People who will have access to the project team at will and who must be consulted during the course of the project.
- People whose approval is needed at various stages of the project or who will determine the project's effectiveness based on the indicators of success.
- People who are expected to be on the project team or available to be on the team as needed. I recommend a light touch on this one, particularly if you are bringing in a consultant, because you do not want to bias the approach by presuming which personnel the consultant will need from your organization. Once the consultant is chosen and the project begins, you will have the opportunity to ensure that the right stakeholders are on the team.

• **Money.** Money is always a touchy subject when it comes to consulting projects, and my position must be pretty clear by now: value and ROI, not cash, should determine whether or not to conduct a project and, in most cases, which consultant to choose. Nevertheless, sometimes you have unavoidable money parameters, and if that's the case, you are best off noting them up front rather than hiding them in hopes that it will all work out. The two money parameters tend to be:

- Budget limitations, which can happen if you have limited control over your budget and no ability to influence those who do have budget control
- Timing of cash flow, which is sometimes a concern for start-ups, small companies, and executives dealing with quarterly or annual budget cycles

What Is Not in the Context Document?

If you are thinking of the Context Document as if it's an RFP, you may be tempted to include information such as detailed specifications on how you expect the project to be done or expectations for how you want the consultant to work. Leave that out. Unless you are looking for an execution-oriented consultant to implement a comprehensive plan you have already developed, it is counterproductive to specify how the consultant should achieve your objectives. Even in the case of execution projects, leave your instructions at the level of "Here's what must be implemented" and avoid specifying how it should be implemented.

In other words, don't assume you know the best approach to achieving your objectives. Maybe you do and maybe you don't, but since you are hiring an expert, it's worth your while to let him tell you how he thinks the job should be done. If you disagree, you can always choose not to hire him or his firm! Suppose you are headed into open heart surgery; you may read a book about it in advance or download some explicit images from the Internet, but you're not going to give your surgeon instructions on how many sutures to put in place and tell her when, in the procedure, she should use suction. When you are talking with an advisor with decades of experience solving a particular problem, the same principle applies.

The Context Document is also not the place to put in contract structures or nail down fees. All of that will happen later, when you are negotiating the approach and the ultimate contract. For now, your intention is to arm prospective outside experts with all the information they will need to develop the optimal path for achieving your objectives.

The six areas above are the ones that work best for setting up conversations about your projects with consultants. Anything less delays the process or lowers your odds of success; anything more muddies the issues and, again, lowers your odds of success.

What Do You Do with Your Context Document?

At this point you should have in hand a single document that incorporates the six sections we went through above: Situation, Desired Outcomes, Indicators of Success, Perceived Risks, Value, and Parameters. What do you do with it? You send it to prospective consultants as a first step in getting the right outside expert to do an outstanding job on your project.

Good consultants will probably have questions, even if your Context Document is extremely well written. You have assumptions in there that the consultant will want to understand; if there are people parameters, the consultant will want to chat through the nuances. The best consultants will help you refine the document and position you for a higher risk-adjusted return.

In net, you have the perfect starting point for your discussions with outside experts. You can approach them knowing that you have fully thought through all the pieces that will inform their approach and that you have forestalled a great many of the issues that derail projects, create strife, and spawn disappointing results. In your bag of tools for achieving outstanding consulting gigs, the well-written Context Document is one of the most important and one you should take the time to master.

Summary

The old saying is that if you don't know where you're going, any road will do. Most client-consultant engagements start with only a vague idea of where they are going; no idea what time they're supposed to arrive; no speedometer, tachometer, odometer, windshield wipers, or spare tire; nary a look at the weather conditions; and little idea who is coming along. Other than that, they're off to a good start.

Too many consultants are happy to head out on the open road of your project without knowing the risks or the parameters that will affect success. They are quite happy to have clients without clear indicators of success, since that frees them to make up a few that fit what they deliver. By drawing up a thorough Context Document before you contact any consultants, you are setting the course for success from the outset and giving excellent consultants the freedom of a tightly written brief. You are also doubling the likelihood that you will select the right consulting firm and be ecstatic with the results it achieves.

You may find that top-notch consultants will help refine the Context Document, which is a great sign. Where do you find those top-notch consultants? That's what we'll turn to next, starting with eight questions that will guide you to the right outside expert.

Finding and Choosing the Right Consultant

Who's Our Partner?

Finding and Selecting Great Consultants

In This Chapter

Your goal is to find the consultant who will deliver the best results with the lowest risk of failure; however, separating the wheat from the chaff is no mean feat when it comes to consultants. In contrast to hiring an employee, where you can iron out any unwelcome surprises over time, there is little room to salvage the work of underperforming consultants brought in for a single situation. Does this mean you should undertake a long, complicated bidding process? No. Sometimes your hunt will require a single phone call. This chapter will show you how to find the right partner for your project.

Key concepts in Chapter 4 include the following:
- The triangle of trade-offs
- Characteristics of the right consultant
- Characteristics of the right approach
- The consortium model for finding consultants

Consulting Disasters

In 1993, FoxMeyer Drugs stood at $5 billion in revenue and was the fourth-largest distributor of pharmaceuticals in the United States. That year the company hired Andersen Consulting to lead an efficiency project leveraging new software at an expected project cost of $35 million. The initiative was a total disaster. Within three years FoxMeyer Drugs was bankrupt and eventually was sold to a competitor for a mere $80 million. According to Computergram International, among the primary factors in this astonishing collapse was the consulting team: "Although at the height of the project there were over 50 consultants at FoxMeyer, many of them were inexperienced and turnover was high." Thirty-five million dollars for an overblown team of inexperienced consultants not loyal to FoxMeyer! What's wrong with this picture?

Around the same time in Europe, McKinsey & Company advised Swissair to follow a "hunter" strategy that involved spending nearly $2 billion on smaller, floundering European airlines. The strategy backfired, and many believe it proved to be a major contributor to Swissair's eventual bankruptcy.

Websites that repel visitors, IT systems that do not perform as expected, corporate strategies that torpedo the company—the list of consulting disasters goes on and on. Hiring the wrong consultant can, indisputably, lead to disaster. Frighteningly, outright failures are only the tip of the iceberg. For every debacle, there are handfuls of projects that deliver poor results and dozens judged mediocre because the wrong consultant was brought on board. Consultants contest the blame for disappointing outcomes, and in many cases there is plenty of culpability to go around. If you hire a strategy consultant, who deserves rebuke when that consultant tosses recommendations over the wall to you and the implementation goes poorly? Similarly, if you employ the wrong type of consultant in the first place, such as a strategy consultant to take on implementation, you should hardly be surprised by substandard results.

Finding the right consulting firm and choosing among potential candidates is, therefore, one of the inflection points on a consulting project which will determine its ultimate success. Among the questions executives ask me, "How do I find the right consultant?" is the most common. The eight questions below will guide your search:

1. Do we want a diagnostician or an implementer?
2. What type of expertise will produce superior results?

3. Do we want fast, talented, or inexpensive?

4. What will the right consultant look like?

5. Where's our killer app?

6. How likely is success?

7. Is the ROI still acceptable?

8. Are they the real deal?

1. Do We Want a Diagnostician or an Implementer?

In Chapter 3, when you defined your objectives, you clarified whether the outcome of your project was a recommended decision, a recommended plan for implementation, or implementation of the plan. The first two outcomes require a diagnostician, and the third outcome requires an implementer.

The line between diagnosis and implementation can be blurry, and there's a direct correlation between implementation expertise and diagnostic bias, which makes your choice more complex. If you visit a neurosurgeon for advice on treating your frequent headaches, the likelihood that she'll advise neurosurgery is much higher than if you were to visit a neurologist, who might present surgery as one of a number of options. Your general practitioner might suggest you are dehydrated and leave surgery entirely out of the conversation. The same pattern of bias would occur if you sought advice about improving sales from experts in sales contests, sales force performance, and strategy (see Figure 4-1).

If the outcome of your project is a recommended decision, then the type of consultant you need is very clear: a diagnostician who specializes in the issue you are facing. If you are looking for a recommendation and a plan, then your choice is trickier because risk bias can enter the picture. *You must never hire a consultant to make a recommendation who has a vested interest in one possible decision* (see Figure 4-2). For instance, if you think of your sales improvement project as a series of decisions and plans that will be implemented, you can see that you never want to hire a consultant with an expertise in sales contests to help you determine how to increase sales. Similarly, never hire a consultant who promises to help you both make a decision and fully implement the decision no matter what the recommendation is. I call this type of consultant a chameleon—a firm that changes to fit the situation and claims to be able to do anything; you want to avoid chameleons at all costs.

Figure 4-1 Expertise and Diagnostic Bias

Figure 4-2 Project Flow and Consultant Bias

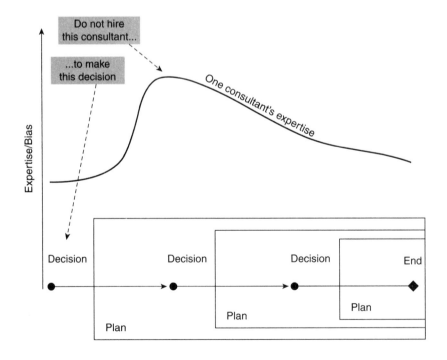

Unfortunately, consultants don't have a box on their website that proclaims, "I'm a diagnostician," with a clear indication of where in the process they start. Further, many consultants are so close to their practice that they don't understand where they fit in terms of decisions, plans, and implementation. As a result, experts may unintentionally mislead you about where they can help you most. The questions below will help you identify the right type of consultant and avoid chameleons.

- **What is your specialty?** If a consultant can't directly answer this question with some level of precision, turn and flee. Excellent consultants have a firm concept of what they do, and they won't spend time trying to fish for what you want before telling you their specialty. Even more important, they know what they don't do.

- **What do you deliver at the end of a typical project?** Another version of this question is, "How is a client typically better off at the end of your projects?" Consultants who recommend decisions will use words like *strategy* and *focus* and *overall direction*. Consultants who specialize in recommending or building a plan will often spontaneously break into song about their beloved processes. Implementation consultants will wax on about *efficiency* and *performance* and *flawless execution*. Chameleons will try to talk about whatever it seems like you want.

If you want a diagnostician *and* an implementer, you have three choices:

1. Reconcile yourself to an outstanding diagnosis with mediocre implementation.
2. Reconcile yourself to a biased diagnosis and outstanding implementation.
3. Hire two consultants and enjoy outstanding diagnosis and implementation.

Even though it may seem counterintuitive, you will usually generate a higher ROI, lower costs, and better results across the board by using two consultants on more narrowly scoped projects than one consultant from end to end. If you hire the consultants properly, there is no additional hassle or expense to find and manage the two experts.

2. What Type of Expertise Will Produce Superior Results?

Executives have a tendency to look for a specialist whose expertise closely matches their problem and situation. If you're a midsize software developer for the insurance industry and having problems with one of your technical supervisor's management style, who could be better than a consultant whose specialty is teaching management techniques to technical managers in midsize insurance software companies? Here's who: a consultant who has developed an extraordinarily effective approach to improving managers' performance; a consultant who has spent 25 years focusing on supervisors in knowledge industries and knows the solutions to the most common problems that position faces; or a teamwork ace whose lessons for personnel working under difficult bosses have resulted in huge boosts in morale and productivity among employees.

A consultant with breakthrough ideas, a superlative approach, or exceptional knowledge can deliver standout success where a run-of-the-mill consultant would produce humdrum results. You are better off searching for a consultant who has mastery of the *outcome* you are trying to achieve than one who has experience with your perceived situation.

There are five types of expertise you should evaluate to determine whether any consultants have superior insights that will dramatically improve your results: industry expertise, high-level process expertise, targeted process expertise, subject expertise, and reason-why expertise.

As an example, suppose you are a clothing distributor and you want to hire a consultant to redesign your website so that your online sales will increase. You could look for a consultancy that has a track record designing clothing websites, but any of the five consulting firms in Table 4-1 would set you on the path to better results.

You will find one of these outstanding consulting firms only if you identify the five types of expertise for your own project and search for breakthrough thinkers. Occasionally you will find a consultant that beats out the rest in two or more categories. When you know which types of expertise make the most difference to your outcome and which types are commonplace, you will be set to go on the hunt for your expert.

Industry experts are usually the least helpful unless you are specifically trying to learn more about your industry than you know already. In most cases, acquiring superior process or subject expertise will generate higher ROI than hiring an industry expert. More examples are provided in Table 4-2 to help you parse your own project into the five categories.

Table 4-1

Expertise	Outstanding Consultant
Industry	A firm on the leading edge of *fashion*; it is able to tell you months in advance the items that will produce bestsellers. You will have to redesign the site, but if you feature the clothing this consultant recommends, your sales will skyrocket.
High-level process	A consultancy with exceptional *design* expertise and sensibilities. Its aesthetic prowess has been applied to consumer products, book covers, and websites, with breathtaking results. You will still need website expertise to translate the firm's design ideas into a website.
Targeted process	A *website design* firm that has an innovative method for designing dynamically changing, "self-learning" websites. Your new, improved site will be online within two weeks of commencing the project, and the design will continuously update and optimize every day.
Subject	A firm that has totally mastered *website* effectiveness. The firm's breakthrough approach to researching traffic conversion has been leveraged across many industries with dramatic results. You will still need a designer who can apply the findings to your specific design.
Reason why	A firm with expertise in *online sales* that has saved companies millions of dollars and months of effort by pinpointing cases where search engine optimization, affiliate marketing, customer relationship management, or other alternatives will be far more effective than website redesign.

Table 4-2

Project	Industry	High-Level Process	Targeted Process	Subject	Reason Why
Decide if we should we close the Lexington plant	Sporting goods	Decision making	Plant evaluations	Plant closings	Cost reduction
Design a pen computer	Technology	Design	High-tech industrial design	Pen computing	Market penetration
Improve our buying group	Retail	Training	Negotiation training	Purchasing	Margin improvement

There is no right way to define each type of expertise for your project; use the five types as a thought starter for your consultant search.

3. Do We Want Fast, Talented, or Inexpensive?

The classic reply when you request someone to perform a service for you is "Do you want it fast, cheap, or good? Pick any two." In consulting projects, the same trade-offs apply (see Figure 4-3). Sometimes, speed is of the essence; and as long as a certain threshold of quality is met, the consultancy that can deliver soonest is your best choice almost regardless of cost. For instance, if you are racing to patent your new medicine, the opportunity cost incurred while you wait for the patent to be in place is so high that even a one-month improvement outweighs any likely difference in fees between one consulting firm and another.

More often, speed and quality are both important. Whereas it's very clear whether or not you get a patent, your decision on whether or not to close your plant in Lexington or whether or not to enter the oil market will be harder to judge. Each month you wait is costing you money. However, it's also important to reach the right conclusion; and therefore, the talent of the consultant becomes more important. As with the previous example, the benefits of getting the best solution as

Figure 4-3   Consultant Triangle of Trade-Offs

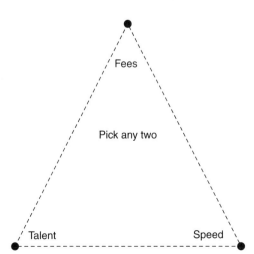

early as possible will typically outweigh any difference in fees between prospective consulting firms.

Occasionally you can set a minimum standard for speed and quality while you minimize fees. For instance, when you are going to distribute tchotchkes at the annual meeting displaying your mission, vision, and values, the firm you choose doesn't have to design handouts worthy of an art museum; any company that can deliver the products before the meeting will work fine. Therefore, you find a few firms that specialize in corporate knickknacks and negotiate the lowest fee. You may have noticed that fee tends to become more important when you are looking for implementation consultants than when you are looking for diagnosticians. The role that fees play and the amount you should pay are covered in more depth in Chapter 8.

4. What Will the Right Consultant Look Like?

Your goal while searching for the best consultant is twofold: (1) maximize the value of a successful project and (2) maximize the likelihood that your project will succeed. The characteristics of the consultant and the consultant's approach will both affect that goal. Therefore, you can construct a checklist of characteristics you are looking for before you start the hunt. The range of situations in which executives bring in outside resources is so vast that there is no single, best checklist; however, below are some of the most common factors to consider.

Characteristics of the Right Consultant

1. **Experience delivering your outcome.** The most important characteristic any consultant you are considering must possess is a track record of delivering your desired outcome. If you are trying to select new markets for growth, then your consultant must have proven successes in identifying lucrative expansion opportunities. If you are seeking expert advice on how to carve raw materials inventory out of your production process, then your consultant must be able to present materials-reduction plans that they developed on behalf of other clients. Otherwise, shoo them along to learn their trade on some other client's dime. You should insist on three case studies of results generated

by the *individual consultant(s)* who will be assigned to your project. You are looking for proof that the specific consultant with whom you will be working can deliver your outcome, not that the firm can.

Note that the consultant's experience in your *industry* isn't always necessary or, in many cases, even important. If your own experience in the industry is lacking, or industry knowledge and a successful outcome are inextricably linked, then industry experience may be required. However, executives tend to put more emphasis on industry experience than is warranted. Years ago the fiddler Charlie Daniels had a TV special, and one segment featured a duet with classical violin virtuoso Isaac Stern. Daniels may have possessed considerably more country music experience, but Stern's skill produced a far better performance. In consulting, as in music, virtuosity trumps familiarity with the genre.

You are looking for expertise in developing an outcome, and often that expertise transcends industries. For instance, a top-notch executive coach can improve the leadership skills of a Wall Street mogul and a Silicon Valley whiz kid with equal finesse.

2. **Willingness to push back.** Robin French, the division president of a global transportation company, speaks fondly of a project in which he had knock-down, drag-out fights with the consultant. "They would never leave a meeting in which there was disagreement between what they thought and what we thought until we hammered out our differences." He contrasted that to a failed project on which the consultant received instructions from the client at arm's length and was precluded from providing input into the project's direction. Robin's story is consistent with those of the dozens of CEOs, division presidents, and other senior executives I have interviewed.

Those discussions reveal that the most consistent characteristic among consultants who delivered successful, high-value projects is their ability to act like a peer rather than a vendor. As you saw in Chapter 1, the best consultants will even push back on whether or not your project is worth undertaking. You know you have the wrong candidate across the desk if he doesn't ask "Why?" when you are describing the project or doesn't suggest how you might improve your objectives, indicators of success, or valuation.

3. **High responsiveness.** Amazingly, some consultants can go AWOL for a week or more, leaving you hanging when some part of their solution is due. This happened on a project contracted by a restaurant chain that had hired a brilliant, but erratic, efficiency expert. While the consultant's work may have been exemplary, the company's inability to get in touch with the consultant and collect timely responses to important questions ultimately led the company to cancel the project at substantial cost. The best consulting firms rapidly return your phone calls and are dependably available to talk through your questions, suggestions, and concerns.

4. **Rapport.** For projects on which the consultants will be working closely with you or your organization, you must be comfortable enough with each other that you will accept their input and recommendations. You don't need to have matching patterns of communication or a desire to hit the pub together after work. In fact, contrary to the vast majority of literature on choosing consultants, you don't need to particularly like your consultants. However, you do need to respect them, you need to be willing to spend time with them creatively problem-solving, and, most importantly, their style cannot inhibit your organization's ability to hear, accept, and adopt their recommendations.

5. **Other, project-specific criteria.** Different types of projects may require very different, project-specific skills, capabilities, and characteristics. For instance, on a design project, you are probably looking for evidence of creativity and out-of-the-box thinking. Training projects may require attention to detail, an engaging on-stage personality, and superb listening skills. Prerequisites for your implementation project may be evidence of project management expertise and the ability to lead a far-flung team. Issues that have stymied your company may require a level of intellectual horsepower commensurate with the challenge. You may need the consultant to exhibit a certain level of gravitas to gain the respect of top executives across the company, or the consultant may need to have spent

time working "on the line" to gain the respect of your rank and file. Usually there are 5 to 10 project-specific characteristics such as the ones mentioned above that you will want on your checklist.

Characteristics of the Right Approach

1. **Optimal project flow.** There are two ways a project can flow: linearly or iteratively. Minutes before I started a grueling, five-hour, project-based exam my freshman year of college, the professor offered sage advice that has served me well throughout my career: "First succeed at passing the exam with a D, then add the components to make it a C and check that it works; then move to a B, then to an A. If you go for an A from the start, your project will never work and you'll fail the exam." Two hours later I walked out with an A, three extra hours to relax, and a new approach to projects: what I now call a *C2B2A approach,* which iteratively improves the outcome and often delivers superior value to the traditional, linear, "waterfall" approach.

A linear project, which is often proposed in formulaic solutions such as Lean, Six Sigma, or TQM, looks something like this:

1. Document the old process in mind-numbing detail.
2. Identify the issues in the old process.
3. Design phases for a new process.
4. Design the details for the new process.
5. Implement the whole thing as one giant project.
6. Hope it works.

In contrast, a C2B2A project searches for a solution that hits the minimum standards for success as rapidly as possible and then iterates through improvements until you achieve excellence (see Figure 4-4). The vast majority of projects, whether they are meant to deliver a recommended decision, a plan, or an implementation, deliver better results with some level of C2B2A iterations built in. However, C2B2A projects require a consultant who is willing to quickly present a mediocre

Figure 4-4   Linear Versus C2B2A Project Approach

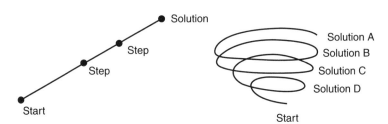

solution and improve on it with your team, rather than the typical consultant who wants to go away until she can present the perfect solution with a flourish and a "ta-da!"

2. **Optimal level of detail.** The approach in execution projects is generally very detailed, because you already have a plan in place. In these initiatives, the tasks, timing, and responsibilities should all be laid out at a granular level. Diagnosticians who are proposing to recommend a decision may also have a moderately detailed approach using a standardized method to arrive at the solution.

   In contrast, for those projects in which you want the consultant to develop a plan for resolving your issue, you will be better served by not requiring the expert to specify precisely, down to the task level, how he will tackle the project. While this may seem counterintuitive, these projects generally require the greatest flexibility in approach, which can be suppressed by a highly detailed project agreement. Projects that grant the consultant considerable latitude yield better results when the proposed approach is described with less specificity.

3. **Realistic assessment of requirements.** Particularly for implementation projects in which the organization will be required to change behaviors, look for a consultant who knows the likely hiccoughs and the right remedies. Consultants who suggest that your culture change initiative or strategic shift can be accomplished in little time with few problems may be looking through rose-colored glasses or trying to sell you on their optimism and (misplaced) confidence.

4. **Excellent change plan.** In addition, for implementation projects, look for an outstanding change management plan. Many of the characteristics of an excellent change plan are discussed in more depth in Chapters 10 and 11.

5. **Appropriate timelines.** Does the approach fit within your desired timing? On decision-recommendation and plan-development projects, superior consultants can often compress timetables to provide more value. Since energy on a project can quickly dissipate, you and the consultant need to create concrete progress quickly in order to maintain momentum. In contrast, for implementation projects, the best consultants may suggest your timelines are unrealistically short given the time it takes to make behavior changes stick.

6. **A long tail.** Does the approach guarantee that the consultants on your project will contribute ongoing advice and input substantially beyond the date they deliver their recommendations? For instance, does it include reviews and fine tuning by the consultant, at reasonable intervals, after the solution has been delivered? Say a consulting team is advising you on whether to enter the home healthcare market; does their proposal include a 6-month review of their recommendation? If a consultant has implemented a coaching program for your marketing directors, will she check in after the coaching is done at 6-, 9-, and 12-month intervals to ensure her handiwork remains in place?

7. **Backup plans.** The best approaches include a description of what the consultant will do if any important stage of the project does not go well, and this should look like more than, "We will do the exercise again until we get it right." Alas, few consultants risk including backup plans in their proposals for fear of looking as though they lack confidence in their approach. Therefore, it is incumbent upon you to ask the consultant to include backup plans. The topic of what can go wrong and what to put in place in advance is covered in depth in Chapters 6 and 7.

Table 4-3 presents a consultant evaluation checklist. You may also find ConsultantChoice™ software to be helpful for sorting among prospective providers. A free copy may be downloaded at http://davidafields.com/resources.

Table 4-3

Consultant Evaluation Checklist			
Consultant Name:	Rating of Consultants		
Characteristics			
Experience delivering desired outcome			
Willingness to push back			
Responsiveness			
Rapport			
Other:			
Other:			
Other:			
Other:			
Approach			
Linear vs. C2B2A approach			
Level of detail			
Understands requirements			
Excellent change plan			
Appropriate timelines			
Long tail			
Backup plans			

5. Where's Our Killer App?

There are six approaches to finding the right consulting firm, five of which are fairly well known and one of which is less common. All six are reviewed below along with their advantages and disadvantages.

Approach 1. Big, One-Stop Shop or Big-Name Consulting Firm

Plenty of executives go with a big consultancy, obviously, or else these firms wouldn't be big! They're easy to find, everyone knows their name, and they carry weight in the boardroom. The biggest advantage to a large consulting firm is that it can put a large number of personnel at your disposal quickly, often with desirable geographic dispersion. If your project requires a large team, which may be the case for implementation projects, then a large firm may represent a good solution. Large consulting firms typically have superlative project management capabilities; therefore, projects that are particularly complex, with a lot of moving parts, play to their strengths.

Large firms definitely have their place and can deliver very good results; however, as Chapter 5 will demonstrate in detail, you are generally better off finding a small firm that specializes in solving the problem you are facing or achieving the improvement to which you aspire.

Many larger firms claim that they are groups of specialists who have come together or work under one banner. Unfortunately, there is a significant problem of bias. Imagine a medical practice that combines a general practitioner with a cardiology group and a surgical center. The GP in that group is far more likely to point his patient toward the cardiologist than other specialists who might be as helpful or more helpful. The cardiologist who has a surgeon on the team is going to be biased toward surgery. Similarly, consulting firms that combine many different areas have financial interests that bias them toward recommending other parts of their own organization.

In addition, there is almost no way to effectively and efficiently combine a group of specialists covering high-level diagnosis, plan development, and implementation because the firm structure required to succeed looks entirely different for those types of consulting projects. When consultants combine everything into a one-stop shop, they end up with a structure that requires you to pay for unnecessary knowledge on implementation projects or unnecessary implementation staff on decision and plan projects.

At best, large firms will deliver marvelous expertise in one area married to merely satisfactory competence in other areas. Therefore, unless your project is particularly large or complex, stick with the smaller, independent firms. If your project is focused on only one of the three possible project outcomes (decision, plan, implementation), then find an independent consultant firm that excels at that outcome. If your project spans all three outcomes, you will do far better by using two best-in-class experts than going with a single, large, "end-to-end" company.

Approach 2. Do-It-Yourself Search for an Independent

This is by far the most common approach to finding consultants. The executive may ask around to find out whether her colleagues or friends have a recommendation and may do a search on the Internet. There are three circumstances in which this approach works well:

1. When someone you know used a consultancy for the same problem you are facing and recommends that consultancy to you

2. When excellence is not terribly important and good enough is okay (i.e., talent is the third priority on the triangle of trade-offs)

3. When it is painfully obvious that the consulting firm you find through this route can achieve your objectives with little or no risk

In my experience, one or more of the three conditions apply in about one-third of all projects, and searching for an independent yourself is the best route. More often, though, this approach will shortchange you and diminish project value. Most companies above a few million dollars in revenue hire executive recruiters to fill key positions and spend considerable time teaching their leaders how to manage internal employees. Yet these same companies try to locate and manage external talent themselves, even when the consultant's impact will far exceed that of one or two or a dozen individual employees. That's a cataclysmic mistake.

Your chances of finding an outstanding independent consulting firm on your own are slim (see Figure 4-5). Most great consultancies are well hidden. Their structure, inclinations, and poor marketing abilities conspire to make them difficult to find. For example, there is an extraordinary consulting firm on the West Coast that reduces SG&A (selling, general and administrative expenses) by 15 to 20 percent through a unique approach that involves suspending corporate culture for a short period of time. If you wanted to reduce your SG&A, how would you find this firm on your own?

It's unlikely that you or one of your colleagues knows the firm because it has worked with fewer than 50 clients. If you were to go onto the Internet and search for a consultant that reduces SG&A expenses, the firm would not appear on any of the first 10 pages of results. To add insult to injury, even if you stumbled upon the company, you wouldn't

Figure 4-5   Universe of Consultants

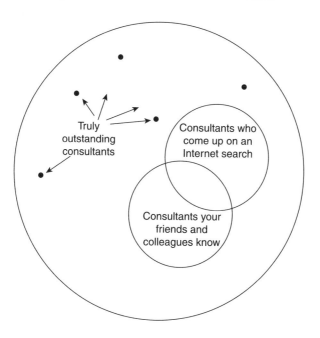

know you had because almost nothing in its materials reveals that it works exactly on your SG&A issue and that its approach is atypical and unusually effective.

A related search technique, which you should strive to avoid, is to recruit a wide range of consultants to present their approaches, from which you isolate the most common approach or the approach that you prefer and then bring in the consultant who has the best track record. This method starts with a limited pool of consultants that come up through a search, and then it introduces the executive's biases and generally includes very limited vetting of the chosen consultant. The results are usually mediocre or disappointing project outcomes.

Approach 3. Informal Consulting Network

The third approach is to tap into one of the growing number of networks of independent consulting firms that recommend one another for projects. In this method you call a consultant you know, who recommends another consultancy in the network. Presumably, good consultants will not associate with poor consultants, and by tapping into the consultants' network, you can avoid providers on the bottom end of the curve. Unfortunately, these groups have little-to-no quality control, and recommendations are based almost exclusively on familiarity and congeniality. No one is rejected on the basis of doing mediocre work because that would involve telling a friend his consultancy isn't good enough to be part of the gang.

These groups have not done any more extensive search to find the best consultants than you or your colleagues would have. In addition, they have a built-in expectation of reciprocity among their members. Thus, the excellent consultant you hired for customer segmentation recommends a sales training firm to you because that firm sent the consultant business another time. Friendships and reciprocal arrangements between consultants may be good for them, but it is certainly not in your best interest.

Approach 4. Clearinghouses

There are a few clearinghouses that have dozens, hundreds, or even thousands of consultants in their talent pool. One type claims it can match you to an outstanding consultant, whereas another type posts your project with the promise that a very wide range of experts will bid on it. Websites such as eLance.com, guru.com, lawyers.com, and similar online feeding places for independent contractors can be useful in a singular set of circumstances.

Specifically, one of these sites may work well for you if you run a small company and have very limited resources or if you are looking strictly for implementation and you are willing to put in the time it takes to sort through dozens of responses. If you are looking for any other type of consultant, however, to help you with a plan or a strategic decision, steer clear of this approach. There is virtually no quality control on these sites, and depending on the site, many of the contractors tend to be amateurs or professionals with very little experience. Although the clearinghouses may say there are strict standards for admittance into their group, I can assure you that the chief qualification is the ability to pay their dues.

Premier consultants typically do not belong to clearinghouses because job boards surface too few projects appropriately aligned to their narrow specialty. Further, their area of expertise is too powerful to be grouped with the generalists and mediocre performers who flock to clearinghouses. As a result, the consultants in these clearinghouses are like the students in the bottom half of their medical school graduating class. When they graduate, you still call them doctor, but ideally, they won't treat your family.

Approach 5. Consulting Brokers

Good consulting brokers work much like an executive recruiter, searching for excellent consulting firms that suit your specific needs. Their mission is to streamline your search process and reduce the risk of hiring a mediocre or poor consultant. On the upside, brokers can address the first challenge of working with independent consultants—finding an exceptional one. The best brokers will conduct an extensive search on your behalf to unearth the optimum firm, or if they specialize in a certain industry or function, they consistently stay on top of which consultants in their area are terrific for different types of assignments. For instance, a number of brokers specialize in the human resources function and constantly evaluate the consultants who target human resource issues.

Not only will good consulting brokers reduce the time it takes to find a consultant, but they will generally find a better consultant because finding is what they do. Rather than relying on the Rolodex of a few colleagues and an Internet search, they conduct a comprehensive search day in and day out—which gives them a far higher likelihood of finding a great consultant than were you to try on your own. The best brokers also carefully evaluate the consultants they present to you.

One red flag with brokers is that many of them operate similarly to clearinghouses, presenting any consultant who meets minimum standards and ponies up a representation fee. A second downside is that the brokers add to the cost of your project. As I have already suggested though, and will discuss more in later chapters, this concern should be low among your worries. If a broker adds 10 percent to the cost of your project, a mere 1 percent improvement in your outcome will more than cover the incremental cost.

The biggest concern with brokers, however, is that they don't help address any of the challenges of working with independent consultants, and in that way, they leave you no better off than if you found the consultant on your own. They are like the salesman who sells a budding ballerina a pair of ballet slippers. He can make sure the slippers fit well, but as for using them and looking graceful on the stage, the ballerina is on her own. If you've seen many aspiring Anna Pavlovas, you know that doesn't always work out so well.

Approach 6. The Consortium Model

The consulting consortium is a twist on the broker approach, set up to solve the challenges inherent in working with independent consultants. The consortium is an independent company that, like a broker, has developed a core competency in finding those few, remarkable consultants buried in the haystack of mediocre and poor providers. In addition, a consortium reduces project risk and commensurately increases the project's ROI by ensuring you are tackling the right project in the first place, then sticking with you to manage the challenges associated with independent consultants throughout the project.

Using a consortium is like having Wolfgang Puck in your kitchen. Not only will he help you plan your dinner menu; but while you prepare the meal, he will give you tips on how to perfectly caramelize the onions, and he'll stop you before you mistakenly add one tablespoon instead of one teaspoon of salt.

Let's go back to the example where you want to reduce your SG&A expenses, which is based on a real example from a division president of a retailer, whom we'll call Sarah. Since Sarah knew that conducting a search on her own was unlikely to turn up the best consultants in this space, she called Bill, a senior director at a consulting consortium, to find an expert in Lean who would aggressively tackle expenses.

The first thing Bill did was help Sarah structure her project optimally by fine-tuning her valuation, thoroughly exploring risks, and building an excellent Context Document. Sarah asked Bill to find someone to build a Lean-based plan for reducing expenses and implement that plan—in other words an implementer specializing in Lean. However, Bill revisited the objectives with Sarah, and they realized there were other, better ways to reach her SG&A goals than finding a Lean expert.

With Context Document in hand, Bill scanned his current stable of consultants, conducted a comprehensive search, and found ABC Associates, a little company in Oregon. ABC's tagline promising rapid, sustainable corporate earnings improvement belied the extraordinary process the company had developed for reducing SG&A. Other consulting firms that might have insisted their rigid approaches were perfect even though they were not quite right for Sarah's assignment never reached her radar.

Bill then helped Sarah develop an outstanding project structure and contract, presenting alternatives that dramatically increased her risk-adjusted ROI. The cost of the project was, admitted Sarah, higher than she originally anticipated; however, the expected return was reassuringly high, and she felt confident her dollars were well spent. The fixed-price fee structure Bill negotiated also seemed ideal for this type of project.

Since Sarah needed her executive committee's approval before launching the project, Bill worked behind the scenes with the owner of ABC Associates, revising his slides and working them into an easy-to-follow, compelling story for the executive committee. As Sarah put it, "It was questionable that ABC would have convinced the executive committee on its own—the original presentation was all over the map."

The SG&A project proceeded well, and Bill kept his fingers in the pie, making suggestions along the way and chipping in ideas from his experience. He was clearly not the expert—ABC Associates led the process—but he was able to add insights and acted as Sarah's surrogate on the project when she couldn't be there herself. Roughly a month into the project, ABC was struggling to keep up with the enormous flow of SG&A reduction efforts it generated. Bill quickly found a highly qualified, additional resource to handle the unanticipated workflow and added her to the team at no cost and without any change-in-scope negotiations required.

Twelve weeks after the project commenced, Sarah was able to present a 16 percent reduction in SG&A, which is more than any of them believed was possible. Bill's fingerprints were all over the final presentation, though he did not participate in the meetings. Sarah was, needless to say, delighted with the experience.

As you can see, the advantage of the consortium model is that it delivers the benefits of using independent consultants while managing the disadvantages. You get the powerhouse thinkers and better project designs, contracts, communication, presentations, and results. This approach enables you to employ cream-of-the-crop consultants without spending time futilely searching for them yourself. Consultants are recommended to you because they are the best, not because they are friends with someone or there is a reciprocal relationship in place.

The consortium's focus is on creating projects that deliver value every time, not on helping build any one consultant's practice. Surprisingly, a consortium doesn't necessarily add cost to a project since it often negotiates better contracts than executives would on their own. As a result, I believe the consortium model will emerge as the dominant way consultants are located, chosen, and brought in by sophisticated executives in the twenty-first century.

Table 4-4 summarizes the advantages and disadvantages of each of the six approaches.

6. How Likely Is Success?

Once you have identified one or more consultancies that specialize in the type of project you are embarking upon, boast the types of expertise needed to deliver superior results, and optimally balance expediency, talent, and cost, you should evaluate the likelihood that the participation of the consulting firm(s) will lead to a successful outcome. The fact is that a consultancy that delivers a slightly better chance of success for your project can easily be worth twice as much as another firm.

The topics of risk and likelihood of success are addressed in more depth in Chapter 6; however, even without turning to that section of the book, you can assign a good, subjective estimate to each consultancy's approach by asking yourself a few questions:

1. Intuitively, how strong does the consulting firm's solution look? On a 1-to-10 scale, how would you rate your confidence in its approach?

2. Is the complexity of the approach well matched to your situation? Is it sophisticated enough? Is it overly complex?

3. On a 1-to-10 scale, how well do you feel the consulting firm's approach applies to your specific situation?

4. Do the consultancy's case studies give strong evidence that it can succeed with your project?

After going through these prompts, use your intuition to develop an estimate of the likelihood each consulting firm will succeed. In most cases, this is going to be a highly subjective exercise. If you are using a

Table 4-4

Ways to Find Your Consultant

	Big-Name Firm	Search Yourself	Consulting Network	Clearinghouse	Broker	Consortium
Easy to find right consultant	●	○	○	◉	●	●
Highest-caliber talent	◉	○	○	◉	●	●
Large project team	●	○	○	○	○	●
Flexible capacity	●	○	○	○	○	●
Geographic coverage	●	○	○	○	○	●
Project management	●	○	○	○	○	●
Low cost	○	●	○	●	◉	◉
Quality control	●	○	○	○	○	●
Risk management	○	○	○	○	○	●

○ Poor   ◉ Mediocre   ● Excellent

broker or consortium partner to find the consultant, she can help you develop stronger estimates based on her experience.

7. Is the ROI Still Acceptable?

In many cases you will need to revise your valuation of the project based on the consultant's approach. The consultant may have compressed the timing or included methods that are easily ported to other divisions or add additional value in numerous other ways. Your estimate of success will also factor into the final valuation. Multiply your final valuation by the likelihood of success to calculate the risk-adjusted value of the project. When you compare the risk-adjusted value to the consulting fees, is the ROI still acceptable? As a general rule of thumb, when a consultant delivers greater than a 7-to-1 risk-adjusted ROI, you still have a strong project. This rule of thumb is discussed more in Chapter 8.

8. Are They the Real Deal?

Finally, ask for at least 10 references from the consultant. It is critical that those references be for the *specific consultant working on your project*, not for the consulting firm in general. You can be flexible on the number of references, but do not bend on those references being for the individual rather than the consultancy in general. A firm does not work on your project, and a firm's overall success is mostly irrelevant. The success of your project is dependent on the individuals doing the work. Pick 3 of the references from the list of 10 the firm provides and call them.

Don't skip this step! It probably won't change your mind on whether or not to use the consultant; however, it may surface important warning signs to keep in mind as the project progresses. If the consulting firm can't provide 10 references for the individual consultant, then reduce the likelihood of success and reevaluate that firm's attractiveness.

Summary

Your ability to find an outstanding consultant is a key contributor to your project's ultimate success. Many an initiative has generated disappointing results because the consultants didn't live up to their billing or promises. The information age has ushered in vast new opportunities to use superior experts, and at the same time, it has made finding those pearls immensely more difficult.

By understanding your project's trade-offs and the optimal consultant's characteristics and approach, you put yourself in a strong position to recognize the right experts when they cross your path. You can then set about the search for your perfect partner, turning to a consortium in most cases or a broker, an online clearinghouse, or a large firm in special circumstances.

If you are turning to a consortium, then your next step is to dive into risks or contracts and fees. However, if you are leaning toward hiring a large, well-known firm rather than an independent, you should be aware of why a small, independent firm is usually a better choice. The next chapter explains how the differences between large and small firms affect your project and, ultimately, the value the project will deliver.

Big or Small?

The Surprising Value of Independent Consultants

In This Chapter

The choice between a large consulting firm and a small one turns out to have a large bearing on most projects' outcome. This chapter delves into the pros and cons of different-size consultancies and addresses many of the concerns you may have about working with an obscure, boutique consulting firm.

Key concepts in Chapter 5 include the following:

- The knowledge economy
- The "apps" phenomenon
- Consultants' conflicting customers
- Small consultancy advantages
- Small consultancy drawbacks

From Big to Small

In August 2002, Donna, a division vice president at a global chemical company, reached out to a handful of consulting companies to contend for her new-markets initiative. Her broad, cross-functional project team invited three large, well-known consulting companies consistently staffed with the best and the brightest from elite business schools. In addition, Donna asked for proposals from a midsize firm with an excellent reputation that was headquartered nearby and from an obscure, boutique firm recommended by executives from a sister division that had undertaken a similar project the year before. After two rounds of interviews and four weeks of negotiations, Donna and her team selected one of the big guns to be their consulting team. The project kicked off on October 8 with a meeting attended by all the internal team members and the eight consultants who would be working the project.

However, on October 1, shortly before the project commenced, the company made some personnel shifts, and Matthew, a young, rapidly rising vice president of marketing, was asked to lead the new-markets project. Matthew, whose sunny disposition and ex-football player frame thinly veiled a no-nonsense, iron will to make progress, had different ideas on how the project should move forward. The day after the kickoff meeting, Matthew summarily dismissed the big-name consulting firm and brought the boutique consultancy in to lead the project with him. Why?

Why would a global company leave a well-known, highly respected consultancy to work with a small consulting firm no one on the team had ever heard of? Was the incumbent doing a poor job? No, the project was barely under way. Did someone at the big firm irritate a key figure? No, everyone liked the members of the consulting team just fine. Perhaps the small firm would do the work at a substantial discount; was that it? No, the boutique firm was actually charging *more* for the initiative. Maybe something fishy was going on—like Matthew was somehow related to one of the consultants at the boutique firm. No, that wasn't the case, either.

Matthew was surging up the corporate ladder for many good reasons. Among them was a solid understanding of why it usually makes more sense to use small, independent consultancies than megafirms in the twenty-first century. By the end of this chapter, you'll appreciate Matthew's knowledge; and like Matthew, you will most likely decide to set aside the famous, large companies in favor of small, laser-targeted consulting firms.

Defining Big and Small

There are no official guidelines on segmenting consulting companies, and different people may argue for different striations; however, for our purposes the definitions below will work well:

Small, Independent Consulting Firms

- **Solo.** This is a one-person shop. Sometimes individual consultants are truly working on their own, and sometimes they may have staff such as an administrator or an analyst. Either way, the consulting horsepower rests with a single individual.

- **Group.** A group is bigger than a solo firm, but it usually has fewer than 25 people in total. Of that number, a group may have 15 consultants, though more often it has only 3 or 4 consultants developing innovative intellectual property, with a team of analysts and implementers supporting them.

- **Boutique.** A boutique has 25 to 50 people in total. At this point, many firms begin to reflect a traditional hierarchy, with multiple levels of consultants in addition to support staff. Some boutique firms are the union of two or more groups, each of which is led by a breakthrough thinker.

Large Consulting Firms

- **Midsize.** A midsize firm consists of 50 to 150 people in total. While some may feel that a consultancy of this size is still a boutique, most firms of this size take on the same general organizational structure as larger firms. Since structure has a large bearing on value, firms of this size fit better in the "large" bucket.

- **Big.** This is a firm that employs 150 to 500 people. A big consulting firm usually has many partners, many levels of consultants, and multiple locations. The locations may or may not be in

Table 5-1

Number of Firms by Size		
Firm Type (No. of Personnel)	Management Consulting Firms	All Advisory Firms
Solo (1+ staff)	85,862	493,595
Group (2–25)	12,536	130,181
Boutique (25–50)	1,611	16,445
Midsize (50–150)	1,066	10,414
Big (150–500)	452	3,962
Mega (500+)	415	2,981

multiple countries, and the firm may not be widely known outside its area of expertise.

- **Mega.** A megafirm has more than 500 people. Some of these consultancies have 10,000 people or more scattered across the globe. They have well-recognized names and generally consult on a wide range of problems.

The important split is between the three small types and the three large types of firms. Throughout the book, the terms *large firms, big firms,* or *megafirms* are used interchangeably to mean any of the three large sizes. Unsurprisingly, there are almost 50 times as many small consultancies as large consultancies. Table 5-1 shows how many of each type of firm there are in the United States based on the latest economic census.

Big or Small?

In general, you should turn to small, independent consultancies when you are looking for the best thinkers, and you should consider larger firms if you need a battalion of doers. For decades, the largest, most well-known consulting firms have been considered the best solution (if you could afford their steep fees). While that may have been the case in the past, it is no longer true. A small, independent consulting firm should be your first choice on most projects.

Am I suggesting that large firms deliver shoddy work or don't utilize good approaches? Not at all! The top consulting firms are staffed with extremely smart, conscientious professionals who perform at a high level. Their processes, in particular, can be excellent, and their employees are well trained. In net, they deliver very good work. But you can contract better than "very good." By turning to the right small consultancy, you will enjoy outstanding results and phenomenal value.

If you are already convinced that independents are your go-to consulting choice, jump to the next section; however, if you are skeptical, consider the following five factors that support the benefits of independents.

1. The Knowledge Economy

The industrial revolution of the eighteenth and nineteenth centuries shifted us from an agrarian economy to a production economy. Much of the way we live is still rooted in that production landscape. However, the past two to three decades have ushered us into a knowledge-driven economy, a seismic shift on par with the industrial revolution What does that mean for you as you consider different consultants? Everything. The design of large consulting companies is most effective in a production economy, not a knowledge economy.

In a production economy, economies of scale were a key driver of success. Integrating vertically and aggregating a wide range of capabilities paid handsomely. Better products could be produced for lower prices, and everyone was a winner. In contrast, there are few economies of scale in knowledge. Whereas the paper industry kept on building bigger mills to lower production costs, knowledge companies can't just build bigger brains. Five hundred mediocre strategists do not have better ideas than a solo strategic genius. They just reach more people with their mediocre ideas. Moreover, thanks to technology, one person can now conduct virtual workshops with hundreds or even thousands of participants (see Figure 5-1).

Collecting a wide range of related manufacturing capabilities under one roof suits a production economy, which, after all, is why assembly lines work. In contrast, owning intellectual expertise in a wide range of specialized areas amounts to buying expensive, nonscalable knowledge machines. Each person in the company is an asset who must be utilized fully to guarantee the greatest profit. Therefore, when you are talking to

Figure 5-1 Strength in Numbers?

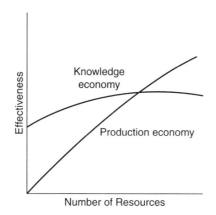

one of the big consulting firms, remember that a huge conglomeration of consultants takes on all the risk of idle assets without a commensurate gain in efficiency. In the knowledge economy it is far more efficient to maintain expertise in many places, where it can be tapped into only when needed.

2. Rising Entrepreneurialism

Mention the term *corporate man*, and most people will describe the stereotype of 1970s IBM salesmen: men in blue suits, starched white shirts, dark ties, and fedoras, working consistently long hours over a 30-year career at Big Blue. Today, employees are not seeking long-term relationships with employers. Median job tenure has plummeted below five years, meaning a typical employee will work for six to seven companies over the course of a career.

Succeeding in a giant corporation takes different talents than those needed to succeed in a small firm, and large businesses don't comfortably house big thinkers chasing autonomy. There are, of course, exceptionally bright people in large corporations; nevertheless, breakthrough thinkers generally eschew corporate environments. Whereas the corporate man brilliantly works the system, individualists reshape systems to fit their brilliance. Their high level of variation, instability, and unpredictability is simply untenable within a large company.

Figure 5-2   Who Is Published by *Harvard Business Review*?

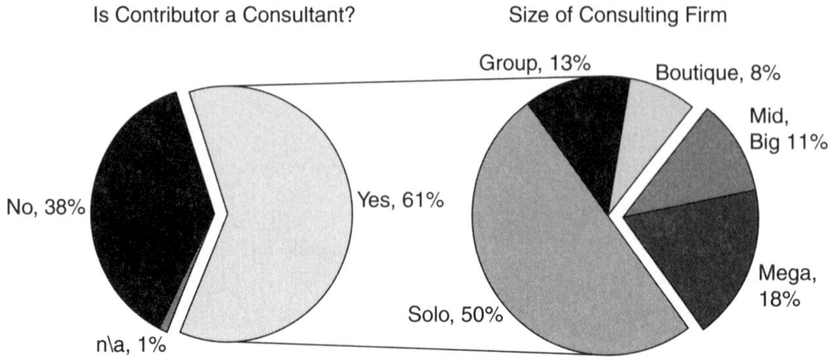

To test this proposition, I turned to the *Harvard Business Review*, which is a bastion of thought leadership and is widely considered the ultimate propagator of powerful new business approaches. Many broadly adopted ideas first surfaced in this venerable publication, from Ansoff's Matrix in 1957 to Blue-Ocean Strategy in 1997. Where does all this thought leadership come from? Are the authors of articles in the *Harvard Business Review* from the large consulting companies that profess to have the world's finest talent? No. In fact, quite the opposite is true, as is evident in Figure 5-2.

Over 70 percent of the contributors to *Harvard Business Review* during the 12-month stretch I reviewed[1] hail from small, independent consulting firms. Fully half of these thought leaders are in solo consultancies. By contrast, only 18 percent of the contributors come from big-name megaconsultancies. The evidence suggests you find the groundbreaking ideas in small firms.

The biggest names in innovative thinking regularly leave the confines of the large firms to form their own groups. Examples include Tom Peters (author of *In Search of Excellence* after leaving McKinsey & Co.) and Clayton Christensen (author of *Innovator's Dilemma* after leaving Boston Consulting Group). Other gurus whose thinking has shaped the business environment never joined large consulting companies at all: Peter Drucker (*Drucker on Management*), Michael Hammer (*Reengineering the Corporation*), and Stephen Covey (*Seven Habits of Highly Effective People*), to name just a few.

3. The Apps Phenomenon

As of this writing, Apple has sold close to 100 million iPhones. This ingenious device has transformed daily living. People are awakened by their iPhone (or iTouch) first thing in the morning. A couple of deft finger moves reveal the morning news, e-mails that came in overnight, changes in the stock market, the day's travel plans, scheduled meetings, the weather, and on and on.

While the technology, form factor, and usability are all important elements in Apple's success, the true core of the iPhone's power is its 1 million+ apps. There is an app for virtually anything you can imagine doing that involves some kind of data—be it written, visual, or audio.

Big companies are not the source of most of those apps. An app can be written by anyone who knows the coding, and a lone programmer in a Mongolian yurt can easily defeat the legions at Microsoft. The best execution of a good idea wins. Company size no longer matters. Talent overshadows scale, and that talent can be anywhere in the world.

The same fundamental shift has occurred in the world of consulting, for largely the same reason. Thanks to new technology, breakthrough thinkers in independent firms can be tapped just as easily as large firms. Consultants are the business version of apps. The best ideas win out. Corporations are no longer forced to turn to megafirms to access talent.

Not long ago, the executive team at a Boston-based company wanted to meet an independent expert in strategic account management. Unfortunately, on the day the executive team was scheduled to get together, the consultant was in Greece running a meeting with another client. After his meeting ended in Greece, he and the executive team each went to a nearby Cisco Tele-Presence facility, and they held the meeting as if everyone were in the same room. It made no difference that the consultant ran a tiny firm and was in a meeting halfway around the world. He was, metaphorically, the best app, so he won the business.

4. Access to the Expert

The amount of value you get from a consulting project depends a great deal on the individuals who are on your consulting team. To achieve peak results, you must staff your team with the expert who has the best command of the processes that will be utilized in your initiative.

In theory, golf is a pretty simple game based on a single process: hitting a small white ball with a club. Anyone who has spent much time on the links is painfully aware of how tough that process is to master. Golfing greats Tiger Woods, Phil Mickelson, Ernie Els, and Greg Norman have all mastered the sport. Do you know what they have in common? A man named Butch Harmon has coached them all. All four reached the pinnacle of their sport by using him and other coaches to continually improve their process. Thousands of hours of practice and a continually improving process separate champions from duffers.

Butch Harmon has written at least two books on playing golf, and he has capably laid out his process for playing well without holding back any critical pieces or secrets. Do the very best golfers settle for reading the book? Of course they don't. They go to the source, because that's where the power resides. Similarly, your best bet is to work with the person who developed or specializes in the approach you need on your project.

A large company with an outstanding idea or process must migrate that thinking across the organization. The organization must be taught over a long period of time, and the process will necessarily be implemented with varying levels of proficiency. When you bring in an independent, on the other hand, you are working with the top thinker, the person who knows the process inside and out—and who knows how to apply it. The difference is appreciable (see Figure 5-3).

Figure 5-3 Your Consultant's Grasp of the Big Idea

If a new, better process comes along, you can choose the consultant who devised that new process. Big consulting companies, on the other hand, naturally resist new ideas because they are still in the process of adopting (and selling) the previous way of solving a problem. The consultants you encounter from large firms are a long way from the original source of thinking on the approaches they will attempt to apply. They do not have the same depth of knowledge and understanding. It's like working with an apprentice to an apprentice to Butch Harmon.

5. Your Goals Versus Consultants' Goals

Young consultants at large consultancies have the same goal as other ubersmart, aggressive, talented businesspeople: to rise quickly in the organization. Their key to rapid advancement is the same as in most other companies: pleasing the boss. Ideally, the consultants would make their manager happy by delighting you. However, the reality is that the manager is rewarded based on a number of factors, including how hard consultants on his team work (i.e., the number of hours), how well new consultants are picking up the corporate processes they're supposed to be learning and implementing, and how well they are exhibiting other behaviors that will mark them for advancement. While the success of your project and your satisfaction are definitely in the picture, they're far from the only driving forces in the consultants' success.

As you continue up the chain of management at the large consulting firm, each consultant's customer is the higher-level person handing out raises, promotions, and bonuses. That person is never you. In addition to his work for you, the manager on your project is evaluated on how well he manages his team, how well he develops people and coordinates resources, and so forth. These are good qualities, but they're not solely directed at creating phenomenal value for you.

In contrast, when you are working with a solo consultant or one of the owners of a small consulting firm, she only has one way to succeed and grow: by making her *clients* happy. If she does a good job for you, you'll use her again, recommend her to others, or both. Your success and her success can be 100 percent aligned, particularly if you structure the project correctly. (See Figure 5-4.)

Large consulting firms are also structured like traditional production companies, with militaristic hierarchies. Smart, inexperienced talent enters at the bottom. Often the consultants in this layer of the

Figure 5-4   Your Consultant's Customer

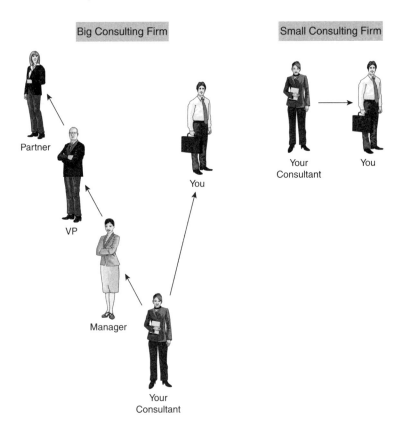

organization are hired right out of business school, though sometimes they have spent a few years at a corporate job. They apply their high intellect with an unfocused, undisciplined, inexperienced hand on clients during their early years while learning the ropes from the more senior consultants on the team. Who is paying for this learning experience? You, the client. Who is it benefiting? The consulting company.

Since the megafirm brings in rafts of these junior personnel, it has to cover their salaries. Just as airlines know that any empty seats on an airplane are wasted assets, consulting firms know that any day a consultant doesn't have every working hour filled by a project, they have underutilized their expensive investment. As a result, the most important metrics at megafirms are utilization and productivity, just like at any other manufacturing company. Similarly, to be efficient the megafirm must deploy its assets whenever possible, whether or not that deployment is in the best interest of the client.

The team of supersmart, talented individuals that the megafirm wants to put on your project was not carefully selected based on each consultant's expertise in the process you need; nor were the team members chosen because of their proven ability to implement that process in situations like yours. Most of them were selected because they had extra capacity and the firm needed to assign them to the next project that came up. Whoops, that's yours!

When Big Is Better

For all the reasons above, as well as the advantages covered in Chapter 4, a small, independent consulting firm should be your first choice on most projects. However, small consultants do come with their own set of drawbacks, three of which will point you back to a large firm.

Drawback 1. Small Consultancies Lack Cachet

There is no denying that in most cases small consulting firms do not have the prestige associated with "brand-name" consultancies that are frequently seen in the boardroom. There are certainly exceptions—what senior executive has not heard of Jim Collins, Clayton Christensen, or Ken Blanchard, all of whom have small consulting firms? Nevertheless, if having a big name in your corner is more important than achieving the best possible results, a small consultancy may not fit the bill for you.

Drawback 2. Small Consultancies Lack the Project Management Expertise and Dedicated Project Managers Found in Large Consultancies

One area where the large consultancies are definitely superior to most small firms is project management. They have personnel whose primary expertise is in project management and who have extensive experience coordinating large projects with many moving parts. Without question, it takes a certain type of person to look at a project map with

1,500 hundred tasks on it, gather information from people working on disparate parts of the plan, and update the progress week after week. Those people are usually not found inside a solo or boutique firm.

Therefore, for execution-oriented projects that require superlative project management skills and that encompass a large number of moving parts, a large consulting firm may outperform its smaller competitors.

Drawback 3. Small Consultancies Have Limited Capacity and Limited Geographic Reach

An outside expert's prowess is of little value if you cannot avail yourself of his talent because he is fully booked. For instance, there is a phenomenal executive recruiter in Connecticut who specializes in finding senior executives to run firms owned by private equity firms. Her results, measured by the long-term success of the people she places, are far superior to those of the large recruiting firms. However, she operates on her own, and she takes on fewer than a dozen assignments each year. A prospective client who hesitates when she says she has availability will often lose the opportunity to work with her for months.

You may love an independent consultancy's cutting-edge approach; however, it may lack the resources to apply its solution to all seven divisions of your company in the time frame you want. Similarly, some implementation projects encompass a very broad scope, particularly if the implementation covers a wide range of geographies or requires an enormous number of tasks to be completed concurrently. IT implementation projects where multiple, on-site adjustments are required or where numerous components must be coded in parallel are a good example. While the Internet and emerging technology such as web conferencing have improved small consultants' ability to operate remotely, for huge, widespread implementation projects, large firms have a distinct advantage, and they are often the best choice. As mentioned earlier, small consultancies are the best choice to find thinkers, and larger firms may be preferable when the project requires a legion of doers.

Dismissible Concerns

Two concerns executives express about small consultancies can be dismissed fairly easily:

Dismissible Concern 1. How Can Small Consultancies Match the Big Firms' Raw Horsepower?

Some executives lean toward large consulting firms on the premise that their consultants, hired from Harvard, Wharton, Stanford, and other elite schools, must surely be smarter (and more effective) than the consultants with less impressive pedigrees populating small firms. This is a false challenge based on a spurious assumption. Earlier in the chapter, I discussed why top talent has fled megafirms to found small, independent firms. Even were that not the case, as an experienced executive you have doubtless found that an A student from a second-tier university consistently outperforms a B or C student from one of the country's top schools. Enthusiasm, dedication, and attention win over raw horsepower in most cases. With small firms you can get the smartest and the best attitude in one package.

Dismissible Concern 2. A Small Consultancy May Not Be Around in Five Years (or at the End of the Project)

Some executives have a bias against small vendors, be they consultants or any other small firm, because of worries about the company's longevity. Since Dell has been around for years, you are confident it will stand behind its computers, but what about Eagle Computers? If the computer malfunctions in a year, will there be any support? Similarly, on the consulting side, you can be confident that Booz Allen, with a century of history, will be around to service the long tail on your project, but will Rinkydink Associates still be in business to fine-tune its plan as you go through the rollout process?

The first answer to this concern is to select an outside expert with proven success over a number of years. Successful consultants who are making money at their craft and steadily acquiring repeat business are unlikely to disappear anytime soon. The second answer if you have this concern is to rethink your approach to entering into business relationships. The demise of Arthur Andersen and Lehman Brothers shows that any size firm can suddenly disappear; therefore, choose the best consultant based on the firm's track record and move forward with confidence.

Working Through Consultant Challenges

Executives frequently encounter a number of other challenges when hiring a consulting firm, some of which are more pronounced in small consultancies, while others are equally problematic in large and small firms. Across the board, these issues can be addressed by turning to a consulting consortium that specializes in building outstanding projects, finding the best consultancies, and working with you across the duration of the project to ensure success.

Challenge 1. The Best Small Consultancies Are Difficult to Find

Finding the best consulting firm for your project—the one that will give you exceptional results and outstanding risk-adjusted return— is definitely a needle-in-a-haystack quandary. There are over 100,000 small management consulting firms, and the majority of them are either chameleons, whom you want to avoid for any project, or mediocre performers who will do a perfectly fine job but won't deliver outstanding risk-adjusted ROI. Even if you are looking for a specialty consultant, your pool of prospective providers contains hundreds of candidates. One or two or, at most, five of these firms are at the level you should be seeking, the ones that are going to give you a breakthrough or best-in-class result with at least a 7-to-1 risk-adjusted ROI (see Figure 5-5).

As if the numbers weren't daunting enough, the problem of finding outstanding small consulting firms is exacerbated by the unfortunate fact that most of them are poor marketers. They are not trying actively to stay hidden, but neither do they have the skill sets, marketing departments, or assets to become well known.

Figure 5-5 The Consultants You Want

You can overcome this challenge by turning to consulting brokers or to consortiums.

Challenge 2. Small Consultants Are Sometimes Harder to Work with Because They Are Not as Professionally Managed as Big Firms

It turns out that the nonconformist geniuses who didn't fit well into the button-down, traditional company environment are just as difficult to deal with when they are hired hands rather than permanent employees. For instance, when a brilliant but bullheaded streamlining expert engaged by a Midwest food producer resisted his client's requests for a fourth time, the exasperated executive canceled the project and grew bitter about consultants in general.

One possible response to this concern is to screen for cultural fit when you are interviewing prospective consultants. In some cases, this may preclude you from going with the best and brightest or arriving at the optimal outcomes; however, your projects will be less stressful and painful to manage. A second possible response is to grin and bear it; i.e., select consultants based on the power of their ideas, deal with their less-than-ideal behavior, and thank your lucky stars that they aren't permanent employees.

The third possible response, which is usually your best course, is to tap into an intermediary who straddles your world and the consultant's. These intermediaries, who are not on your staff full-time, yet understand the language and dynamics of your corporate culture, can be found in consortiums. In fact, the presence of these professional project leaders is one of the major benefits of the consortium model and part of why consortiums will become more and more prevalent.

Challenge 3. Small Consultancies Don't Communicate Their Ideas Well

Unfortunately, the world of powerful thinkers is populated by individuals whose expertise is so deep in their area of specialty that they struggle to put their ideas into terms that everyday businesspeople understand. Similarly, when project meetings are held, adjustments are made, ideas and recommendations are batted around, and problems are addressed, these interactions require excellent communication skills that can be lacking in consultants whose focus is in an area of expertise, not team leadership.

A senior executive at one large company recounted his experience with a boutique consulting firm brought in to tackle the company's reorganization. The consultants were whip smart and had an impressive track record to bolster their quality assertions. However, within days of starting the engagement, they publically announced that most of the vice presidents in the organization were "stupid and should never have been put in their jobs." Morale across the company plummeted, and the best employees started jumping ship to competitors. This type of blundering is fairly common with wildly smart people whose soft skills tend to be weak.

The communication challenge is very similar to the previous concern with professionalism in its cause and solution. Once again, the consortium model will help you overcome the limitations of a small consultancy while enjoying the advantages of its powerful thinking and laser-targeted skill set.

Challenge 4. Consultants Large and Small Suffer from "Problem Myopia" and Process Rigidity

Setting chameleons aside, most consultants have a solution they deliver and a proven process or approach to delivering that solution. Metaphorically, their solution is attaching one thing to another, and their process is a hammer and nail. As a result they develop the myopic view that companies face only two types of problems: the problem of attaching things (which can be solved with a large enough nail and a well-wielded hammer) and everything else.

To a sales training company, the range of problems that can be solved via sales training is extremely wide. Its consultants know that morale problems, flagging market share, and late deliveries could each be resolved by the right type of sales training. Rarely will those consultants admit you are headed in the wrong direction entirely and advise you that, instead of hiring a sales trainer, you should address your organizational design, fix your product and your message, or solve the operations problem on your hands.

Most consultants follow the process they employed in the previous three engagements that went well because it is "proven" and because, more importantly, they are invested in it; however, that process may not be best for your particular situation. In addition, many projects face a significant, midcourse twist that changes how the consultant should work. Will a carpenter in love with his hammer and nail even recognize his bias when a screw and cordless drill would be more effective?

The first step in bypassing these challenges is thoroughly defining your project objectives and the indicators of success. If you are very clear on what success looks like, then it will be easier to see whether a hammer and nail will do the trick or whether a paintbrush is a better answer. As with the other challenges in this section, the consortium provides another option for addressing the issue. Since a consortium's focus is on defining the need and then finding the best consultant, its expertise is in seeing the world as it is, not as a problem in search of the consultant's solution. A consortium will tell you when you need an organizational design expert rather than a sales trainer.

Challenge 5. Small Consultancies Have Limited Capabilities

The advantage of a small consultancy often resides in its unique, high-power solution developed over many years and projects. On the flip side, its solution is typically very narrow, and the breadth of its strengths is limited. When a West Coast fabric company sought outside advice on whether to outsource a portion of its weaving operations, the company found a perfect consultancy to provide counsel. However, that consulting firm had to stretch when the project morphed into a vendor selection exercise, and it was totally out of its depth when integration expertise was required.

Scope evolves and shifts on most projects. In an ideal situation, you would be able to switch out one expert for another if your needs changed dramatically. One solution is to stick with a large firm that has mediocre performers across the full range of issues you may face; however, a better solution is to work with a provider that can access the best independent consultants in the world but is not beholden to any of them. In this model, your provider ensures you always have superlative talent on your project even if your needs alter dramatically.

Challenge 6. Consultants Can Be Too Theoretical Rather Than Practical

One of the common complaints about big-name consulting firms is that their solutions sound good in theory but don't work well in reality. The same holds true for many small, independent consultancies too, though often for a different reason. Many of the big-name firms hire the best and the brightest directly from graduate school. These young consultants receive their practical training on the job, through working on client projects. The fact is, you don't know what it's like to be in a pool if all you do is dip your hand in and read the temperature. Consultants who have not lived through the business problem they are solving are working on theory, and their solutions often don't survive a confrontation with reality.

In the world of independents, you will most often find consultants who have spent many years in corporations and have lived with their recommendations when they were on the executive's side of the desk. However, that doesn't mean their great ideas always work, particularly in the realm of breakthrough thinking, where many of the best consultants can be found. On the one hand, you want a consultant with game-changing ideas that will exceed your expectations and help you leapfrog the competition. On the other hand, you want solutions that have survived the crucible of real-world application across numerous client situations.

In other words, you want the cure for cancer but you don't want to be the guinea pig on which a new drug is tested. That is, indeed, a challenge. The solution is to find those consultants whose breakthrough ideas are proven but not yet widely adopted. You want to be slightly ahead of the wave—but not so far ahead that you don't know if it's big enough to carry you and not riding the crest along with your competitors.

Challenge 7. Very Few Consultants, Large or Small, Manage Project Risk

Every consulting project comes with a wide range of risks, most of which are poorly recognized and even more poorly managed. The next two chapters of this book give you techniques for managing risk in a way that gives an enormous boost to the value of your projects. Unfortunately, at this point very few consulting firms, big or small, know these techniques, which means you bear the entire burden of understanding and applying the concepts well.

I anticipate that large firms and consortiums will start adopting project risk management techniques earlier and more broadly than small firms. In a few years you may be able to overcome the project risk management challenge by turning back to the large firms if you are willing to accept their many disadvantages. Your other choice is to partner with an expert in project risk management, who is most likely to be found at a consortium.

Summary

One of the choices most executives struggle with is whether to hire a large, well-known firm or a boutique firm that has less of a reputation but, potentially, a more innovative solution. In the vast majority of cases, you stand to enjoy a better outcome and a higher ROI by working with a small consulting firm. The exceptions to this rule are large implementation projects, particularly those that require best-in-class project management skills or demand broad, geographic representation.

It's unlikely that you are going to dismiss a consultant a few days into a project, like Matthew did at the chemical company; however, if you do follow in his footsteps, you'll tread with full understanding of the benefits. Whether you choose a small firm or a large firm, consultants walk through your doors carrying a host of challenges that you must manage in order to maximize your value. Many of these challenges are best handled by turning to a consortium, as described in the previous chapter.

One set of challenges in particular, managing project risk, is understood by very few consultants; yet it holds the promise to dramatically increase the expected value of your projects. The next two chapters explore project risk and the opportunity it presents for you when you hire consultants.

Risk, Fees, and Contracts

What Could Go Wrong?

Reducing Risk

In This Chapter

This is the first of two chapters dealing specifically with risk. Both chapters build on the pioneering work of Bob Endres and his company, Synaptic Decisions. Bob opened my eyes to two business-changing concepts: (1) risk is embedded in contracts, and the allocation and valuation of that risk is largely overlooked, and (2) risk can be valued and reallocated by cleverly introducing variations during negotiation.

In this chapter, I outline the most common risks encountered in projects with coaches, consultants, trainers, and other outside experts, and I show you how to dramatically enhance the value of your projects by reducing the risk of something going wrong. One method of mitigating risk—namely, transferring the burden from you to the consultant—opens the door for sophisticated negotiations and is tackled in the following chapter.

Key concepts in Chapter 6 include:
- Risk-adjusted value and risk-adjusted cost
- What risks are important to consider
- The sources of risk
- How to mitigate risks

Tourist Attractions

If there is truth in the adage that every person has a unique ability that should be celebrated, then the geographic parallel is that every place has its own special features that should draw tourists. For residents of Bedford, Indiana, their town's distinction was obvious: Bedford is the limestone capital of the world. Armed with this precious honor and boundless passion, the town won a federal grant to start constructing a theme park dedicated to the wonders of limestone. Key attractions included a 95-foot-high limestone replica of the Great Pyramid of Cheops and an 800-foot-long likeness of the Great Wall of China. A mere $700,000 was poured (chopped?) into this project before rising concerns over the tourist pulling power of the park halted construction. Alas, the crumbling remains of the venue draw few visitors.

Funding a limestone theme park seems frivolous when the money could have been directed instead to an important scientific project—for instance, one that would allow scientists to replicate the big bang and gain awesome insight into the fundamental nature of the universe. Just such a project, called the Superconducting Super Collider (SSC), was conceived and started in the 1980s. The 54-mile particle-accelerator loop was projected to cost $4 billion to $5 billion, a hefty price tag, which nonetheless paled when held up against the untold benefits of scientific exploration, particularly during the cold war when scientific prowess and bragging rights were important national priorities.

The SSC was no small-town pipe dream. The project was studied for four years before site selection began, and even the Congressional Budget Office issued a 130-page report, replete with graphs, tables, and pie charts analyzing all aspects of the project. In 1993, a mere two years after breaking ground on the project, the cold war was over and the projected cost of the SSC had ballooned to over $12 billion. The project was canceled with only one-quarter of the loop completed and $2 billion irretrievably sunk into the ground. To add insult to indignity, fewer people visit the remains of the SSC than travel to the limestone debacle in Indiana. The site was sold for an estimated $6.5 million to a chemical company in 2012.[1]

Some projects rest on faulty assumptions at the outset. Others face a shifting landscape, changing priorities, or unexpected costs. No matter what the project, there are risks, many of which are well hidden, and the last thing you want on your hands is an embarrassing limestone theme park or an expensive-but-worthless aborted project.

What Could Go Wrong?

Consulting projects are risky.[2] A few risks are handled consistently and explicitly, such as when you safeguard your trade secrets by asking a consultant to sign a confidentiality agreement before you reveal sensitive information. The cost risk is virtually always front and center, though it is consistently mishandled because it hides dozens of other points of exposure. Other risks are ignored or come to the surface and are then inadequately addressed—for instance, when you ask the consultant how much of your internal staff's time the project will take and he gives a vague, comforting reply about minimizing the drain on your resources.

Whether you address the risks explicitly or never even think of them, one way or another they are embedded in your contract with the outside expert. Usually they are tied into your agreement through omission, rather than commission. To a large degree, that's fine. Negotiating and drawing up contracts would become totally unwieldy if you strived to address every possible risk explicitly. However, huge amounts of value are left on the table because important risks are not appropriately managed.

Risk-Adjusted Cost and Risk-Adjusted Value

Take a moment and write down the cost of a project you have under way or are considering.

Cost of project:_____

In your estimate you probably included the fees the consultant is charging, the nonconsulting expenses such as travel, and, perhaps, the prorated, fully loaded cost of the time your employees are dedicating to the project. Chances are you didn't include the fees for an expanded scope if the project turns out to be far more complex than you originally thought, the additional employee time in that same scenario, or the cost of extra stress and aggravation caused by midproject renegotiations. The key word in the costs you left out is *if*, which is a surefire indicator that a risk is involved.

Figure 6-1 Risk-Adjusted Cost

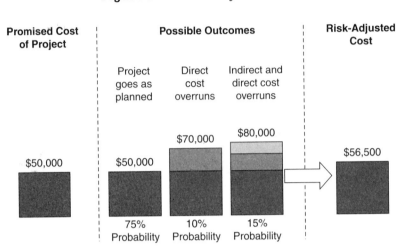

A better metric than cost is *risk-adjusted cost,* which incorporates other direct and indirect costs that could accrue to your project adjusted for the probability that they will occur (see Figure 6-1). Cost risks are squishy and tough to get a handle on; nevertheless, they may alter the success of your project.

Thinking of the same project as before, take a moment to write down the estimated value of the project:

Project value:_____

Since you read Chapter 1, you probably have a well-defined sense of the upside your project can deliver. You have included hard benefits and soft benefits, direct and indirect value. However, chances are you did not include the value of the project if it fails completely, the value if your initiative finishes a month or two behind schedule, or the opportunity lost if you had applied your resources to a better project. As with costs, the *if* indicates a risk you should be incorporating into your valuation of the project. The *risk-adjusted value* of a project incorporates the most likely and impactful risks (see Figure 6-2).

When you look at the value of a project with all the risks fully analyzed, you may decide the project isn't worth doing at all, or you may realize it has to be done much more urgently.

Figure 6-2   Illustration of Risk-Adjusted Value

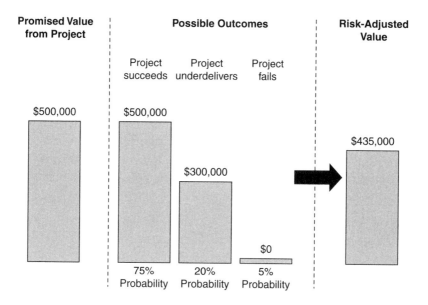

What Are Our Important Risks?

The operative word in this question is *important*. If you worry about every risk, no matter how remote and no matter how inconsequential the effects, you will paralyze yourself and stop every project before it even begins. Below I outline the most common risks, though there are certainly others you may encounter. As stated earlier in the previous footnote, for simplicity I have conflated causes and effects under the rubric of risk.

The Project Does Not Work

There is always a chance no tourists will flock to the limestone theme park. A succession plan may fall to pieces when a key individual leaves, a new approach might be rejected by your organization, or a consultant may not have the promised expertise to complete the project. For innumerable reasons, a project could fail partially or completely.

The Project Does Not Deliver the Expected Value

This is the risk that a project delivers against the objectives, but the value does not materialize. For instance, the cost reduction project reveals fewer savings opportunities than you had anticipated.

The Project Takes Too Long or Misses Key Dates

Often a strict timeline must be met, and the worry here is that, for one reason or another, the project fails to meet that timeline. Alternatively, the project may simply drag out, reducing the value significantly. An extra month's delay can mean tens of millions of dollars in lost profits for a pharmaceutical company introducing a new medicine.

The Project Is More Expensive Than Anticipated

If you have set up a budget for the project, there is always the chance that the costs will exceed that budget, which could be very uncomfortable for you. Similarly, the project may require more internal personnel resources than you anticipated. The causes of this problem range from underestimating the amount of data needed to underestimating travel costs to forgetting about some important hardware, just to name a few examples.

The Project Is Painful to Manage or Has Many Midproject Negotiations

Some projects and some consultants demand much more handholding than you expected—for example, when you feel like you are headed into revision after revision of a training presentation because the trainer just doesn't get what you're after. In addition to the extra resources this requires, these projects drain positive energy from the project.

The Project Becomes Irrelevant

Sometimes changes in the environment suddenly render an initiative irrelevant. The technology world presses this lesson upon us all the time. How do you think the team working on the latest generation of the Sony Walkman felt when Apple introduced the first iPod?

The Project Alienates Some Personnel

Personnel often leap off the company ship when some consultant is wreaking havoc. A disgruntled employee who was left out of the loop or treated poorly by a consultant may slow down or sabotage the project. Organizational acceptance is a constant risk that I address in more depth in Chapter 10.

The Project Makes You Look Bad

This brings many of the other risks to a personal level. If something goes awry in the project, it reflects poorly on the project's sponsors and leaders, regardless of assurances that failure is an unavoidable part of making forward progress.

Key Information Is Given to Competitors

If you are investing heavily to bring your manufacturing costs down, could your carefully designed processes, developed in tandem with the consultant, be introduced to your competitors? An inadvertent statement by your consultant might clue in a competitor.

The Project Scope Does Not Maximize Value

In the ERQuip example earlier in this book, the sales training project that the vice president originally requested would have delivered a fraction of the return that the larger, culture change project drove. Too broad a scope can be just as deleterious to value. One company I worked with wanted to identify markets affected by climate change. My immediate question was, "What market *isn't* affected by climate change?" There was no way to point the company to lucrative new markets quickly and for a reasonable fee until the scope was narrowed.

The Best Consultant Isn't Chosen or the Best Solution Isn't Delivered

Some solutions work, whereas others are truly outstanding. While Dogpile and Altavista suffice as Internet search engines, Google is, well, Google! There are certainly times when a good enough solution is all you need. More often, though, it pays substantial dividends to find the provider who is a breakthrough thinker or absolutely best in class within the area you need. Far too many companies underappreciate this risk, and it shows in their tepid performance.

Resources Could Have Been Utilized Elsewhere to Better Effect

This is the risk that you shouldn't have embarked upon the project at all because some other initiative would have provided a higher return. Alternatively, this can reflect a failure to dedicate internal and external resources where each will give the greatest results.

As you walk through the most common risks, pay particular attention to the likelihood of each risk and its level of impact. *Likelihood* is the probability that the risk will occur. *Level of impact* is how much it really matters if the risk occurs. In the checklist in Table 6-1, you can note a range of impacts and likelihoods. For quantitative risks, multiply the impact times the likelihood to determine the net risk. For qualitative risks, simply highlight those with both high impact and likelihood.

Are There Important Consultant Risks?

Truly sophisticated clients who want to negotiate powerful contracts with outside experts take the time to deduce the other side's risks. Why? Because, one way or another, consulting firms are charging you for the risks they are bearing. When you understand the consulting firm's risks, you can reallocate them to your advantage and take simple steps that keep your consultants' energy focused on your issue rather than letting them get sidetracked by their own worries. What follows are the most common risks faced by consultants.

The Project Takes More Resources Than Expected

Unless you agree to a terrible fee structure, a project requiring extra consulting time or staff is bad news for the consulting firm. You both might underestimate the complexity, or the project might require endless revisions, or the project manager you assigned isn't living up to his commitments. Some consultancies add a "pain in the neck" charge onto projects with clients known to take extra time and effort. This is a prime example

Table 6-1

Common Risk Checklist				
Common Risks	**Possible Impact/Likelihood**			**Net Risk**
	Low	**Med**	**High**	
The project does not work	/	/	/	
The project does not deliver expected value	/	/	/	
The project takes too long or misses key dates	/	/	/	
The project is more expensive than anticipated	/	/	/	
The project is painful to manage or requires mid-project negotiations	/	/	/	
The project becomes irrelevant	/	/	/	
The project alienates some personnel	/	/	/	
The project makes me look bad	/	/	/	
Information is taken to competitors	/	/	/	
The project scope does not maximize value	/	/	/	
The best consultant isn't chosen or the best solution isn't delivered	/	/	/	
Resources could have been utilized better elsewhere	/	/	/	
Other:	/	/	/	

of the consultant's perceived risk being embedded into the contract by way of an extra charge.

The Project Takes Resources from Other Important Tasks

If the consulting firm is already near capacity, then unexpected resource requirements on a project can jeopardize other efforts. In a worst-case scenario, unexpected requirements at one client endanger the work being done for another client.

A Poor Outcome Hurts Reputation

Failure is just as painful for consultants as it is for clients. In a service business, reputation is everything, and the demise of Arthur Andersen may be the largest and most famous example of this risk coming to roost. Andersen's reprehensible work with Enron eventually was revealed, and other clients subsequently fled the firm. One reason top-notch consultants turn down certain projects is that they realize the requirements are outside their skill set and the reputation risk is too high. Mediocre consultants believe they can do anything and will tell you as much. Usually they do not recognize the reputation risk or don't have much of a reputation to begin with.

Project Fees or Rewards Are Below Expectations

Fee structures with a variable component add risk for the consultant. Even fixed fee projects can have reward risk. For instance, phase 2 of the project may never commence; the client could be very slow in paying; or referrals, which are like gold for a consultant, are not forthcoming.

A Key Employee Is Lost to a Client

Senior executives at many companies were formerly employees at consulting firms. When a consultant sets a brilliant strategy for a new division, the board may make an extremely lucrative offer for her to come onboard and lead that division full time. For the consulting firm, that is a mixed blessing. On the one hand, that employee tends to be loyal to the consulting firm and will, if possible, direct more projects to the alma mater. On the flip side, the consultant has now lost the capability to apply that genius at scores of other clients, which is often a far greater loss.

The Project Ties Up Resources That Could Deliver More Profit Elsewhere

For example this may be a consultant agreeing to keynote your annual meeting for $7,500 then having to turn down a request to facilitate a board meeting for another client on the same date. Or it could be taking on your six-month project for a good fee which then precludes the year-long engagement opportunity that arises later.

The Project Is Not Set Up to Deliver Phenomenal Value

This book shows why 90 percent of projects could deliver more value. The unexceptional results most initiatives produce might meet expectations; however, they don't engender loyal clients, glowing referrals, and big bonuses. Think of this risk as cruising along in a BMW rather than a Bentley. The BMW may perform up to specifications, but it doesn't deliver the rewards that would have accompanied the more expensive car.

The Consultant Could Have Received a Higher Reward Relative to Value

This, oversimplified, is this risk of underpricing a project—for instance, when a design group agrees to a flat fee regardless of the new product's success and the new product turns out to be a blockbuster. The risk goes beyond pricing, however. For example, a valuable opportunity is missed when the client's vice president of operations agrees to copresent a case study at an industry convention; then it turns out that the well-known chairman of the board was so impressed that she would have been the copresenter had she been asked. These risks are summed up in Table 6-2.

What Are the Sources of Our Risk?

There are three sources of risk:

1. **Your company (the client).** For instance, you may fail to provide key information during the scoping process, or a critical employee on the initiative could leave.

Table 6-2

Summary of Consultant Risks
The project takes more resources than expected
The project takes more resources from other tasks than expected
A poor outcome hurts reputation
Project fees or rewards are below expectations
A key employee is lost to the client
The project ties up resources that could be have delivered more profit elsewhere
The consultant could have done a better project to deliver more value
The consultant could have received higher reward relative to value
Other:

2. **The consultant.** For instance, the consultant could misrepresent his depth of expertise, or the subject-matter expert could be hired away by a competitor, or the consultant may treat personnel poorly and unnecessarily spark resistance to change.

3. **The environment.** For instance, the FDA could reject the submission regardless of how much work the team put in to develop it, or the exchange rate between yen and dollars could shift dramatically, causing the cost of the Japanese resources to skyrocket.

There are seemingly endless sources of risk. Not all risks are important, however; and as I mentioned earlier, small, unimportant risks should be dismissed. Go back to the list of risks for your project and note the most likely sources of those risks, skipping the risks that are low likelihood and low impact. You can use the checklist in Table 6-3 as a guide.

How Can We Reduce the Likelihood of Our Risks?

The most wonderful aspect of risk is that the offending event hasn't happened yet! For every unfortunate event or outcome you identify, there are numerous ways to lessen the chance that it will occur or the effect

Table 6-3

Common Risks Checklist	
Common Risks	**Most Likely Sources of Risk**
The project does not work	
The project does not deliver expected value	
The project takes too long or misses key dates	
The project is more expensive than anticipated	
The project is painful to manage or requires mid-project negotiations	
The project becomes irrelevant	
The project alienates some personnel	
The project makes me look bad	
Information is taken to competitors	
The project scope does not maximize value	
The best consultant isn't chosen or the best solution isn't delivered	
Resources could have been utilized better elsewhere	

it will have if it does occur. For instance, the risk of hiring a consultant who doesn't possess the necessary skills can be mitigated by doing a better job vetting the consultants up front. The effect of that risk could also be lessened by populating your project team with internal resources who evince the critical skills. Below are some suggestions for how to mitigate the most common risks. This is by no means a comprehensive review. In fact, your ability to devise creative risk abatement mechanisms is a large factor in how much you can increase the risk-adjusted value of the project and lower the risk-adjusted cost.

Table 6-4

Risk	Preventive Action
The project doesn't work	Identify and address the most likely source of failure
The project doesn't deliver the expected value	Identify and address potential revenue dampeners
The project takes too long or misses key dates	Identify and address potential time sinks
The project is more expensive than anticipated	Identify and address the most likely areas of cost overruns
The project becomes irrelevant	Identify and monitor critical external factors that could affect the project's relevance

Use Preventive Actions

This is heading off the most likely causes of failure in advance. For example, if there's a decent chance that the members of the board of directors could reject the results, then they should be very carefully consulted before the project begins and at numerous points along the way. Table 6-4 clarifies how to use this strategy for many risks.

Institute Metrics and Checkpoints

I talked about specifying metrics for success in Chapter 3, and one place those metrics really come into play is in reducing risk. While the project is in progress, you can get a good idea of whether it is measuring up if you have a good yardstick for success. For instance, if round after round of ideas from the advertising agency makes you yawn, you're on your way to a boring commercial. To use metrics well, three pieces need to be in place:

1. The metric you choose has to be a good indicator of the *results* you are trying to achieve, given the process you are using to achieve them. For example, if a business development expert told you she is going to spend the first two months compiling

a database, then looking at the number of leads generated during that time isn't a good indicator. Looking at the size of the database, however, may be. Similarly, positive feedback from attendees at a training session is a poor metric, whereas changed behavior is a good one. The key is to keep your metric focused on progress, not activities.

2. You must have checkpoints. In other words, you must pay attention to the metrics over the course of your project. For example, "customer awareness" may be a great progress metric for measuring the success of your brand-building project; however, that metric won't abate risk if you have no way to regularly collect customer awareness or if you don't look at the change in awareness until the end of the project.

3. You must have an action standard. If you institute a metric to help mitigate risk, you must define *in advance* what performance should spur action and what that action should be. For instance, you could agree that a business development project will be canceled and a full refund given if the consultant doesn't generate 20 new "A-level" leads by the end of the second month.

It's okay to use a qualitative metric as long as it's valid, you have checkpoints, and you know your action standard in advance. Board approval, positive feedback, and perception of lower tension between departments are all qualitative metrics, and they all can be perfectly legitimate ways to lower risk. Metrics and checkpoints work best when you develop them with the consultant and build them into the contract. That way there's no confusion and your efforts to lower risk are hardwired into the project. Table 6-5 clarifies how to use metrics for many risks.

Estimate Project Value Correctly at the Outset

The most consistent cause of disappointing results is poor understanding of the project's impact and the requirements at the outset. Arbitrarily set targets and hoped-for results increase the risk of project failure. Use the approaches from Chapter 1 to gauge the impact of your projects and check your assumptions to ensure the value is not overestimated. Table 6-6 shows how you can correctly estimate project value to lower risk.

Table 6-5

Risk	Metrics and Monitoring Action
The project doesn't work	Monitor metrics closely aligned to the desired outcome
The project doesn't deliver the expected value	Monitor the value delivered (or indicators of the value that will be delivered) regularly throughout the project
The project takes too long or misses key dates	Monitor progress checkpoints well in advance of key dates
The project is more expensive than anticipated	Monitor and review costs at regular intervals
The project alienates personnel	Institute a feedback mechanism with minimal risk for the whistle-blower
The project makes you look bad	All the above actions

Scope and Resource the Project Correctly

Give adequate time and latitude for success, ensure unequivocal support from project sponsors, and staff the effort with the best available outside experts. Time, budget, personnel, and talent are the resources to scrutinize when you are putting a project together. For instance, a process change initiative will deliver superior results if your internal, administrative support is relieved of other duties rather than if new responsibilities are dumped onto an already full plate.

Table 6-6

Risk	Action to Mitigate Risk
The project doesn't deliver the expected value	Ensure a solid estimate of the likely value at the outset
The project makes you look bad	Communicate the realistic estimate of project outcomes upward and outward

Table 6-7

Risk	Action
The project does not work	Agree with the consultant on the time, budget, and personnel necessary to achieve project success; find the best outside talent available
The project does not deliver expected value	Ensure that the required resources are available; monitor and modify resources if necessary to support the initiative
The project takes too long or misses key dates	Write key dates into the contract
The project makes you look bad	Scope the project correctly before jumping in

As with the other methods for reducing risk, your best chance of applying this strategy successfully is writing it into the contract. While it won't help if you poorly scope the project, it will at least make you and the consultant both accountable for providing the proper support. Table 6-7 clarifies how to use this risk mitigation strategy.

Use the Correct Fee Structure

Since Chapter 8 is dedicated to fee structures, I won't spend much time on it here. However, I do want to reinforce the point that choosing the correct fee structure is a great way to reduce the risk of cost overruns. See Table 6-8 for an example of how to mitigate this risk.

Table 6-8

Risk	Action
The project is more expensive than anticipated	Use a contract structure that locks in the proper return on investment and, if appropriate, caps expenses

Table 6-9

Risk	Action
The project is painful to manage or requires many midproject negotiations	• Include a well-written Context Document in your contracts • Don't hire difficult consultants expecting them to be easier to work with later on • Let the experts do their job • Be reasonable in the number and nature of your change requests

Build Better Contracts; Don't Hire Problems

Spend extra time up front building an outstanding project agreement with your outside expert. Always start with the Context Document as the first part of your contract because it frames your project. The approach section of your contract should reflect the amount of leeway you are giving your consultant; being overly specific about the approach in the contract may result in a very inflexible project, which causes a stream of renegotiations when conditions change.

Equally as important as building a solid contract is avoiding problem consultants. An outside expert who is aggravating during the dating process isn't going to be any better once you're married to each other in a project. Similarly, don't be a problem client. If you are caught in a seemingly endless series of midproject negotiations, check whether your side of the table is responsible for the changes and stress. It's not unusual for executives to hire an outside wizard and then insert themselves as an "amateur expert" who micromanages the magic. Table 6-9 captures these risk-reduction strategies.

Include People Management as Part of the Approach

People issues commonly sink a project. Informing the consultant that your employees must "either get with the new program or get off the bus" is posturing. Proposing that you will manage people issues on a case-by-case basis is sticking your head in the sand. As Table 6-10 underscores, you must put plans in place to address employees' concerns or to

Table 6-10

Risk	Action
The project alienates some within the company	Develop plans to address people issues before the project commences and refine those plans during and after the project (for more, see Part IV)

ensure the desired behavior changes take root. I discuss people management in more detail in the final section of this book.

Monitor What Information Is Shared; Have a Strong Confidentiality Agreement in Place

Most executives who are concerned about information being leaked have already brought legal counsel into the mix and have developed nondisclosure agreements. It almost goes without saying that you should never hire a consultant who has shared confidential information "out of school" with you. A consultant who shows you other clients' information in detail in her credentials presentation is likely to show your results to someone else too. (Two actions you can take to reduce this risk are captured in Table 6-11.)

Write an "Early Warning" Obligation into the Contract

Sometimes either you or the consultant can see a storm brewing on the horizon. Perhaps the consultant can see that your rollout plan for the upgraded laptops will run into problems due to the variety of

Table 6-11

Risk	Action
Information is taken to competitors	• Use strong nondisclosure agreements with realistic, enforceable terms • Only share sensitive information that is critical to the project's success

Table 6-12

Risk	Action
The project does not work	Obligate both sides to give early warning if it appears that project success is in jeopardy
The project does not deliver expected value	Obligate both sides to give early warning if expected value is in jeopardy
The project takes too long or misses key dates	Obligate both sides to give early warning if a milestone will be missed
The project is more expensive than anticipated	Obligate both sides to give early warning if project cost may exceed budget
The project alienates some personnel	Obligate both sides to raise personnel issues as soon as they surface

operating systems your employees use around the world. By stipulating that both sides are obligated to bring material issues to the other's attention as early as possible, you avoid exasperated cries of "Why didn't you tell us two months ago when we could have done something about it?" Table 6-12 specifies actions for mitigating these kinds of risk.

Read the Other Chapters in This Book

One of the major goals of *The Executive's Guide to Consultants* is to reveal opportunities to elevate your project's value. As a client, you can enjoy greater ROI by implementing the suggestions I've given throughout these pages (see Table 6-13).

Now go back to the list you made earlier of high-likelihood–high-impact risks and the sources of those risks. Quickly brainstorm each mitigation strategy that will help you reduce the likelihood of those risks occurring. Be as detailed as possible with your ideas, jotting down specific people, departments, dates, or restrictions.

How Can We Reduce the Impact of Our Risks?

You can reasonably expect to encounter a serious problem in one project or another. Bad things happen, and that's why it's called a risk. In this section, I am going to show you three powerful strategies for reducing

Table 6-13

Risk	Action
The project scope does not maximize value	Read and implement Chapters 1–4
The best consultant isn't chosen or the best solution isn't delivered	Read and implement Chapters 5–6
Resources could have been utilized better elsewhere	Read and implement Chapters 1–2

the detrimental effects that result when unfortunate events materialize. A fourth strategy for reducing negative effects—the most powerful strategy of all, and touched on briefly here—is the subject of the next chapter.

Strategy 1. Create Backup Plans

Backup plans are generally absent in small and large companies alike. Executives naturally resist creating backup plans because (1) "We fear that developing alternatives makes us appear unsure of what we are doing" and (2) creating them takes a lot more work. Get over this resistance. Below are examples of how to use backup plans to mitigate many of the most common risks:

- **The project does not work**. What will you do if the project is an utter failure? If your entry into the new market fails, do you have other approaches you could try? If the plant throughput project does not increase the output enough to meet orders, do you have a secondary supplier you can buy from? There is always a chance a project simply will not accomplish the objective. If there are other options you can put in place that would get you at least partway to the desired outcomes, identify those in advance and consider how you would deploy those options should they be needed.

- **The project does not deliver expected value**. The same backup plans you put in place for total failure will reduce the negative impact of this risk. In other words, if there are additional ways to capture the value you are targeting with your project, then have those identified and ready to act on from the outset.

- **The project takes too long or misses key dates.** Well-prepared backup plans to diminish this risk can save you mountains of grief down the road. It can be as easy as having an alternative presentation ready in case the results from the market research project don't come in on time. Or it could be having a "tiger team" preidentified and ready to jump in if a critical date is in jeopardy. Your backup plan only needs to be thought through in general terms, discussed with the stakeholders who would be affected, and written into your overall project plan.

- **The project is more expensive than anticipated.** The only real backup plan in this case is to have an alternate source of funds in case the budget for this project doesn't work out. An executive who knows how she will fund a project that runs over budget can react far more nimbly and competently than one who is scrambling in the face of every round of financial stress.

- **The project makes you look bad.** The backup plans you put in place in case of project failure, project underdelivery, missed deadlines, and budget issues will serve your reputation in good stead should some external event throw your big project into a downward spiral.

Strategy 2. Run Parallel Projects

This risk mitigation strategy is similar to putting backup plans in place but is more proactive in its deployment. It is the business equivalent of not having all your eggs in one basket, and it is a strategy I highly recommend when the risks are substantial. The examples below illustrate how this strategy is used to mitigate two of the most common risks:

- **The project does not work.** Run more than one effort at a time if the risk is nonnegligible and the impact of failure is severe. For example, if your project is entering a new market, how do you mitigate the risk of failure? By having multiple new market initiatives going on at any one time. Similarly, if the board of directors rejects your recommendation, the damage will be far less if you have some alternatives already in development. A succession plan won't crumble into uselessness when a key employee leaves if you are grooming multiple potential successors at the next level of the organization.

- **The project does not deliver expected value.** Using parallel projects is similar to buying multiple stocks to diversify (and lower the risk in) your financial portfolio. As with stocks, the risk will decline as long as all your projects are valued on a portfolio basis. For example, if you have three cost-cutting projects under way, each of which is supposed to deliver $1 million, you should be discounting the total value of all three projects by the probability that they, as a group, do not deliver up to expectation. If $1 million is an optimistic expectation for each project, then perhaps you should only be expecting $2.5 million from all three as a portfolio.

Strategy 3. Keep Internal Relations Programs at the Ready

The third strategy for reducing the negative impact of your risks is targeted squarely at the concern about personnel becoming alienated or upset by the project. I show you how to reduce the likelihood of this risk primarily in the final part of this book. The way you reduce the impact of people issues is by having internal relations programs "in the can." For instance, you'll lose fewer midlevel executives to the havoc potentially wrought by a reorganization project if you have an All-Hands Process Review presentation ready to go in case the need arises. You don't need to deliver the presentation if no discord develops, just because it's written. Have it there in case it's needed.

Require your consulting firm to have a protocol in place to take care of employees who are rubbed the wrong way by some personality conflicts with one of the consulting staff. Again, a prepared letter or phone-call script will make a world of difference because it can be issued quickly and thereby nip the downside effects in the bud. The fact is, we are all human and occasionally the consultant is going to step on someone's toes. As a smart client, you should insist the consultant keep an ice pack handy for just such an occasion. This is a risk for which an ounce of preparation can forestall a ton of hurt.

Strategy 4. Contractually Reallocate Risks

The fourth strategy for reducing the negative impact of your risks is using your contract and innovative mechanisms such as options. This sophisticated approach can be relatively complex; therefore, the entire next chapter is dedicated to the subject.

Table 6-14 provides a list of the risk mitigation strategies.

Table 6-14

Summary of Risk Mitigation Strategies
Reduce likelihood:
• Identify most likely sources of downside and use preventive actions
• Use effective metrics and checkpoints
• Get better estimate of project value
• Scope and resource the project correctly
• Use the correct fee structure
• Build better contracts; don't hire problems
• Include people management as part of the approach
• Monitor information sharing; use nondisclosure agreements
• Write an early warning obligation into the contract
• Read the other chapters in this book
Reduce negative effect:
• Create backup plans
• Run parallel projects
• Have internal relations programs in the can
Contractually reallocate risk

Summary

Identifying and addressing risks is one of the most powerful, underutilized methods for increasing the value of your projects and reducing the cost. Clients and consultants alike start each new project with high hopes and great expectations, only to wake up one morning with a half-built limestone theme park or a 14-mile-long rusting scar in the ground. Disasters like these can be avoided if the risks are better identified up front and prevention and mitigation strategies are put in place.

Your ERP project that is six months late, with specifications spiraling out of control, may be only a bad dream if your Context Document is written well, you have the right progress checkpoints in place, and the approach isn't overspecified. Similarly, if your marketing project meant to acquire new customers via MySpace fails, that won't sink the company if you are also targeting Facebook and you have a telesales campaign in the works too. By working through the checklists above and employing the mitigation strategies in this chapter and ones to follow, you will dramatically increase the risk-adjusted value of your projects.

One question many executives ask is, "How can I make the consultant take on some of the risk?" That question is at the heart of a mitigation strategy that is so powerful it deserves a chapter of its own: employing options. What you will see in the next few pages is a mostly unexplored method for creating better, more valuable contracts with consultants.

What Are Our Options?

Value Wizardry and Sophisticated Contract Negotiation

In This Chapter

In this second chapter dedicated to risk, I review an approach to real-locating risk between you and your consultant that, employed properly, can lead to highly sophisticated, value-creating negotiations. The next few pages reveal how to develop win-win contracts that increase the value of your projects, lower the risk, and, often, lower the costs too.

Key concepts in Chapter 7 include:
- The power of variations
- 14 Contract Tuning Keys
- 10-step process for reallocating risk

Getting Snowed

In many parts of the country, the winter of 2010–2011 seemed like one long snowstorm. While children rejoiced the string of school cancellations, their parents grew increasingly frustrated with longer and longer delays before beleaguered plow services could clear their driveways. At the state and municipal levels, snow removal costs spun out of control, compromising other priorities. For example, Amesbury, Massachusetts, had set aside $225,000 for snow removal that season, and by the end of February its spending had risen to over $650,000.[1]

However, in at least one municipality, budget woes were averted through sophisticated risk reallocation. According to reinsurance company Swiss Re, the city of Fort Wayne, Indiana, historically spent $3 million annually to clear the foot of snow that fell over a typical winter. City officials knew that for every half inch of snow above that 12-inch mark, their costs would rise by $250,000 and, as in Amesbury, a bad winter could bankrupt the city.[2] Rather than bear that risk, they reallocated it by purchasing a "call option" on snow plowing for $500,000. If the snow fell more than 12 inches in one season, they could run their plows and it wouldn't cost them a dime extra (as long as it didn't snow more than 20 inches, which was more than any winter on record). Hence, while each falling flake added to the snowdrift of worry in Amesbury, city officials in Fort Wayne could frolic in the powder with their kids, knowing their budget was intact.

Problems in a consulting project can pile up beyond any reasonable expectations like snowdrifts in the Rocky Mountains, and as you saw in the previous chapter, more than your budget is at stake; consulting projects are rife with risks. You can do your best to prevent them and mitigate them, but when the blizzard hits, would you rather be the mayor of Amesbury or Fort Wayne?

Who's Paying for Risk?

Let's say you want to dive into social media and you have estimated that attracting 100,000 fans on Facebook will bring an incremental $1 million to your business. You identify two consultancies that appear to be identical in size, approach, expertise, and experience, and you ask each to give you a proposal. However, you tell one firm that you will pay it 100 percent up front for the project without any possibility of cancellation, and you tell the other firm that you will pay it for whatever work it completes and that the project can be canceled at any time without notice. Which consultancy do you think will ask for the higher fee? The second one, of course, because that firm is facing far more risk that the project won't enrich its coffers the full amount, plus it will be out of pocket for the costs of its services while the project is under way.

The point is that you are charged for risk, whether or not the price is immediately apparent. When your consultant bears more risk, one way or another the risk will be reflected in your contract. The trick is to tease out who is bearing which risks, what is being charged to carry them, and whether reallocating them makes sense. Sometimes, a gain for one side directly corresponds to a loss for the other, as if your friend suggests you flip a coin to see who picks up the tab for dinner and you, instead, pull out a die and say you'll pick up the tab if he rolls a six. You've reallocated the expected cost of dinner directly from you to your dinner companion. Often, however, you can find a trade that's good for both sides. For instance, you might offer to pick up the tab for dinner since your friend's credit card is almost maxed out, and in return, he'll drive you home so you can enjoy an extra glass of wine. This way you lower his risk of having his credit card embarrassingly declined, and he reduces your risk of drunk driving.

What's the Secret to Reallocating Risk? Variation

The plan for you to pick up dinner in exchange for a ride home comes to fruition because you and your friend have information about what each other wants and what risks you are facing. Similarly, to reallocate risks in a consulting project, you need information, and there are two ways to get it: (1) ask for it or (2) create an "information net" to capture it.

If you want to know what a guitar sounds like, you could pluck one string, or you could strum all six strings while forming a variety of chords on the fretboard. The former approach will hint at the guitar's acoustics, whereas the latter will grant you a richer feel for the instrument. Similarly, when you are listening for information from consultants, you could issue a traditional RFP, from which you will get back a single piece of information, or you can create an information net that rewards you with a wide range of insights into your prospective consultant's perceptions of risk. The key to building an information net is understanding the special string used for its construction: variation.

Introducing risk variations into your conversation with the consultant is like playing chords on the guitar, and the more you try, the wider the information net you are weaving.

One way to understand this is to think about term life insurance. The reason term life insurance works is that the insurance companies can vary their premiums based on factors such how old you are, how long you want the insurance, and how big a policy you purchase. An insurance agent will present a number of alternatives with different premiums based on the size and the duration of the policy. If you quit smoking, you lower your risk of dying *and* you lower your premiums. That's a double win, and that's what we're going to strive for on the consulting side: lower risk and a higher return on investment.

What Can We Vary? The Contract Tuning Keys

Guitars feature pegs or keys to change how each string sounds. By fiddling with these keys, guitar players use "drop D" tuning, "open tuning," or dozens of other variations to create the optimal sound for certain songs. For consulting projects, there are 14 different Tuning Keys (shown in Table 7-1) that can be varied to help you get the optimal contract with your consultant—a contract that creates the best balance of risk and value.

Some of the Tuning Keys overlap, and you may think of others I have not included. These 14 will serve as an excellent starting point, however, and will give you ample room to create the variance you need

Table 7-1

The Contract Tuning Keys	
Access to the consultant	Flexibility
Access to future projects	Intrusiveness
Cancelability	Publicity
Duration	Scope
Fee and terms	Skill transference
Fee structure	Timing
Incentives	Timing flexibility

to lower your risk and increase your value from consultants. The place to start is usually by varying *scope*. After that, you should look to *fee structure* and *incentives*; then, depending on your situation, some of the other Tuning Keys may be helpful too. However, as I'll explain later, too many variations will render your negotiations unwieldy and clumsy.

How Can We Vary the Scope?

You should always ask prospective consultants to give you at least three scope alternatives. If you are considering a few different consultants, you should determine the alternatives in advance and ask each of the consultants to provide three pieces of information for each project scope: (1) their approach, (2) the likelihood of achieving the project's outcomes, and (3) fees. When developing the scope alternatives, focus more on the results and outcomes you want the consultant to deliver and less on the consultant's specific activities and approaches.

By asking three consultants for feedback on three different scope alternatives, you will have nine sets of approaches, estimates of success, and prices to compare. You will know how much value each consultant puts on each part of the scope, the consultant's self-perceived strengths, and the market rate for different outcomes. Soliciting information in this fashion is based on the "commercial menu" approach to structuring, bundling, and tendering variations in contracts, an approach developed and perfected by Bob Endres at Synaptic Decisions.

The factors that can be varied as part of scope are myriad. You can include or exclude teams, divisions, geographies, or product lines. You can ask the consultant to start earlier in the process or jump in later, to lead tasks or merely offer advice. You can ask for the consultant's work to be captured in an online wiki or a hard-copy binder or a PowerPoint presentation, to name a few ways.

Let's go back to the example where you are asking a consultant to help you attract Facebook fans. You could have the consultant build only the plan, or also give you real-time guidance while you implement the plan, or build the plan and lead implementation. You identify three excellent consultants and ask them to give you their approach, the estimated likelihood of success, and the fee for the three different scope alternatives. Once the information comes back, you create your own estimates of success by using your knowledge, looking at the various approaches, and talking to the consultants.

Table 7-2

	Scope Alternatives		
	1. Build Plan	2. Build and Guide	3. Build and Implement
Value of success	$1 million	$1 million	$1 million
Likelihood of success	55%	65%	70%
Expected value	$550,000	$650,000	$700,000
Fee estimate	*$50,000*	*$75,000*	*$100,000*
Expected return	**$500,000**	**$575,000**	**$600,000**

With this information in hand, you can calculate the expected return from each alternative by multiplying the likelihood of each outcome by the value of that outcome, then subtracting the consultant's fees. Table 7-2, for the sake of simplicity, shows how this might look for one consultant.

On the basis of these calculations, your best bet is to have the consultant lead the whole initiative, including implementation. The ROI is still very high, and the absolute dollar return you can expect is higher than any of the other alternatives. You could, of course, get more sophisticated by estimating the value of differing levels of success; however, that generally becomes too complex for all but the largest projects.

By varying scope, you build an excellent information net that gives you insight into the likelihood of success (or risk of failure) with different scopes, approaches, and consultants. That in and of itself is a huge step up compared with how most executives approach consultants. If you want to take the next step in reallocating risk, then the next Contract Tuning Keys in your sights should be fee structures and incentives.

How Can We Vary the Fee Structure and Incentives?

Sometimes executives strive to reallocate risks by asking consultants to be paid based on their performance. This is the proverbial carrot-and-stick approach where the consultants play the role of the donkey. On the Facebook project, you could suggest a contract in which the consultants get paid $100,000 if they surpass 100,000 fans but receive no compensation if they fall short of that level of success. Such a contract transfers 100 percent of the value-to-cost risk to the consultants since they only get paid if they deliver the outcome they promised.

Few consultants will agree to a contract with a risk of getting nothing at the end.[3] No matter how good the consultants are and how cooperative a client you are, the consultants can't control the risks you introduce, nor can they control the exogenous risks; yet they have to earn a living from their efforts.

One way to align your interests and change the risk profile would be to tell the consultants that you will pay them $1 per Facebook fan they acquire. It's as if your stick's size varies depending on how far the donkey travels. If you don't cap the payment that the consultant can receive, then your stick becomes a carrot that grows as the donkey covers more miles. This looks a lot like the piece-rate contract structure I will discuss in Chapter 8, and in fact, that is exactly when such an incentive system is most appropriate.

A reasonable percentage of fees at risk that many consultants will accept is somewhere between 10 and 50 percent. Most consultants will want a commensurate reward balancing out the penalties. The upside in moving to a variable-fee structure is that you are providing ample encouragement for the consultants to mitigate every impediment to success they possibly can and increase your likelihood of an outstanding outcome.

You work with this Tuning Key by asking your prospective consultants whether a variable-fee structure could change the likelihood of success on the project. Some consultants may say, "No. We always give our very best effort, and that's what we've shown you." Most consultants, though, when faced with a significant enough carrot or stick, will find *something* they can do to eke out a better chance of success. For the Facebook example, let's assume your preferred consultant tells you he could potentially change the odds of success under a penalty-reward scenario. Table 7-3 summarizes the fee structures, the probability of success, and the expected value of the project.

As you can see, clever incentive plans can create a win-win scenario for you and consultants if the incentives encourage the consultants to mitigate more risks on their end or take other measures that would increase the likelihood of success. In this example, the total return you can expect from your investment increases even though you are offering almost twice the fee to the consultant. Plus you have reduced your odds

Table 7-3

	Flat Fee	Penalty-Reward
Value of success	$1 million	$1 million
Fee if fails	$100,000	$60,000
Fee if successful	$100,000	$180,000
Likelihood of success	75%	85%
Expected fee	$100,000	$162,000
Expected value	$750,000	$850,000
Expected return	*$650,000*	*$688,000*

of spearheading a fiasco while increasing your chances of being recognized for an outstanding initiative.

This type of arrangement can work because the consultants come out ahead. They can count on receiving enough fees if the project falls far short of expectations to allay their fears of working for nothing; and perhaps most importantly, they have a shot of increasing their fees 80 percent versus the flat-fee structure.

Incentive-type plans work even better when there is more than one level of success. For instance, let's say that if you attract any fewer than 80,000 Facebook fans, the project will totally fail because you won't have critical mass; however, if you attract 120,000 fans, the value to you will be $1.5 million. In this scenario, adding one extra level of incentive payout makes a huge difference, as shown in Table 7-4.

Concerns related to fee structure and incentives include:

- **Cash flow issues.** Occasionally there is a legitimate concern about cash flow. In the Facebook example, perhaps not enough cash is available to cover the consultant's $100,000 bonus should the project succeed beyond expectations. However, the consultant may be open to receiving the bonus on some sort of payment plan that alleviates your cash flow concerns. Remember, the consultant is only earning an extra $100,000 if the project is so successful that you are enjoying an incremental $500,000.

- **Complexity issues.** Payment based on results requires you to track the level of success you actually achieve on the project, which sits uncomfortably with many executives. Nevertheless, if you

Table 7-4

No. of Fans	Value	Flat Fee		Penalty-Reward	
		Fee	Likelihood	Fee	Likelihood
<80,000	$0	$100,000	25%	$50,000	15%
100,000	$1 million	$100,000	70%	$100,000	75%
>120,000	$1.5 million	$100,000	5%	$200,000	10%
Expected return			*$675,000*		*$797,500*

constructed a solid Context Document, then you have excellent, measurable, trackable indicators of success. If you are not confident in your indicators of success, you need to address that problem before bringing on a consultant.

- **Fairness issues.** If the consultant earns $100,000 on a project that nets you $1 million, it feels fair. Whereas paying another $100,000 for delivering an extra $500,000 rubs some executives the wrong way. Somehow you have to put this fairness issue aside. Set up incentive plans that help you achieve your objectives, and stop worrying about whether they help other people "more" than you. Of course, ensure you are keeping the total value of the project at a level where it's worth doing. In the Facebook example, if you hit the 120,000-fan mark, you will gain an incremental $500,000 at an incremental cost of $100,000. The percentage ROI on the incremental success might not look quite as good, but the real value to the company is enormous.

Parenthetically, a substantial advantage of insisting on a penalty-reward fee structure is that you will attract consultants who are most likely to succeed. In this way, the structure itself engenders a virtuous circle that brings down project risk even further.

Varying scope and fee structure and incentives may be as much complexity as you can handle. Together, they create an information net vastly superior to the traditional RFP process and allow you to dramatically increase your risk-adjusted value. Remember that you don't have to do everything in one step. You can create scope alternatives, collect that information, and then go back to the consultant with varied incentive plans.

What Else Could We Vary?

The remaining Contract Tuning Keys will handle most of the risks we examined in the previous chapter and introduce the opportunity to be more creative in your contracts. Fiddling with these keys is where you can introduce sophisticated alternatives such as a call option on consultant capacity to reduce the risk of missing a key date, a cancellation option for future phases, or an option for the consultant to delay the project by three weeks in return for a discounted fee.

To keep this chapter a reasonable length, I will present only an overview and some examples of each of the remaining Contract Tuning Keys. Keep in mind that each of the keys can be used with the same amount of nuance as scope, fee structure, and incentives.

Access to the Consultant

How easy it is for you to get in touch with your consultant? Who is allowed to call upon the consultant? And how often can you call upon the consultant and about what subjects? These are all questions of access. If you want anyone in your company at any location in the world to be able to call upon the consultant 24 hours a day, 7 days a week, an unlimited number of times for any reason, that's going to cost you a lot more than if only the CEO can contact the consultant, and only on certain topics and only during business hours.

Access to Future Projects

Will the consultants automatically get notified about other projects you are doing where they might add value? Remember, you can also tune the consultant's side of the project to create more or less value. Offering notification of upcoming projects reduces the consultant's risk of finding future business, and that can be very attractive. The most straightforward version of this is when you break a project into phases and the consultant can reasonably expect to get the work on Phase II of the project if she does a good job on Phase I.

Cancelability

Can you cancel the project and, if so, with how much notice and at what cost? As a matter of principle, you may presume that you should be able to cancel a consulting project at any time for any reason and just pay for the work that is done up to that point. You will pay for that principle. Total cancelability creates considerable risk for consultants, and one way or another, to stay in business they have to cover that risk with their fees.

If you are 99 percent sure that your project will be completed from start to finish, then you could agree to a no-cancellation clause in the contract. It makes very little difference to you because you know you are going to do the project; however, the consultant gets to set aside a large worry and may reflect that with a substantial discount. Everyone wins.

Duration

How long is the consultant available to you? Varying duration gives both sides of the discussion an interesting window into the other's world. Some consultants are so busy that being locked into one client for a long time creates additional upside risk. Others have unsteady business, in which case knowing revenue will be coming in for a longer period of time may be extremely valuable.

For open-ended types of projects, such as coaching or intermittent advice and direction, you can vary the minimum duration of the engagement. For instance, you might agree to a minimum of six months of coaching or to a two-year retainer agreement for as-needed advice. You could also include renewal options in the agreement. You may find that a longer-duration contract creates more value and lowers risk for both sides. Perfect!

Payment Terms

How much will you pay the consultant, and what are the terms of payment? The fee section of a consultant's proposal has some sort of magnetic charm. Every executive flips to it first, no matter what else is in the proposal. It's as if the rest of the proposal is just the wrapping paper around a Christmas present that's been sitting under the tree for a week and the anticipation of seeing what's inside is unbearable. *Hooray, the fee is lower than you feared!* or *Oh no! The fee is more than you can afford.* Fortunately, there is a lot more to the proposal than fees, and there's a lot more to fees than the dollar amount.

The terms of how you pay your fees are a great way to vary the value and risk in a project. Paying the entire project up front appears to shift a lot of risk to you; however, if you are given a discount for up-front payment by a small firm worried about cash flow, your net return may increase. Tying payments to deliverables or completion of the project may lower your risk; even so, a consultant worried that he would have to wait for you to finish the project may raise his fees. Other ways you can vary fees and terms include the payment currency (on international projects) and in-kind services or products instead of cash.

Flexibility

How much can the project approach change without requiring renegotiation of the contract? This is an easy way to add value on both sides. Constant delays to renegotiate statements of work are expensive, time consuming, frustrating, and detrimental to the overall value of the project. For instance, specifying that the consultant must conduct at least 15 customer interviews is very inflexible. What if only 5 interviews are necessary to see a consistent pattern? Or what if, after conducting 15 interviews, you and the consultant agree that a focus group is really needed to fully understand the feedback? By locking the approach down so tightly, you are reducing flexibility. Make your outcomes inviolable and experiment with different levels of flexibility in the approach.

Intrusiveness

How much is your organization affected before the rollout of the final solution? For instance, megaconsulting firms are known for blanketing their clients with dozens of junior-level consultants who can create a lot of disruption during the assessment and design phases of their projects. On the other end of the spectrum live the consultants who like to do the work out of sight, applying their secret, black-box method, and then come back at the end of the project with their recommendation.

There's no right or wrong level of intrusiveness. If your organization needs to be shaken out of its complacency, you might want the consultants to be more visible and active in creating waves during the project; however, the consultants may see that as driving up costs because they need to spend more time on-site. Conversely, your team could be running full tilt and have no time for outsiders' interruptions. Lower intrusiveness could be viewed by consultants as increasing risk because they get less input and buy-in prior to delivering their recommendation.

Publicity

To what extent can the collaboration between you and the consultant be made public? Many executives aren't aware of the value consulting firms place on publicity, which is a critical lever in their marketing plans. While large companies often prohibit publicity in their standard contracts with vendors, you still have a lot of room to create variance.

You can, for instance, make an informed decision to relax the no-publicity rules for a project based on the specific situation. In addition, agreeing to recommend the consultant to colleagues in two different companies may be viewed as a big publicity win for the consultant. Similarly, providing a testimonial that consultants can use on their website or in their marketing materials may stay within the bounds of your no-publicity rules while creating a reward or incentive for the consultants.

Skill Transference

To what extent will your organization be able to repeat what the outside experts did after they leave? If you bring in the experts from a consulting firm to help you prioritize your new market initiatives, you may want them to teach you how to use their forms and processes so that you can conduct the prioritization exercise without them next year. On the other hand, you may have no interest whatsoever in learning Java programming from the techies you hired to build your website, and if you need to make changes, you're happy to call them in again to do the work.

The consultants may view their approach and tools as valuable proprietary intellectual property and charge a high premium for leaving it in your hands. Alternatively, they may view skill transference as a way to increase your level of sophistication so that you will better appreciate their more valuable offerings. You won't know unless you gather information in your net.

Timing

How rapidly will the project be completed? For instance, if the consultant is supposed to prepare materials within six weeks for the February 15 annual corporate meeting, it's unacceptable if the materials will not be ready until March 1. On the other hand, if your consultant is collecting feedback from your customers to help your promotion agency develop a better trade show booth, there may be no urgency since the next trade show is six months down the road.

All the guidelines I outlined under the incentives Tuning Key can be worked into timing, including adding penalties and rewards for achieving certain results within certain time frames. For instance, you might offer a 10 percent bonus if your product designer finishes the new mechanical drawings two weeks early, and you might include a $5,000-per-day penalty for each day post deadline for which the drawings are not completed.

Timing Flexibility

How fixed are the starting and ending dates and any midproject milestones? A project that will definitely start August 1 and run until a "hard stop" on December 31 harbors less uncertainty for the consultant than a project that could start any time within the next six months and run roughly six to eight months depending on unforeseeable factors. If there is no penalty for repeatedly changing the date of the preliminary results presentation at the last moment, that is more risk than if, once you're within a week of the meeting, the date cannot be changed without incurring additional costs.

Adding timing flexibility increases or lowers risk depending on who gets the flexibility. As a client, the more you can wrap a project around your priorities and needs, the better it is for you; similarly, if the consultant can schedule your work around other engagements and commitments, that can be an attractive benefit to the consultant. As a result, timing flexibility can be an excellent Contract Tuning Key for increasing value and lowering risk for both the client and the consultant.

How Do We Make All This Work? Ten Steps for Reallocating Risk

You just read about an extensive number of possible variations. If it strikes you as impossible, infeasible, and unworkable to introduce so many variations to your consultant, you're absolutely right! The 10 steps that follow are a down-and-dirty, practical approach to packing the optimal combination of value and risk into a consulting project.

When I am hiring consultants to help on my own business, I use only the first five steps of the process most of the time. Varying scope and one other Tuning Key such as timing leads to a far superior arrangement with the consultant than if I had merely issued an RFP, and it is quick and easy. For larger projects that have greater impact on the business, I use all 10 steps—and the resulting increase in risk-adjusted value never fails to amaze me.

Step 1. Context

Work through all the steps outlined in Chapter 3 to develop an excellent Context Document for your project, including the Situation, Objectives, Indicators of Success, Risks and Concerns, Parameters, and Value sections.

Step 2. Levels of Success and Risk

Revisit your risks and concerns as well as your desired outcome and indicators of success to identify the major factors that could drive success or failure on this project. If there are varying levels of success on your project that depend on how well you achieve the desired outcome or how those risks play out, make note of them. There may only be two levels: succeed or don't succeed. On the other hand, there may be a range between abject failure and nirvana.

Step 3. Revised Valuation

Revisit your estimate of the project's value and use your best judgment to assign values based on the levels of success and risks you identified in Step 2. An example of the second and third steps for the Facebook fans project is shown in Table 7-5.

Table 7-5

Result	Indicator of Success	Value
Project fails	<80,000 fans	$0
Target	100,000 fans	$1 million
Huge success	>120,000 fans	$1.5 million
Perceived Risk	**Indicator/Event**	**Effect on Value**
Timing	Completed ≤8 weeks	None
	Completed 8–16 weeks	-$100,000/month
	Completed >16 weeks	Project fails

Step 4. Identify Your Contract Tuning Keys

Choose the two, three, or, at most, four Contract Tuning Keys in addition to scope that you believe could have the greatest impact on increasing value or decreasing risk for your project. For each Tuning Key, create a few variations you could present to the consultant. Don't overthink it; just create the variation that you believe will have the largest impact and move on. You don't want paralysis by analysis! Table 7-6 shows how you might summarize the variations on the Facebook fans project.

Step 5. Identify the Preferred Consultant

Use the tips in Chapter 4 to identify one or more consultants who could deliver excellent ROI on this project. To accomplish this, you will most likely refine your Context Document and your estimates of the project's value. As part of this step, you present the consultants with your scope variations and then decide on the consultant and scope that offer the best combination of approach, likelihood of success, and initial fee.

   If you are not going to use any additional Contract Tuning Keys, you would stop here. As I mentioned above, these first five steps are sufficient for most small initiatives, and on their own they will generate a stronger, more powerful project.

Table 7-6

Summary of Tuning Key Variations on Facebook Project			
Contract Tuning Key	**Variation 1**	**Variation 2**	**Variation 3**
Incentives	None	Penalty for <100,000 fans	Large penalty for <80,000 fans; bonus for 120,000+ fans
Timing	Start immediately; finish within 8 weeks	Start immediately; finish within 12 weeks	Start at your convenience; finish within 12 weeks
Duration	4–8 weeks; based on implementation and internal timetable	4–12 weeks; based on implementation of final deliverable	Option to renew for 4–10 weeks as needed to reach 120,000 fans

Step 6. Identify the Consultant's Contract Tuning Keys

Interview your preferred consultant to home in on what the consultant perceives as the greatest risks and value-creation opportunities. Marching consultants through the 14 Contract Tuning Keys to get a sense for their hot buttons is quick work. During the interview process, the consultants will usually tell you exactly what variations would be helpful for them. Table 7-7 shows the information that a conversation with the preferred consultant in the Facebook fans project might yield.

Consultants may also respond well to "compensation events" that reduce their risk. This concept, developed by the Institution of Civil Engineers as part of their New Engineering Contract, embeds each side's responsibilities explicitly into the contract by specifying what triggers a change in compensation. For instance, if you promise a full-time project leader during negotiations and renege on that obligation then the

Table 7-7

Summary of Consultant's Tuning Key Variations on Facebook Project				
Contract Tuning Key	Variation 1	Variation 2	Variation 3	Variation 4
Terms	20% up front; 80% upon completion	30% up front; 30% at project midpoint; 40% at completion	50% up front; 25% in 30 days; 25% in 60 days	100% up front
Publicity	No publicity rights	May use company name and logo in marketing materials	Use of name and logo; also will provide written testimonial	Same as Variation 3, and will approve quotes in a case study

consultant's fee would be increased. Or, if the consultant pledges to deliver research results by May 1 and the date passes without a report, then the fee is reduced. Compensation events reward good behavior and, because they reduce risk, they can reduce your costs while increasing the likelihood of success.

Step 7. Create Contract Bundles

Creating a "commercial menu" is the magic in Bob Endres's negotiation approach, and it is where artfulness and experience come into play. You need to look at all the variations you are considering across all the Contract Tuning Keys and develop just a few—usually three or four—bundles that combine the variations in a meaningful way. For example, you could design bundles to generate the lowest out-of-pocket costs, the lowest risk, or the highest level of success. Table 7-8 shows how you could combine variations for the Facebook fans project.

Table 7-8

Contract Tuning Key	Facebook Project Contract Bundles		
	Low Cost	Low Risk	Most Fans
Incentives	None	Large penalty for <80,000 fans; bonus for 120,000+ fans	Large penalty for <80,000 fans; bonus for 120,000+ fans
Timing	Start immediately; finish within 12 weeks	Start immediately; finish within 8 weeks	Start at your convenience; finish within 12 weeks
Duration	4–10 weeks; based on implementation of final deliverable	4–10 weeks; based on implementation of final deliverable	Option to renew for 4–10 weeks as needed to reach 120,000 fans
Terms	100% up front	20% up front; 80% upon completion	Consultant's choice of terms
Publicity	Use of name and logo; also will provide written testimonial and will approve quotes in a case study	No rights	Use of name and logo; also will provide written testimonial and will approve quotes in a case study

Step 8. Solicit Revised Estimates

At this point, you provide your preferred consultant with the different bundles and get his feedback on fees and how he thinks each structure will affect your likelihood of achieving success. To accomplish this step, you could use a variation on the simple letter below.

Dear Joe,

As we have discussed, I am impressed by your group and believe you may be able to help us achieve our objectives. We want to put together a contract with you that creates the best mix of risk reduction and wins for both sides. Without changing the scope we have agreed to, would you please let us know what your revised fee would be under the three alternative structures outlined below? We know that the contract often influences how likely we are to achieve success; therefore, please provide your best estimate of how successful you think we will be under each structure.

Structure #1. In this contract structure you will receive a flat fee for the project, paid 100 percent up front. You will receive your fee whether or not we attract 100,000 fans, and you have no obligation to provide additional consulting should your original work fail to deliver 100,000 fans. We expect you to kick off the project immediately, and you have up to 12 weeks to complete the project. In addition, we will allow you to use our name and logo in marketing materials and will allow you to quote us (with our approval, of course) in a case study that you write.

Structure #2. In this contract structure we expect you to start immediately and finish the project within eight weeks. In this structure the use of our name or logo in marketing materials is prohibited. Your fee will depend on how many incremental fans you attract. Therefore, we need to know three fees: (1) if the project attracts fewer than 80,000 fans; (2) if the project attracts 80,000–120,000 fans; (3) if the project attracts more than 120,000 fans. We will give you 20 percent of the middle fee as an up-front payment and will pay you the remaining fees based on your level of success within four weeks of the project's completion.

Structure #3. In this contract structure you may start at your convenience, as long as your work on the project is completed within 12 weeks. In addition, we will extend the performance period for measuring the number of fans we attract 10 weeks after you finish the project. We will allow you to use our name and logo in marketing materials and will allow you to quote us (with our approval, of course) in a case study that you write. As in structure #2, we need to know three fees based on achieving fewer than 80,000 fans, 80,000–120,000 fans, and over 120,000 fans. You may specify the up-front fees. (Of course, if your performance warrants lower fees than we gave you up front, you will have to return the difference.)

Below are two summary tables: one for you to submit your fees and the other for your estimated likelihood of success.

	Your Fee		
Level of Success (# fans)	**Structure #1:** Guaranteed flat fee; 100% up front; up to 12 weeks; publicity	**Structure #2:** Variable fee; 20% up front; up to 8 weeks	**Structure #3:** Variable fee; your terms; up to 12 weeks; case study
<80,000	$_____	$_____	$_____
80–120,000		$_____	$_____
>120,000		$_____	$_____

	Likelihood of Success		
Level of Success (# Fans)	**Structure #1:** Guaranteed flat fee; 100% up front; up to 12 weeks; publicity	**Structure #2:** Variable fee; 20% up front; up to 8 weeks	**Structure #3:** Variable fee; your terms; up to 12 weeks; case study
<80,000	_____%	_____%	_____%
80–120,000	_____%	_____%	_____%
>120,000	_____%	_____%	_____%

Step 9. Evaluate and Tweak

Evaluate the fees and likelihoods of success that your consultant presents. You will learn a considerable amount from this approach about how much each consultant truly values flexibility, guarantees, money up front, publicity, and other Contract Tuning Keys. Of course, you will have to reflect on the consultant's answers and use your own experience and judgment to refine the consultant's estimates.

Using these data, you calculate the expected value, cost, and return for each bundle. Often you learn enough to create a fourth bundle that is some different combination that creates the best of all worlds for you and your consultant.

A lot of executives wonder whether consultants will go through what appears to be a giant hassle. The answer is simple: yes! Most of the time, consultants are delighted to participate in the design of alternative project structures that can lower risk and increase value on both sides of the equation. Remember, you are not trying to find ways to gouge the consultants; rather, you are looking for places where you both win. Some consultants are stuck in their ways and simply respond, "This is how we price projects, and these are our terms." Run away from those consultants as fast as your feet will carry you. Those are the same consultants who will be inflexible in applying their approach and unable or unwilling to adapt to the real world when it doesn't match expectations.

Step 10. Choose and Move Forward

If you follow this process correctly, it will add very little (or no) time to your negotiation timetable. Yes, there is more work involved; yet by doing your homework up front and being thorough in how you consider both sides' Contract Tuning Keys, you actually speed up the negotiating part of the process. There's far less back-and-forth on little details and a lot more excitement to get moving on both sides.

You might want to add an eleventh step, which is celebrating the hard work you did to construct a truly outstanding project structure. Why bother going through all this work? Because you can routinely add 10 to 20 percent to the expected value of your project while bringing down the costs. On a project that's supposed to deliver $1 million in benefit, the incremental $100,000 to $200,000 warrants a day or two of extra effort. Plus, of course, you increase your likelihood of outstanding results that you and the consultant can celebrate.

Summary

Identifying and mitigating risks is only the starting point for increasing project value and decreasing cost. By creatively and skillfully reallocating risk, you can hire better consultants for lower fees and enjoy greater rewards at the project's end. Rather than worrying whether another snowfall of unforeseen events is going to break your budget or sink the project, you can rest easy, knowing that your contract structure shifted the worry to the consultant's side of the table. Plus when you use these techniques, you will bask in the glow of having traded a few low-cost favors in return for lower fees or higher odds of success.

In the past your RFP for a new product-design project would return three bewilderingly different fees and approaches from three different design consultants. This chapter trades in the traditional process for an approach that will reveal that one designer is 100 percent confident in her outcomes and has little time to devote to your project, whereas another designer is short of work, hungry for new projects, and willing to put in overtime to get it right. In fact, you will have dozens of insights into each consultant's true strengths and the rationale behind the consultant's fees.

Are those fees fair? Are they a good deal? Is the consulting firm being paid for the work it takes on or the results it produces? When should the consulting firm be paid? While we've talked a lot about fees, we haven't answered those questions in depth or addressed how you should structure your contract with the consultant to get the results you desire. Therefore, the entire next chapter is devoted to fees and contract structures.

What's the Deal?

Fees and Contracts for Consultants

In This Chapter

It's time to wrap up everything you have done to frame a great project, find the right consultant, and increase the risk-adjusted value into a contract. How much, on what basis, and when you should pay the consultant are the most critical pieces remaining to be nailed down.

Key concepts in Chapter 8 include the following:
- Rule of thumb for how much to pay
- The problems with VTM contracts
- Leeway and boundedness
- Value-based, FTM, stipend, and piece-rate contracts
- Phased, earned, and calendared payment schedules

A Great, Terrible Project

In the fall of 2004, the CEO of the Magard Company finally succumbed to the lure of installing an enterprise resource planning (ERP) system. The midsize manufacturer of turbine parts for windmills was nestled in the wooded suburbs 90 minutes outside of Detroit, where it had grown steadily since "Pop" Magard founded the company as an auto parts supplier roughly 60 years earlier. Magard Co. proudly touted itself as a family-owned company with family values, and to the executive team that meant keeping as much of the work inside the company walls as possible.

For three years, Jim had postponed the inevitable while he staffed the in-house IT workforce and directed an internal effort to overhaul the company's systems. Nevertheless, by the end of 2004, Jim started searching for an outside expert. Jim, Sarah Stevens, his COO of almost three decades, and the Magard IT staff interviewed four well-known ERP providers between Thanksgiving and Christmas of 2004. The consultants' solutions ranged from an $850,000 bare-bones system to a $3.6 million custom-software bundle packed with bells and whistles. Even at the low end, this was a huge spend for Magard, dwarfing any other project the company had pursued since expanding its office building in the late 1980s. Ultimately, Magard chose the consulting firm that seemed to have the most experience with the company's type of operation and whose recommended solution was neither the most simple nor the most complex. The estimated fee? A hair over $2 million for a system that would take 18 months to install.

Two-and-a-half years later, Jim Magard waved farewell to the last ERP consultants, who, all told, had cost him $1 million in extra consulting fees beyond the original estimates. When I interviewed Jim, the new system was approaching its fifth anniversary and running as smoothly as one of his finely tuned turbines. Yes, the project ran 50 percent over budget, he reflected, "Though in the big picture the extra cost wasn't dramatic. The payback with inventory control exceeded our hopes and has allowed us to keep growing steadily."

Can you imagine your most expensive consulting project running 50 percent over budget and thinking it's not a big deal? Two lessons hidden in Magard's experience are at the heart of this chapter: (1) the cost of a good consulting project is often inconsequential compared with the benefit, and (2) you need the right contract structures in place at the start to avoid financial surprises later.

How Much Should We Pay?

The second question most executives ask a prospective consultant—right after they inquire about whether the consultant can do what they need—is how much it will cost. How much *should* you pay a consultant? If you are looking for advice on what day rate to pay or how much you can expect to pay for a strategy project, you will find no precise rates table here. As you'll see later in the chapter, often you shouldn't be looking at day rates (or hourly rates) at all, and a strategy project for GE can't be put on the same fee scale as a strategy project for ABC Plumbing.

The quick rule of thumb is to cap project fees at around 15 percent of the risk-adjusted value of the project. Some companies end up spending far, far more than that, particularly on huge IT projects; however, that is often because they don't know what their risk-adjusted return is in the first place and they haven't used the correct contract structure. In general, a 7-to-1 risk-adjusted return is much higher than you will achieve from other investments.

The other rule of thumb is to spend more time focused on the results a consultant will generate than on the fee. A quick example will demonstrate why: Suppose you are undertaking a project that you have valued at $1 million. The first consultancy you talk to submits its recommended approach and quotes a fee of $85,000. After reviewing the approach, you estimate the likelihood of the project succeeding at 85 percent, which means the fees are 10 percent of the risk-adjusted value. The second consulting firm you interview seems more experienced and suggests a different approach that, while simpler, costs significantly more: $120,000. How much more likely to succeed does the second consultancy have to be for its expected results to exceed the extra fees? Just 4 percent. That's all. If the second consulting firm, which is more experienced, increases the project's likelihood of success from 85 to 89 percent, your value from the project will justify fees that are almost 1½ times as high as its competitor's! (See Table 8-1.)

You could spend your time trying to negotiate down the second consulting firm's $35,000 premium, or you could channel that energy into working with it to increase the overall value of the project and the likelihood of success. The former approach will yield, at most, $35,000, whereas the latter approach could yield $100,000 or more—for instance, if the consultant proposes ways to increase value 10 percent in addition to decreasing risk. (See Table 8-2.)

Table 8-1

	Consultant 1	Consultant 2
Project value	$1 million	$1 million
Likelihood of success	85%	89%
Expected return	$850,000	$890,000
Fee	$85,000	$120,000
Net expected return	$765,000	$770,000

As a business owner who frequently contracts outside experts, I understand the draw of lower fees. My experience has always been that when I overcome my natural frugality and invest in an expert who improves the result of my project, it pays out in spades. The point is not that paying higher fees is always a better choice, nor is it that the consultancy that quotes the highest fee is the best firm. Rather, your key learning should be that results, not fees, should be your primary focus when choosing and negotiating with a consultant.

What about comparing the consultant's fees with the cost of using internal employees? If a six-month project costs $400,000, then some executives react by saying, "For that money, I could devote four of my full-time employees to the project, complete it in six months, and

Table 8-2

	Consultant 2			
	Original Fee	Negotiate Price	Mitigate Risks	Improve Outcome
Project value	$1 million	$1 million	$1 million	$1.1 million
Likelihood of success	89%	89%	95%	89%
Expected return	$890,000	$890,000	$950,000	$979,000
Fee	$120,000	$100,000	$120,000	$120,000
Net	$770,000	$790,000	$830,000	$859,000

have half the year of those employees' productivity left to play with." Unfortunately, this reasoning is incomplete and misleading. A number of factors have been left out of the equation:

1. What is the fully loaded cost of those employees, including benefits? In the United States the cost of benefits for the average employees is a bit more than 40 percent of their salary. An apples-to-apples comparison would also include indirect employee costs such as hiring, training, infrastructure, and allocated overhead.

2. What is the current ROI from those employees? Many executives do not know what return they can expect on any one employee. Therefore, I advise using return on labor costs (RoLC), which you can easily calculate by dividing your total annual revenue by your annual payroll plus benefits. Although not every employee directly generates revenue, every employee's activities should be connected to the bottom line. You could refine the RoLC by position or function; however, an average number works well for most companies.

   As a point of reference, in the United States we expect about $6 of revenue to be produced for each dollar of payroll. In this example, diverting employees to work on the project whose combined compensation is $200,000 for six months may save $400,000 in consulting fees, but it costs $1.2 million in lost productivity ($200,000 × 6 = $1.2 million)!

3. What is the risk-adjusted value of having the project completed by experts compared with internal resources? Often (though not always), the likelihood of success on a project is much higher when you use experts who specialize in your issue. As you saw earlier, a very small improvement in your odds of success can outweigh a huge difference in costs.

4. What else could you do with the money you would allocate to consulting fees? If you have prioritized well, no other project will give as high a return.

An executive's gut feeling that the consultant's fees are out of line with the cost of employees is exacerbated by the short time frame in which this princely sum is expended. If his $400,000 project took one month instead of six, then his impression that he should utilize internal resources would be even stronger. But his intuition is leading him astray. It is often worth far more to have a project completed in a shorter time frame; for instance when you are working on a product launch or a cost-savings project. Again, keep your eye on the value, not the cost. On many projects the consultant could charge you a higher total fee for one month than for six months, and you would benefit handsomely.

Contract Structure: On What Basis Should We Pay the Consultant?

Choosing the right contract structure is like choosing the right knot to tie in a rope. Most of us still tie our shoes with the granny knot we learned as kids, even though it's not a terribly good knot—often our laces don't stay tied; and we use the same knot for just about everything else, too. We know there are numerous knots that are better suited for one situation or another, but we may not feel comfortable tying a bowline, a sheet bend, or a clove hitch.

Many executives are still using an old, ineffective knot to bind consultants to their companies. The contractual equivalent of the granny knot is the variable time and materials (VTM) contract in which you pay the consultant an hourly or daily rate that varies depending on the seniority or skill set of the individual on the project. The consulting company may give you a blended "team rate" rather than a rate for individuals; nevertheless, it is still a time-based fee.

At the end of the project, the consulting firm tallies up the number of hours contributed by the personnel on your project team and presents you a final bill. You may have paid some portion of an estimated fee prior to the project's conclusion; however, any contract in which fees are adjusted at the end based on the amount of time actually worked is a VTM project. This includes cost-plus projects, which are standard fare for government-sponsored projects.

These types of contracts are highly problematic, and you should refuse to enter into them. Consultants who expect to invoice for VTM, as well as purchasing departments that want to bill that way, are resorting to an archaic and highly flawed contract structure. Among the problems with VTM contracts are the following:

- **There is a moral hazard.** Consultants are better off if they work more hours or assign higher-priced resources, regardless of whether that extra time or level of resource is in the client's best interest. Most consultants are trustworthy and don't seek to take advantage of their clients; however, an engagement with diametrically opposed interests, as is the case with VTM agreements, is a poor solution.

- **Emphasis is on activity rather than solutions.** Because the fee structure is based on how long it takes to complete the work, tasks become the center of attention. The objective of bringing in an outside expert, though, is to achieve an end, not to pay for the means.

- **Focus is on cost rather than value.** Since the meter is constantly running, it becomes a focal point and a distraction. Preproject negotiations immediately zero in on the day rates, and executives may hesitate to call the consultant with a question midproject or to request a minor addition (such as an extra presentation) when they know every conversation adds cost to the project.

- **Burden of due diligence falls to you rather than the expert.** Although the consultant has more experience judging how much activity will be necessary on your project, you are the one responsible for estimating correctly. The consultant has little incentive to nail the time and activity required to get you to your goal. After all, the consultant doesn't suffer if her estimate is low, and it's unlikely she will take less time than her estimate. As Figure 8-1

Figure 8-1   A Big Problem with VTM Contracts

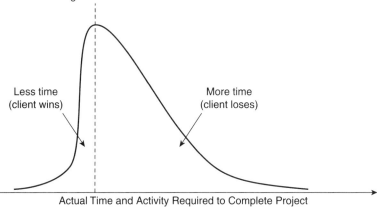

depicts, the risk profile in these types of contracts is asymmetrical in a way that is not propitious to you, the client.

- **Risk is increased.** While the value of a project may be fixed, in a VTM contract the cost is, by definition, variable. If the consulting firm takes significantly longer to do its job than either of you anticipated, it still gets paid (more than it had counted on), whereas your ROI on the project plummets. The entire risk of higher-than-anticipated activity falls on you.

- If you cap the project fee or have a "not-to-exceed" clause, then you have shifted risk back to the consulting firm; however, it will counteract the increased risk by quoting higher variable rates, which, again, redirects the risk back to you (see Figure 8-2). Provisions such as this can undo all the work we did in Chapter 7 to find the true value of project risks.

Figure 8-2   Why Caps Don't Work

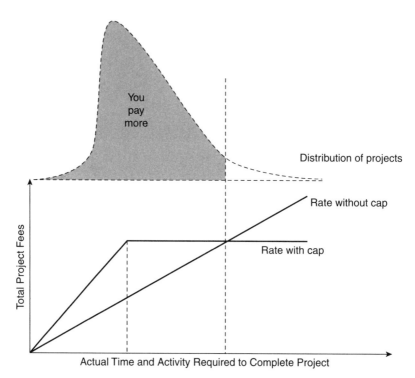

- **There is the risk of an adversarial relationship.** The reasons above amount to misaligned interests between you and the consultant, seeding distrust and setting the stage for an adversarial relationship. When you are investing tens of thousands or even millions of dollars into an initiative, distrust and internecine issues are the last thing you can afford.

There are four basic contract structures that will serve you substantially better than the VTM approach, and all of them are designed to align the consultant's interests to yours. They are the clever, effective twists of rope you can substitute for your old granny knots, and they are, for many companies, a huge leap forward in the way business can be conducted with an outside expert. The four contract structures are distinguished on two dimensions: project leeway and project boundedness.

Project Leeway

On some projects, the outside expert's work is tightly prescribed, down to the precise steps she should take and the way those steps should be taken. For instance, when you hire an accountant to pull together your annual taxes, the steps the accountant needs to take are well known. Tax codes are the same for everyone, and every accountant follows those codes (at least we hope so). CPAs don't get to pick and choose which tax forms to fill out or make up new ones to submit to the government. Certainly some financial analysts have a better command of the nuances of tax codes or have more experience or even more creativity. However, there is very little leeway in what steps an accountant has to take and how those steps must be taken. Further, the core intellectual capital underlying the project—in this case the tax codes—is constant, regardless of the accountant.

In contrast, some projects are wide open, such as when a large Verizon Wireless franchisee wanted help improving the performance of his store managers. The consultant he chose had full discretion over the implementation, the approach, and even the focus, as long as the desired end result was reached: improved performance. Every aspect of the project was in play, and the core intellectual capital underpinning the approach could vary from consultant to consultant.

The examples in Figure 8-3 may help clarify the concept of leeway.

Figure 8-3   Examples of Project Leeway

Leeway			
More ↑	Train our sales force on consultative selling	Recommend where we should focus to improve morale	Help us significantly reduce downtime at the Camden plant
Less ↓	Train our sales force on the SPIN method using the official SPIN materials	Conduct an interview with each department head, then one or two focus groups with each department. Then report back your findings and your recommendation on where to focus to improve morale	Use the "official" Six Sigma black-belt process and tools to reduce the downtime at the Camden plant by at least 15%

The more commoditylike the purchase, the more you will look at the consultant's costs (i.e., time and materials), whereas the more intensively the project relies on the consultant's exclusive intellectual property, the more you will turn to the value the consultant provides. This will become clearer after we review project boundedness.

Project Boundedness

The second factor that will help you identify the best possible contract structure is the project's *achievement boundary*. Think of the boundary as the finish line to a running race. For some projects, the tape is clearly visible and a predetermined distance from the start. Like a 100-yard dash or a 4-mile relay, tightly bounded projects have well-defined end points, deliverables, and timing. For instance, if you hire a website pro to update the look of your home page, then by a predetermined date, web surfers will land on your new home page, and the initiative will be completed.

Other projects are more like scavenger hunts, where you have a goal, but you could go about it in different ways and finish at different times and in different places if you finish at all. Unbounded projects have undefined end points, variable deliverables, and flexible timing. If you ask the website pro to be an on-call resource who gives advice and periodic recommendations based on competitive sites, you are setting up an unbounded project. You might agree to a yearlong contract, or you might agree to keep the service in place unless at some point

Figure 8-4 Examples of Bounded and Unbounded Projects

Achievement Boundary

Bounded ← → Unbounded

Write a plan for increasing sales	Help us increase sales
Redesign the sales team	Help our sales team function well over time
Conduct 6 training seminars for 30 people in 3 cities	Train all new employees on emotional intelligence, as the need arises

you no longer feel it adds value. Some months you might call on the consultant many times, whereas other months you might not talk with him at all.

The examples in Figure 8-4 show more-bounded versus less-bounded projects.

The Four Basic Fee Structures

Combining the amount of leeway and the project's boundedness indicates what fee structure will align interests and promote the greatest possible value. As Figure 8-5 shows, the four basic fee structures are value-based fees, stipends, fixed-price time and materials, and piece rate.

Figure 8-5 The Four Basic Fee Structures

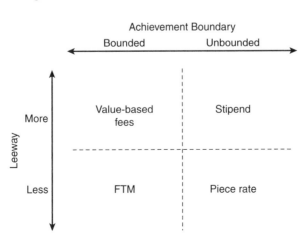

Achievement Boundary

Bounded   Unbounded

More: Value-based fees | Stipend

Less: FTM | Piece rate

Leeway

Value-Based Fee Contracts

In value-based fee contracts, the consulting firm's compensation is based on the amount of value you expect it to contribute. The extensive value-determining process in Chapter 1 and the sophisticated risk-reallocation work in Chapters 6 and 7 put you in an excellent position to know whether or not the fees the consultant is asking for are worthwhile. As mentioned earlier, a good rule of thumb is to attain at least a 7-to-1 risk-adjusted return on the consultant's fees.

As I also mentioned earlier, your decision on which consultant to hire for this type of initiative should rarely come down to cost or fees. In projects of this nature, the quality, experience, intellectual property, and approach of the consultant make a huge difference in the outcome. Even a small reduction in risk or improvement in expected outcome can outweigh a significant fee gap between two consultants.

Most strategy and process consulting engagements fall into this high-leeway–high-boundedness combination, and therefore you should resort to this type of contract most often. If you want to know more about how value-based fees look from the consultant's side, I highly recommend reading books by Dr. Alan Weiss including, for instance, *Value-Based Fees.*

Stipend Fee Structures

In stipend contracts you pay the consultants a fixed, periodic sum (a "stipend") for as-needed access to their expertise, ingenuity, and intellectual capital. The amount of that fee is also loosely based on value; however, in unbounded projects the value is much harder or impossible to quantify. Therefore, the amount of the stipend tends to be judged on a "reasonableness" standard against a rough idea of the magnitude of value. That value may be affected by the consultant's expertise, experience, availability, and response time, among other variables.

A critical component of the successful stipend project is that the periodic payment is fixed, regardless of the amount of time put in. Your interests and your efforts are perfectly aligned under this structure, boosting your revenue as efficiently and quickly as possible. Another key element of the stipend is that the outputs are not narrowly defined. Once you start to introduce tightly bounded objectives and end points, you are moving into the territory where a fixed fee (value based or time and materials) is appropriate.

Stipend contracts can last many years and even transcend corporate boundaries. The CEO of one large consumer electronics firm has retained a single PR firm on a monthly basis for over two decades during his trip through three different companies. The firm gives him general advice and recommendations, helps him think through external communication strategy, and provides feedback on his internal missives. Over the years the level of trust and understanding has grown; and even though the CEO had to reduce the firm's stipend during some lean years, the firm's counsel has grown continuously more valuable. When a large, well-defined PR need arises, he creates a separate contract to handle it.

Fixed-Price Time and Materials

When the project is tightly bounded and the consultant is given very little leeway, a *fixed-price* time-and-materials (FTM) contract is most appropriate. This kind of contract is well suited to implementation projects because you are dictating exactly what must be done and are just looking for some skilled bodies to execute the tasks. The more common the skill, the more qualified contractors you will find, and the more you can, and should, start looking at time and materials rather than value. Often these are projects in which you are not looking for best-in-class or breakthrough solutions (at least, not due to the consultant); rather, you are looking for competent performance.

IT implementation projects often fall into this category, as do many training exercises and approaches that use rigid, well-defined systems, such as Six Sigma. You may find implementers who are more or less qualified or skilled, just as you can find bricklayers who are more or less qualified or skilled; and the higher-end consultants will charge more per hour or day. However, they are still following your overall direction with little leeway in what gets done when and how.

To build an FTM contract, your consultant should propose how much time at each skill level he is allocating based on a detailed outline from you. Then you agree on a total rate for the entire project, and that becomes fixed. This realigns your interests and the consultant's so that for the remainder of the project both sides become focused on efficiently and effectively achieving your desired outcome. How resources are allocated and how efficiently your goal is achieved are the consultant's problems.

The fee for the training project becomes $15,000 for three days of training. Period. The fee for the IT project becomes $1.5 million for worldwide implementation of the new procurement system. No overages allowed. For complex projects, the fee may be the sum of a number of smaller, fixed-price components, particularly if you are not exactly sure up front which pieces will be needed. Take an example where you are preparing a new line of products for approval by the EPA and you hire a consultant to create labels that meet EPA standards. An FTM contract is best since there is little leeway and the project is tightly bounded; however, the EPA sometimes requires a second set of labeling, and that is hard to predict in advance. Therefore you should agree to a fixed price to develop the labels based on the consultant's estimates of the time required and her daily rate and agree to a separate fixed price for the secondary labeling, which will be added if necessary.

I have heard consultants complain that projects are too unpredictable, which shifts all the risk in an FTM contract onto their side, or that FTM contracts create a bad situation for the client if they don't "budget enough" to cover for unexpected project requirements. Look at the Magard example, they might say. That took a full year of extra effort and $1 million in extra consultant fees that wouldn't have been covered in an FTM project.

Nonsense. First of all, the Magard project should not have been a time-and-materials project in the first place. The consulting firm was given tremendous leeway on how to achieve the desired result, and the contract should have been structured as a value-based fee. Had Magard paid the consulting firm $3 million or even $4 million from the outset, the consultants would have done just as good a job or even better, and the project's ROI, by the CEO's own admission, would still have been outstanding.

Second, even if the consulting firm were paid on an FTM basis, for which it undoubtedly would have built in a buffer of $250,000 or more, I'm willing to bet it would have finished Magard's system earlier and with as much quality or more since extending the project would now be penalized rather than rewarded. The incentive to achieve your objective earlier is another advantage of an FTM contract compared with a VTM project with a cap (see Figure 8-6).

Yes, projects are tough to predict—particularly larger projects. Therefore, determine fixed prices in advance for the most likely situations that may arise, such as designing the second set of labels in the FDA example above. Similarly, you can predetermine a fixed cost for different scenarios, such as if phase I of a project reveals that four, six

Figure 8-6 FTM Versus VTM with Cap

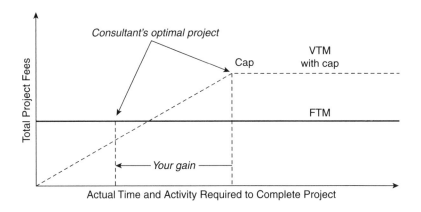

or eight production lines must be overhauled. In addition, FTM contracts should contain a clause that protects both sides in the event that some unforeseen circumstance dramatically alters the scope of the project. Keep it at a high level, though, to avoid frequent negotiations over changes in scope.

Should you worry that a consultant will skimp on the quality if the fee is fixed or bail altogether if the project is going belly-up? Not if you choose an excellent consultant in the first place. No consultant can build a good reputation by taking shortcuts that deleteriously affect the clients' outcomes; and just like the builders in your town who use flimsy materials and cut corners in construction, a bit of due diligence before you bring them on board will quickly reveal their true nature.

Piece-Rate Contracts

Finally, there are projects that give the consultant very little leeway but are unbounded. An example would be if you were to contract a training company to run a boot camp for each new sales representative, in which the representative would obtain product knowledge and selling skills. The content of the training is predefined, and there is very little leeway for the outside expert; however, the number of people brought through this boot camp over the course of a two-year contract may vary considerably. Therefore, you agree to a fixed price per trainee—a piece rate.

Piece-rate contracts are very different from contracts in which you are paying an hourly or daily rate. In a piece-rate contract you are paying by the deliverable, where the content of the deliverables is standardized but the quantity is undetermined. Once you agree upon a fixed price per deliverable, it is up to the consulting firm to manage the amount and quality of manpower required to deliver each time.

For instance, suppose you are paying for an IT company to install a new system across all divisions, but it is difficult to determine in advance how many fresh installations will be needed versus upgrades. In this case, you would create a piece rate for each type of installation, and the total contract would end up being whatever the combination of fresh installs and upgrades turns out to be. In this example, what you have really done is combined two piece-rate projects—one for fresh installations and one for upgrades. Each is unbounded because the number of deliverables is undefined at the start.

Other Contract Options

While many other contract structures are used between consultants and clients, the two that I most often receive questions about are skin-in-the-game contracts and equity-equivalent contracts.

Skin-in-the-Game Contracts

Skin-in-the game arrangements are sometimes referred to as *performance-based fees*, and as a client, you may be thinking that this is exactly what you want: pay consultants if they succeed, and don't pay if they don't produce value. For instance, let's say you are hiring a consultant to help you negotiate contracts with your suppliers of raw materials. The consultant claims she can save you 10 percent on your raw materials costs if you let her work her magic. Should you suggest a skin-in-the game contract in which she would get paid based on the actual savings she produces? There are pros and cons to this type of contract, and before putting one together, you should consider both sides.

- **Lowers your short-term risk.** The big pro for this type of project is the massive shift of short-term risk from you to the consultant. In a situation where the risk is very high or you have very little faith in the consultant, shifting the risk may become quite attractive. If your raw materials costs don't go down at all, there are no consulting fees to pay. All you've lost is some sweat equity, and you've gained more confidence that you already had great rates for your raw materials.

- **Increases complexity.** These types of contracts require more precise measurements of progress and outcomes, which can be very complex. In the raw materials example, you have to agree on how to establish a baseline price, and you also have to control for exogenous factors. For instance, if the market price of raw materials declines in general, does the consultant reap the benefit of the cost savings? What if the consultant negotiates a contract with options in it that make the dollar savings difficult to determine up front?

- **Raises measurement difficulties.** You can only create success-based rewards if you can accurately measure success. Profitability is notoriously tough to estimate, and even seemingly simple metrics like sales or payroll costs can be a challenge. The consultant may say that he should be remunerated on the basis of the actual cost of the raw material and not, for instance, the freight charge since that is outside his control and his process; however, suppliers may not habitually break out freight charges, and suddenly the measuring has become more challenging.

- **Leads to disagreements.** In our example, you would think there is little room for disagreement; however, what if your raw materials requirements drop? The consultant might insist that you compensate him based on the savings you would have had if you had used the same amount of raw materials as last year; however, to you, the actual savings is not very much, and the ROI on the project will drop significantly if you have to pay based on theoretical savings rather than real savings.

- **Increases cost.** Any time you shift risk away from you, there will be a price attached. Whereas on a value-based contract you may get a 10-to-1 return, you will get a lower return on a skin-in-the-game contract for the exact same project.

Let's say the consultant promises $200,000 in savings on raw materials, and you estimate there's a 50-50 chance that his approach will work. The risk-adjusted value to you is $100,000, and you are amenable to his $10,000 fee. For a skin-in-the-game contract to work out for this consultant, he would probably charge 15 percent, which means if his approach works, you will pay $30,000. As always, in the grand scheme of things, the cost of a project is small potatoes compared with the gain even when the fees are three times as high. Nevertheless, be aware that you may pay three times as much for the same work.

- **Increases long-term risk.** A subtle downside to these types of contracts is the incentive to work the project in a way that maximizes performance on the success metric rather than achieving the actual long-term objective. If you cannot find an accurate, easy-to-measure indicator of success that is tied to your long-term outcomes, stay away from this type of contract. For instance, if the consultant creates a 10 percent decrease in raw materials costs but, in the process, burns your bridges with virtually every supplier in the industry, that may come back to haunt you when your current supplier is no longer willing to lowball. Consultants who come in on a skin-in-the-game basis and lower costs by reducing headcount create costly, value-reducing, long-term problems almost without exception.

What do I recommend? Reallocating risk is a great idea, and the different ways you can do it are shown in detail in the previous two chapters. For that reason, I like skin-in-the-game contracts if you do them right. Here are the keys to setting up a great contract of this variety:

- **Only put a portion at risk.** Massive shifts in risk exacerbate all the downsides of this type of contract. At most you should designate 50 percent of the total value of the contract as variable based on actual results.

- **Stipulate up front how exogenous factors will be controlled or addressed.** This means you have to think through in advance what else beyond the consultant's work could affect the outcome of your project and then state explicitly how that will be measured and worked into the calculations. Where this is not possible, don't use skin-in-the-game contracts.

- **Use valid, leading indicators.** Actual performance in the marketplace is often a lagging indicator. Profit, for instance, is a lagging indicator. In the example of the cost savings on raw materials, the lagging indicator could be the actual dollars paid to the supplier through the end of the year; the leading indicator would be the projected costs based on the negotiated price and the expected amount of raw materials that will be used. Lagging indicators are generally harder to measure, involve more exogenous noise, and delay payment (which will increase costs and apprehension). However, make sure the leading indicator is valid. Reduction in payroll costs in the short term, for instance, has proved not to be a good indicator of profit savings over the long term.

- **Use metrics that are clear and indisputable.** A gut feeling that the project is successful, or the subjective rating of the consultant's performance, is too open to debate.

- **Set up performance hurdles rather than a linear scale.** Rather than paying 10 percent of savings, agree to pay $10,000 if the savings are above $75,000 and $15,000 if the savings are above $150,000. On a training program, pay a bonus for each trainee who scores above 70 percent on an exam. You pay nothing for a score of 69 percent, and you pay the same for a trainee who scores 100 percent as one who scores 71 percent. This eases the requirements for precise measurements and mitigates that downside of skin-in-the-game contracts. The best hurdles are action standards because they are typically binary. You go forward with Phase II or you don't. You roll the program out or you don't.

Equity-Equivalent Contracts

Equity and equity-equivalent contracts are a special form of skin-in-the-game contract applied to unbounded projects. In these contracts the consultant is given equity in the company (which is most common in start-ups) or given the equivalent of equity via shadow stock or a percentage of EBITDA or some similar metric.

For example, there is an excellent consultant in Pittsburgh who takes on only three clients at a time, and he works for those three clients as their de facto vice president of sales. His clients are smallish companies that cannot afford a senior leader of his caliber full-time, and they pay him a stipend plus some equity in their company. In return, he delivers the blue chip experience, leadership, and expertise of a 25-year veteran with an impeccable track record.

Equity-equivalent projects avoid most of the downsides of a skin-in-the-game contract because there are no measurement issues. In addition, these kinds of projects encourage a long-term view, and they totally align the consultant's objectives with your own. However, since the value of the equity depends on so many factors outside the consultant's control, a consultant will rarely accept it as the primary form of compensation. For an unbounded, extremely high-leeway project at the most senior level, the equity-equivalent piece can be a nice addition to a consulting contract. The example of the consultant in Pittsburgh is the best one I've encountered and serves as a good model.

When Should the Consultant Get Paid? A Question of Timing

If consultants do work before they are paid, they take on risk; if consultants receive payment before the work is completed, risk shifts to the client's side. Therefore, timing is an excellent candidate for the risk reallocation techniques described in the previous two chapters.

Up-Front Payment

Usually consulting firms will ask for at least some portion of their fee to be paid up front. Is this reasonable considering you haven't received a lick of value? Yes. Before commencing your project, the consulting firm has most likely eliminated the possibility of working with your direct competitors, has blocked out time, and may have pulled together teams, materials, and processes. There is generally a significant opportunity cost and investment taken on by a consultancy before the project begins.

In addition, when a consulting firm brings a lot of intellectual property to the table, the value it is contributing to you tends to be very front-loaded, and so the payments should be too. Once the consultants share their ideas, approaches, processes, models, or other jewels, it's possible for the client to terminate the project and tackle the implementation on its own. No ethical client would do this; however, not all clients prove to be ethical, and consultants are understandably wary of giving away their assets before receiving compensation.

How much is paid up front is open to negotiation, of course, and is part of the total risk allocation package. For example, you might opt to

Table 8-3

Contract Type	Percentage Up-Front Payment
Value-based fee	20–50%
Stipend	100% before each period starts
Fixed time and materials	15–40%
Piece rate	0–10%

pay a consultant 100 percent up front in exchange for a lower fee or a guarantee of early delivery. The figures in Table 8-3 are a rough rule of thumb.

Payment Based on Phases

Large projects often have multiple phases that involve distinct streams of activity. A recent contract I reviewed called for six distinct phases over eight months and a total fee of roughly $3 million. You can apportion the payments of each phase as a separate project with associated installments at commencement and completion. You and the consultant will have to negotiate how much of the total value is delivered by each phase of the contract. Of course, you should be doing this anyway to ensure that every phase is actually delivering enough value to be worth doing.

Tables 8-4 and 8-5 show how a $500,000 multiphase project might be paid.

Table 8-4

Phasing			
Phase	Value	Payment at Commencement	Payment at Completion
Assessment	10%	100%	–
Macro design	40%	50%	50%
Micro design	30%	50%	50%
Rollout	20%	20%	80%

Table 8-5

Payments			
Payment	Phase Commencing	Phase Completing	Total Payment
1	Assessment		$50,000
2	Macro design	Assessment	$100,000
3	Micro design	Macro design	$175,000
4	Rollout	Micro design	$95,000
5		Rollout	$80,000

Timing Based on Deliverables

This is the most common basis for payment, and while it has some advantages—namely, you don't pay for work unless you get what you paid for—it has a couple of disadvantages too. The two big disadvantages of paying based on deliverables are:

1. It focuses the consultant's attention onto deliverables rather than desired outcomes. When you describe your indicators of success as traditional deliverables such as reports or presentations, too much energy is spent on preparing and presenting materials. This is energy that would be better used in the service of reaching your desired outcome.

2. It increases the risk for the consultant that payment will be delayed and, therefore, increases your cost. Keep in mind that the timing of completing a project may be outside the control of the consultant. In fact, it is common for clients to delay projects for internal reasons such as personnel changes, availability of key constituents, and conflicting priorities. These add unexpected and uncontrollable costs to the project for the consultant and, ultimately, you.

Therefore, if you are going to use deliverables-based timing for payments, (1) make sure you and the consultant spend time designing excellent indicators for success that are indisputable and clearly measurable and (2) insert a clause into the contract that reallocates risk back to you for delays caused by you rather than by the consultant. The language you use may look something like this.

Fees are payable as follows: $X on January 4, 2010, $Y upon achievement of the indicators of success for Phase 1, and $Z upon completion of Phase 2. Unless the consultant is the cause of significant delays, all payments must be completed prior to May 1, 2012.

If your gut protests against a clause like this, remember that your goal is to increase value, lower cost, and improve the odds of success. This clause looks on the surface like it is merely a boon to the consultants; however, on closer examination, you will see that it reduces your cost (because the consultant will offer a lower fee in return for this payment provision) and it rewards both sides for getting the project done on time.

Timing Based on Calendar

An excellent, though less common, timing arrangement is calendar-based payments—for instance, 50 percent upon commencement, 25 percent after 30 days, and 25 percent after 60 days. At first blush, you might view this as a terrible way to pay a consultant since it is not based on any type of deliverable. It turns out you already make payments this way. To whom? Your employees. Your employees are paid on a regular, calendar basis regardless of when they complete their work. Yes, they are expected to accomplish certain tasks, achieve certain objectives, and perform at an acceptable level; however, the timing of their work and the timing of their payment are poorly linked.

Since your relationship with a consultant—particularly a senior-level consultant working on a high-leeway project—is closer to a partnership or employer-employee relationship than a client-vendor relationship, an employee-type payment schedule may be appropriate.

Use of Escrows to Hold Payments

Escrow accounts are one of the best solutions to the question of when to pay the consultant. They reduce risk on both sides of the table at once while adding virtually no cost. In an escrow arrangement you deposit fees up front, on a phased or calendar basis, and then release the fees when certain conditions are met. For example, in the $500,000 phased project discussed earlier, the consultant may be uncomfortable starting the entire initiative with only 10 percent being paid up front. Therefore, you could make the first payment to the consultant of $50,000 when the project commences and, at the same time, deposit the second payment ($100,000) into an escrow account. The conditions of the escrow account are set so that when the consultant finishes the "assessment" phase and starts the "micro design" phase, the money is released to the consultant. If the consultant never finishes the assessment phase or doesn't finish it to some predetermined level of success, then the money reverts to you.

Since the money leaves your control when it goes into escrow, the consultant can feel much more assured that she will get paid if she delivers the work. Similarly, since the money is not yet in the consultant's hands when it goes into escrow, you can feel more confident that you will get the promised work before the funds are irrevocably spent.

Summary

Determining how much to pay your consultants is important, and yet in the grand scheme of your project, it turns out to be less important than knowing when and on what basis you will pay them. When you turn your attention from cost to value, from fee reduction to risk reduction, and from competing interests to aligned interests, you set yourself up for a successful project.

With the right contract structure in place, the nightmare project that balloons from $1 million in consulting fees to $2 million and beyond will never happen. You may end up agreeing to $2 million from the start; however, you will know it's a good deal, and you'll know that the consultant is striving diligently to deliver the value as early and with as little risk as possible. That can only be good for you. With five years of retrospection, Magard came to realize that even a project that ran 50 percent over budget can be spectacularly successful. The real loss was the extra year it took for the project to be completed—and most of that year probably could have been avoided had the consultant not been paid on a VTM basis.

After the prework, searching, choosing, and negotiating, you are finally ready to get the project started. The next section of the book covers what you can do before, during, and after the consulting project to maximize your value.

Successful
Implementation

How Do We Prep for Success?

Readying Your Company Before the Project Starts

In This Chapter

Now that you have an agreement with an outstanding consultant and a handle on your project's risks, you are undoubtedly excited to get your new, expert partners up and running at high gear. Before you hand over the keys to the consultant, it's important to lay the groundwork for phenomenal results.

Key concepts in Chapter 9 include the following:
- Buy-in
- Decision-making styles
- Communication levels
- Planning for scarce resources
- The FARCI method

Maine's Fiasco

In 2001 the state of Maine embarked on a project similar to ones in other states around the country: upgrade its health claims processing system to clear claims faster, track costs more accurately, and offer more accurate information to healthcare providers while meeting new federal requirements for privacy. The state's head of procurement inked the $15 million agreement with a consultant in October to build the new system by the looming, federally mandated deadline 12 months away.

More than three years later, on Friday, January 21, 2005, the state finally flipped the go-live switch on its new web-based Medicaid claims system. The cost for development up to that point had ballooned to $25 million. Within days of activation, millions of dollars of claims had been handled improperly, and the scale of the impending meltdown was starting to emerge. By the end of March, the state was holding on to approximately 300,000 mismanaged claims, healthcare providers were seeking emergency loans or going out of business due to lack of funds, and Medicaid recipients were being turned away from their doctors' offices. In December, the state commissioner who had overseen the project resigned, and the estimates of the new system's cost were approaching $30 million.

What went wrong? A debacle of such proportions does not stem from a single error or decision. Without question, virtually none of the best practices laid out in this book for structuring a project and hiring the right consultant were in place. However, even had the state written a top-tier Context Document and hired a better consultant, the project would have failed. The project team was extremely understaffed, and it did not have the personnel to complete the work that had to be done within the required time frame. In addition, the team unsuccessfully battled to get face time with the state's Medicaid experts. As a result, the team was left to make uninformed decisions on how to meet Medicaid requirements. Perhaps worst of all, the project was set up so that the state's internal programmers and the consulting firm's staff would work on parts of the system without involving each other. With such poor communication on the project, failure was inevitable.[1]

You can hire an exceptional consultant and still face disappointing results if you do not prepare your company for the hired gun's arrival. Your attention and dedication to getting your company's ducks in a row before launching a project will determine how smoothly or painfully the project proceeds and, in some cases, whether you achieve a successful outcome at all.

The answer to "How do I prep for success?" breaks down into four areas of focus:

1. Do we have sufficient buy-in?
2. Are we prepared for the risks?
3. Do we have the right resources at the ready?
4. Do we have guidance mechanisms securely in place?

Do We Have Sufficient Buy-In?

Many executives believe the secret to a successful project is simple: communication, buy-in, and participation. The popular literature would certainly have you accept that with sweeping involvement and collaboration, project life will be hunky-dory. That is not the case. Not every project requires significant buy-in. Different levels and types of inclusion are appropriate at different times, and sometimes an Autocratic decision style is exactly what's needed.

Comparing two examples will illustrate the elements of buy-in and the way they can differ from project to project. The first example involves Dan, a division president within a major entertainment company, who knew that his days were numbered unless he could improve the division's performance. A central component of his plan was improving the output of the production department, which was in total disarray. Productivity was low, competing demands from different product lines made priorities unclear, and communication was poor and disorganized. First, Dan tapped a young, charismatic up-and-coming production director, Paul, to be vice president of production. Dan then hired a consultant and established a simple remit: set Paul up to succeed.

In the second example, Omar, the senior vice president of innovation for a consumer products company, asked the managing director of a consortium to locate a truly outstanding expert to help name a new line of products. The track record of Omar's company using outsiders to name product lines was spotty, and he was skeptical that consultants could reliably produce first-rate product names.

Table 9-1

	Dan's Project	Omar's Project
Project objective	Paul is set up for success	Product line has great name
Type of project	Area of focus/plan	Implementation
Behavior change required	Extensive	Almost none
Impact on people	High	Low
Number of constituents	Many	Few
Ambiguity in project	High	Low
Speed requirements	Sooner is better	Fast is critical

Previous attempts had taken a long time to produce a handful of patently obvious or unusable names. Perhaps, he reasoned, it is just a crapshoot, in which case the task could be taken on internally with as much success, less time, and little expense. After calling the consortium, Omar handed off the project to Charles, who would be leading the project, and Shirah, the market research manager, to work out the details.

These two projects couldn't be further apart in a whole host of ways, including the level of buy-in required for success. Table 9-1 shows some of the differences.

With these two projects in mind, let's take a look at what was needed to gain sufficient buy-in, using the same questions you should use before starting every project.

1. Is There Unwavering Support from the Top?

Every project must have an executive sponsor who supplies unwavering support. An executive sponsor is the manager who is ultimately responsible for securing the resources (money, time, and people) for the project. She acts as a visible champion of the project, keeps her finger on the general pulse, and, when necessary, acts as the final decision maker. The moment it looks like her support is flagging, fear, uncertainty, and doubt set in, work slows down, quality suffers, and outcomes are put in jeopardy.

In both example projects there was a clear executive sponsor: Dan and Omar, respectively. Dan's support of the consultant's work was never in doubt from the moment he made the first call until Paul took the stage to present the final results at an annual division meeting. Omar was a bit more ambivalent about his project, particularly in the beginning, because he wasn't sure it made sense to bring in an outside expert. As a result, Charles was very slow to return consultants' phone calls, and it took longer than necessary to get the initial approvals in place. Were it not for the fact that developing the name was starting to delay the launch of the company's new product, Omar's project would have continued to languish.

If you are the executive sponsor of a project and are uncertain about its viability, then work through your doubts *before* hiring an outside expert and putting together a project team. The chapters at the beginning of the book provide guidance in determining whether a project is valuable, but you will have to make the strategic decisions about what initiatives you will take on. Once you have made your decision, then back it fully, letting the people involved know your commitment. That doesn't mean you can't change your mind if evidence suggests you've made a poor decision; it does mean you show total commitment while staying open-minded.

If you are leading a project but are not the executive sponsor, you need to lock in a high-level champion before you start anything else. Stop the presses *before* the executive sponsor signs on the dotted line if support is not rock solid. Don't confuse a signature with unassailable support. Push back and work through any concerns and objections your executive sponsor has, because her level of ambivalence will directly correspond to your level of pain during the project.

2. Are We Using the Right Level of Inclusion?

In Dan's project to set Paul up for success, Dan and the consultant could have sat in a room for a couple of days and worked through all the pieces they thought would be necessary—the vision Paul would have to articulate, the organizational design, the new chain of command, and so forth. Then they could have revealed their brilliance to the whole organization, including Paul, and striven to force adoption of their vaunted plan. Would that level of noninclusion have worked? Of course not. Paul needed to be involved in the design of his own organization and vision, and realistically, many of the other stakeholders in the company needed to agree to changes in processes that would affect them.

Conversely, Omar could have organized a companywide meeting to gain approval on the product-line names, perhaps granting employees the time to argue through their differences in opinion and then holding a vote to decide on the final name. That democratic process may hold some appeal, but it definitely would not have fit in the timeline, and the resulting name would be suspect. The opinions of the crowd of employees inside a company generally don't accurately represent those of their customer base.

As you can see, there is not a one-size-fits-all rule for how much inclusion is best to create organizational buy-in for your project. The model in Figure 9-1 shows the five types of decision-making styles you can set up for your project and indicates which is most appropriate based on the level of inclusion.

To determine the optimal level of inclusion for your project, look at the time available to make the decision, the breadth of the behavior change your project will require across the organization, the extent to which people's behavior will have to change, and the extent to which secrecy or security is an issue.

The five decision-making styles that grow out of those factors are Autocratic, Evaluative, Participative, Democratic, and Consensus. In Autocratic decision making, the executive sponsor, the project leader, or some small number of people to whom decision-making authority has been delegated make major decisions based on information at hand and their own experiences, perceptions, and knowledge. The organization at large has little-to-no input in this style. If the executive sponsor delegates authority, it is usually to one person or, at most, a small cadre of coleaders.

In the Evaluative and Participative styles, the decision making continues to rest with the executive sponsor or her delegate(s); however, the level of organizational input increases. In the Evaluative style, the decision makers supplement their knowledge and perceptions with the information and ideas from the organization. In the Participative style, the organization also contributes opinions and feedback.

When the responsibility for major decisions moves to a broader group, such as a steering team composed of advocates for various groups, or to the entire organization, either the Democratic or

Figure 9-1 Spectrum of Decision-Making Styles

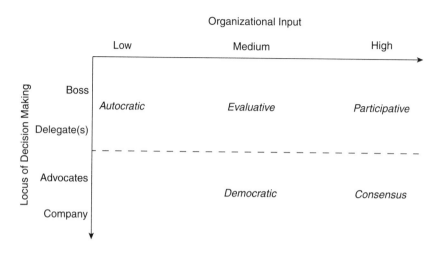

Consensus style can be employed. In the former style, decisions are made on a majority-rules basis; in the latter style, everyone must be brought on board.

Choose your decision-making style based primarily on the breadth of behavior change, which describes how much of the organization will have to work differently as a result of your project, and the extent of behavior change, which is how different the new world will be. The effects of the different styles include the time it takes to make a decision and the number of security issues that arise. (See Figure 9-2.)

Figure 9-2 Drivers of Decision-Making Styles

Autocratic   *Evaluative*   *Participative*

Democratic   *Consensus*

Breadth of Behavior Change

Extent of Behavior Change

Time to Decision

Security/Secrecy of Decision

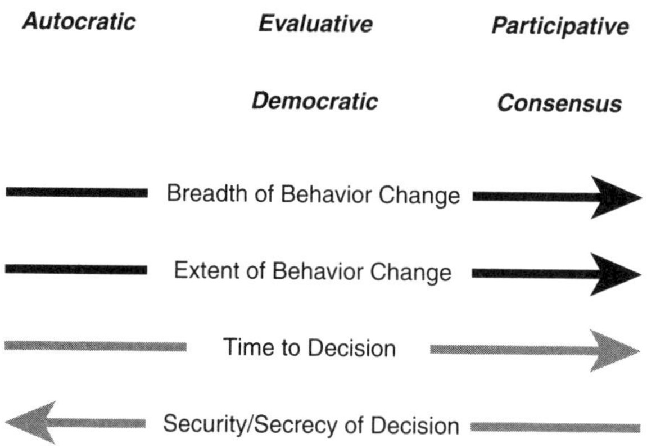

Dan's project to set Paul up for success involved considerable behavior change from Paul and his entire organization, as well as the many different product-line managers. Everyone inside the company knew that Dan was going to transform the production organization, and it didn't matter at all if people outside the company found out. Dan deemed the timeframe to be paramount, however, and sought a speedy process. The best decision-making styles for his project were Participative and Democratic. The Autocratic and Evaluative styles had too little inclusion and would not have garnered enough buy-in from the organization, and the Consensus style would have taken too long. He ended up using the Participative style for aspects of the project that were related to just the production department and a more Democratic style for those parts of the project that required other departments' buy-in to be successful.

In contrast, Omar's product-naming project involved no behavior change, time was of the essence, and it was critical that competitors remained unaware of the new product line. The appropriate style was unquestionably Autocratic. In this case, Omar appointed a small team of delegates including Charles, Shirah, himself, and the vice president of sales, whose opinion he valued. That group made the decision on the name and announced it to the organization. No further buy-in was necessary.

3. Are We Including the Right People?

Sufficient buy-in means you also have the right people supporting the project. Create a list of who will need to be included, at least at some level, during the project by using the following questions:

1. Who will need to work on this project?
2. Who will have to implement the results of this project?
3. Whose work, responsibility, job scope, power, status, or pride will be affected by this project?
4. Who has knowledge that is directly relevant to the decisions being made?
5. Who could sabotage the project, while in process, by diverting resources, conveying misleading information, or injecting negative energy?

6. Who will benefit from the results of the project?

7. Have we included all necessary external stakeholders, e.g., vendors, partners, customers, shareholders, regulators, media?

4. Are We Communicating the Right Information?

You won't get stalwart buy-in from someone who has no clue what you are doing. Therefore, how much you need to share and what you need to share are your key questions after you determine your level of inclusion, i.e., who you are going to include in the project and in what way. Your goal is to decrease the level of worry, since worrying is an internally focused, unproductive state for any employee in any organization.

Worry is ambiguity plus indecision. In contrast, apprehension evaporates when a definitive decision has been made and people have been told where they are going, how they are going to get there, and how they will handle bumps in the road (see Figure 9-3). Hence, to reduce organizational worry, you need to communicate the project's desired outcomes, your overall approach to get there, and your plan for setbacks. The more input people have into the decision, and the more ambiguity there is in the project, the more depth of information you need to convey.

In Dan's project, the level of inclusion and the level of ambiguity were both elevated. The employees inside the production department were not sure how the organization would change or what that would

Figure 9-3 Worry = Ambiguity + Indecision

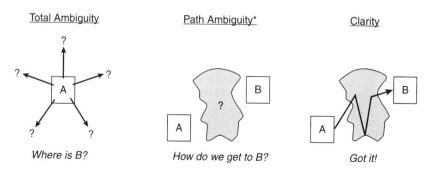

Total Ambiguity	Path Ambiguity*	Clarity
Where is B?	How do we get to B?	Got it!

*Path ambiguity adapted with permission from Dr. Alan Weiss

mean for them. Dan's first order of business, therefore, was to communicate his intentions for the project clearly and concisely. His announcement to the organization sounded like this.

As you know, our division's performance has lagged expectations; therefore we must take steps to change how we do business. Our first priority is to boost the productivity of our production department. We are initiating a project that will improve the way the different business units interact with production, improve communication between production and the business units, and improve processes inside the department that are dampening productivity.

He quickly followed that announcement with another communiqué that spoke to his approach, including Paul's appointment as vice president, the use of consultants, the opportunities for inclusion, and the initiative's timing. Dan led with the announcement about Paul because he knew the biggest question in everyone's mind was who would replace the current vice president. Rather than let speculation siphon energy from the real work at hand, he addressed it immediately. If the ambiguity includes very specific points of concern, address them quickly and concretely.

Trust also mitigates worry. If the employees in your organization trust you and believe you have their best interests at heart, their level of concern decreases. In essence, they are saying their decision is to trust that you know the route to the promised land, can deal with the bumps in the road, and will convey them there safely. Remember that simply because you believe that the employees in the organization *should* trust you or that you are worthy of their trust doesn't mean they share your perception. Your level of communication needs to reflect the reality of their perspective.

5. Is the Project Perceived as Fair and Appropriate?

The final secret to obtaining buy-in is organizational acceptance that your desired outcomes and your approach are reasonable, appropriate, and fair. As Ann Latham, author of *Clear Thoughts*, states:

When people believe the process is fair, they can accept almost anything, even terrible decisions, and move on. When people believe there is no fair process, they become angry and fearful. Even good decisions can raise the hackles if the process is suspect.

Unfortunately, fairness looks different from different vantage points. Dan saw that his current vice president of production was not managing the department well, in which case removing him from the role appeared perfectly fair. The vice president of production and some of his subordinates felt that targeting the role of vice president was scapegoating and patently unfair. Your solution in these situations is ensuring that people feel they are being heard, which can be accomplished with the following four steps:

1. Ascertain who will be threatened by your desired outcome, level of inclusion, or project approach. Whose livelihood or pride is at risk? Soliciting input from colleagues a few steps away from you in the organization is a big help in this step.

2. Strive to understand their point of view. What would their description of fair look like? This is not the time to defend or explain your stance.

3. Honestly explain your vantage point and demonstrate that you understand the other ways of looking at the issue and have considered them.

4. Act consistently.

Are We Prepared for the Risks?

You can handle the second area of focus prior to launching your project quickly: revisit the risks in the project and confirm that you are prepared for them, have mitigated them well, and have backup plans in place. In other words, you should always start a project expecting it to succeed and ready for it to fail. In that way a project is like a single play in a football game. Although the play is designed to gain yards—and, perhaps, even a touchdown—the defense often spoils the play. In these cases the quarterback has backup receivers, or the running back lurches in a different direction. And if the play doesn't work, the athletes move on to something else.

Chapters 6 and 7 cover risk management in depth. Your task at this point is to ensure that you have contingencies in place for when the unexpected happens on your project. You should have backup plans in place for the most probable and most severe problems that could crop up on your project.

Do We Have the Right Resources at the Ready?

In most cases, you don't hand over a bag of cash to a consultant with the admonition, "Come back when everything's done." Generally you or others in your company will be called upon to contribute insights, expertise, or a spare set of arms and legs. The two questions about internal resources you must answer before commencing the project are these:

1. Do we have the right competencies on the team?
2. Have we identified and planned for scarce resources?

1. Do We Have the Right Competencies on the Team?

There's little sense in hiring a brilliant thinker for a project if you yoke him to an internal team lacking in key talents and competencies. Before the project kicks off, your project leader should sit down with the consultant to map out exactly what internal resources are needed. If the only people who *can* work on the job are you and an associate, or the two guys from IT, or the market research manager, this question may be moot. Nevertheless, by scoping out the competencies you *should* have on your team, you will know where you and the consultant have to keep a watchful eye on the project as it progresses. The four buckets of competencies are:

- **Technical.** Will this project require an expert on atmospheric interference? If you are exploring exotic new products, is there a regulatory expert on the team who can keep you within federal guidelines? Will the project benefit from highly creative thinkers (which I lump under the banner of technical competencies)?

   Sometimes you purposely want to avoid having people with related technical competencies playing a role because they suffer from the curse of knowledge. They already "know" what can be done and what can't be done, and as a result, they will steer the project down a predictable path while blind to breakthrough opportunities.

Either way, make a list of the technical competencies that are needed or that you specifically don't want represented on the team; then simply check them off as you staff the project. Any missing competencies go on your "watch-out" list for later.

· **Fiefdom.** By this I mean the full range of stakeholders necessary for the project's success. If you are revising a process that touches finance and accounting, are the sovereign states (i.e., departments) of Corporate Finance and Accounting represented on the team? If you are setting strategy that will affect four business units, are all four of those fiefdoms' interests (and understanding) being considered? This isn't a question of inclusion and buy-in so much as one of knowledge needed for success.

· **Leadership.** A project team without strong leadership is a like a second grader's soccer team: uncoordinated, unplanned, and unlikely to score if faced with the slightest resistance. There are thousands of books written on leadership, and this is hardly the place to present a long tractate on the subject. Suffice it to say, there must be a clearly identified leader who will make good decisions, resolve disputes, steward the project's vision, shepherd the group past distractions, redirect efforts when a contingency plan is needed, and keep the project's energy flowing right to the very end.

· **Communication.** Ideally, the project team's leader is also a good communicator. Of course, ideally *everyone* is a good communicator, but we know that's not the case. Therefore, you must staff your project team with people who can express themselves clearly in two important, distinct directions: to the consultant and to the rest of the organization.

The COO of Matchall, a privately held consumer products company, described a product development project for which the company engaged a well-known, Midwest product-design consultancy: "It was an incredibly frustrating project for everyone because the designers would present a panel of ideas that were totally off base and we would send them back to make revisions; then they would return with more ideas that missed the mark. It really wasn't their fault. The manager I had assigned to the project just couldn't articulate what we wanted."

Similar stories abound with internal communication misses that led to bruised egos at best and, at worst, internecine battles that torpedoed projects. Since every project requires good communication, anticipate the potential for misconnects and ensure that the team is equipped appropriately.

Sometimes a company will staff a project with whoever is available, either because it simply doesn't have the right competencies in-house or because the people with those competencies don't have capacity; there are also times when a company will staff the project with underutilized personnel because it feels it has an obligation to do something with those employees. The first two cases are understandable, and the third is, in my opinion, unconscionable. All three situations, however, should be managed as much as possible by having the consulting firm supplement your team to cover any competency gaps. Make a watch-out list of missing competencies, which you will then reference as you fine-tune your progress dashboard and project health checklist.

2. Have We Identified and Planned for Scarce Resources?

Earlier, when choosing a consultant, you decided how to balance the triangle of trade-offs among speed, talent, and fees. Now you have to make a similar decision for your internal support of the project in terms of time, personnel, and capital. In this case, capital includes money and other capital expenses such as space, equipment, material, technology, and even information. Your job in this area is to make sure that, at most, only one of those points limits your success, not two or three, and that you are managing that one point as well as possible.

Consultants are often frustrated by clients who want fast results but then are not available for meetings or take weeks to circulate a document for approval. That is poor resource planning on the client's part. Ideally, your rate-limiting internal resource is financial capital, which is capped by the risk-adjusted value of the project. This financial limit is where your internal triangle of trade-offs intersects with the consultant triangle of trade-offs (see Figure 9-4). You then manage your personnel, time, and any other capital resources so that the consultant, not anything on your side of the table, is the rate limiter on success.

In other words, since you are paying the consultant to solve your issue or help you achieve your aspiration, don't make it excruciating for her to get to meetings and to get feedback and approvals from you. Similarly, if you manage your deadlines poorly and, as a result, can only give the consultant two weeks to finish a task that would normally be

Figure 9-4 Two Triangles of Trade-Offs

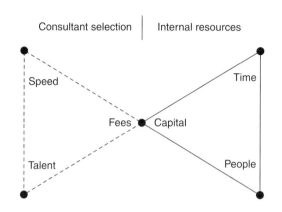

completed in two months, you are unnecessarily compromising the success of your project.

The preventive action in this area is to identify, with your consultant, which resources are likely to be scarce and then to pad them accordingly. For example, if expert input is needed, as was the case in Maine's medical claims project, book extra time with those experts near critical points, so that if hiccoughs occur, you have those people at hand. If it takes two weeks to get any approval through your legal department and that will potentially delay the project, build extra time into your schedule to get legal approval or set up a preapproval process. A project with no padding along the critical path is brittle and unlikely to survive its encounter with the real world.

Do We Have Guidance Mechanisms Securely in Place?

You need to put mechanisms in place to make your indicators of success active and to monitor the health of the project as it progresses. In addition, most projects include some decisions along the way, and all but the fortunate few will involve some changes in approach, scope, timing, or resources versus the original plan. Your two guidance questions are the following:

1. Who are the people involved in which decisions, and how are they involved?

2. How, practically, will we measure progress?

1. Who Are the People Involved in Which Decisions, and How Are They Involved?

Clear decision rights stave off a multitude of problems. They streamline your project and prevent people inside the organization from inappropriately involving themselves where they have little or no knowledge. One of the best frameworks for laying out decision rights on a project is the FARCI approach, in which decision points are mapped out in advance with five roles:

1. **Final approves (F).** This is the one person (most often) or small group (rarely) who has the final say on any disputes that cannot be handled by the designated approver(s).

2. **Approves (A).** The person, or people, authorized to make the decision (i.e., approve). If multiple people are involved, or if a party can dispute the approver's decision, a separate, final approver is necessary.

3. **Recommends (R).** Those people inside your organization and on the consultant's team who make a recommendation for the decision at hand.

4. **Consulted (C).** Those people, inside and outside the organization, whose input is sought but who are not decision makers.

5. **Informed (I).** People who are informed of the decision after it is made.

FARCI takes the question of inclusion down to a tactical level, specifying who will be included in various decisions within the project. For instance, if the project needs the full-time help of two people from the accounting department and the department head says he can only afford to lose one, who gets a say in that decision? Who never even needs to know? Below are typical decisions that are best mapped out in advance using the FARCI process:

Who decides on . . .

- Which resources are initially allocated to the project
- Which resources are allocated if more or different resources are needed midway through the project
- What changes in scope are acceptable within the current parameters of the project

- What changes in the approach or tasks are acceptable
- How much, if at all, the consultant's compensation can be modified
- What the protocol is for changing project parameters such as timing, objectives, and measures of success
- Whether or not the consultant's recommendations at each stage of the project are acceptable
- Whether or not the metrics for success have been met
- When, if ever, the project should be canceled

Often you should have a steering committee in place overseeing the project's progress. The FARCI approach will help you indicate explicitly to your organization who is on the steering committee and what oversight is within the purview of those on the committee. This can be especially important in deciding whether the consultant's recommendations are acceptable. On engagements intended to result in a decision or an implementation plan, a great steering committee will include people who can judge whether the recommendations will actually work for your company once they are implemented. Often these will be technical experts, customers, or other stakeholders. On implementation projects, there are fewer recommendations, and the steering committee should consist of people who can recommend and approve modifications necessary if the implementation is not going as planned.

Memorialize your FARCI framework for the project on a single-page document retained by you, project team members, and stakeholders. The document will contain a table that looks like Table 9-2.

2. How, Practically, Will We Measure Progress?

The output of this question will be a progress dashboard that is one of the key "vitamins and minerals" you'll use to keep your project moving in the right direction. The vitamins-and-minerals component will be explored in the next chapter. Progress comes in two flavors: forward movement on the project and improvement on the indicators of success. Completing a task is forward movement on the project, whereas improving your condition or achieving part of your goal is progress on your indicator of success. Sometimes, but not always, the two are intertwined.

You measure forward movement on the project very simply by putting milestones in place. If you are expecting the consultant to complete

Table 9-2

	VP Finance	VP Operations	Finance Director	Finance Managers
Initial resource allocation	F/A	C	R	I
Midproject resource allocation	F	C	R/A	I
Changes in scope	F	I	R/A	C
Review preliminary recommendations	I	I	F/A	R
Review final recommendations	F	A	R/A	C

an assessment in six weeks and then have final results for you four weeks after that, ask the consultant to break the project down into a few observable steps so that you can keep track of progress. For instance, the assessment may include 40 interviews with internal personnel and with customers over the course of the first two weeks, and in addition it may include a review of your production numbers. In this case, on your progress dashboard, you note the number of interviews conducted and whether the production numbers have (1) been given to the consultant and (2) been reviewed.

On projects with very little consultant leeway, your milestones should be described with precision and tracked very tightly. The example in Table 9-3 shows milestones in an implementation project where the consultant was hired to conduct a customer feedback study.

Your list for each project will look very different. The idea is to keep tabs on the project's progression, not to micromanage the consultant. You want to know when something is going off track so that you and the consultant can quickly jump on it and take corrective or contingent actions.

On projects with more consultant leeway, your milestones should be described less granularly, and the tracking should be more flexible. More importantly, be prepared for the milestones to change on projects with high leeway. For instance, let's say you have hired a consultant

Table 9-3

Milestones on Customer Feedback Study
1. Consultant submits draft questionnaire
2. We submit revisions
3. Consultant submits final questionnaire for approval
4. We give approval
5. Interviewing commences
6. One-quarter (25%) of interviews are completed
7. Half (50%) of interviews are completed
8. Three-quarters (75%) of interviews are completed
9. All interviews are completed
10. Coding of open-ended questions is completed
11. Top-line results are submitted to us
12. Final results are submitted to us

to determine how you should boost morale across the company; the original milestones may include some internal focus groups, one-on-one interviews, and a review of your annual survey. However, what if, midway through the project, the consultant identifies external issues and wants to conduct interviews with a handful of your vendors? Should you dismiss her as incompetent or unable to follow a plan because she wants to deviate from the predetermined milestones?

Of course not. Keep your eye on the goal of the project, and use the milestones as an indicator that you should be asking questions to determine how the project is progressing and how any changes will affect expectations. In the example above, you might ask, "If you go to vendor sites, will that compromise our target delivery date of September 15?"

With your milestones in hand, you can start to build a progress dashboard that you will review on a regular basis over the course of your project. The first section of your progress dashboard contains the project milestones outlined in a table that looks like Table 9-4.

The second flavor of progress will be tracked easily if you spent time working through the indicators of success in your Context Document. Before you start the project, determine how you will review your indicators of success as the initiative moves along. Focus on how easily and

Table 9-4

Section A. Major Milestones	
Milestone	**Projected Date**
Historical track layouts given to consultant	October 15
First-round work session with consultant and cutting-in crew	November 1
Second-round work session with operations and scheduling	November 8
...	

frequently you can observe the indicators rather than on them being concrete, quantitative, or objective. For instance, if your indicator of success is market share, then you could include monthly or quarterly market share on your project dashboard. If your indicator of success is the management team's confidence that it has sufficient information to make a decision on a merger, then put a periodic, informal poll of the management team on the dashboard. Avoid situations where all your indicators of success can only be measured at the end of the project. Instead, find at least one or two methods to determine whether you are headed in the right direction while the consultant is in midstream.

These intermediate indicators of success, which will compose the second section of your project dashboard, may look like the example in Table 9-5.

3. How Will We Know If the Project Is at Risk of Failure?

By the time a project is coming apart at the seams, it is usually too late to save without heroic effort. Maine's Medicaid claim system started falling apart shortly after it commenced, and the deterioration continued for three years until the mess reached titanic proportions. You can prevent a similar, disastrous snowballing effect by regularly reviewing your project's health.

You and your consultant must sit down in advance to make a list of red flags that either side should notice as the project steams along. Don't confuse the project's progress with its health. A perfectly healthy project

Table 9-5

Section B. Goal Progress				
Desired Outcome	Indicators of Success	Midproject Metric	Next Target Value	Current Value
Increased rail-yard capacity	Number of cars in yard	Number of cars in yard during beta test	1,088	1,035
Management approval of investment into rail-yard upgrades	Management gives approval at executive team meeting in March	Number of individual executive team members who agree the change is needed	VP of rolling stock division agrees	3 VPs out of 8 are in agreement

can give you unhappy results if, for instance, there is a major shift in the marketplace that renders your intended solution irrelevant. The converse is not true. There is no way to get great results from a project that unravels or stutters to a halt. Therefore, the third section of your project dashboard is a project health checklist that will give you advance warning if your project in danger of imploding. Table 9-6 illustrates a checklist with 10 excellent indicators of project health plus room for any additional red flags you and your consultant identify.

Summary

To achieve an outstanding result on your project, it's not enough to clearly outline your objectives and hire an excellent consultant. You need to prepare your organization to work with the consultant, and you need to collaboratively establish structures, processes, and a dashboard that engender success.

The ERP project at risk of spiraling out of control can be kept within bounds if the department directors whose input is needed are corralled in

Table 9-6

Section C. Early Warning Project Health Checklist	Date	Date	Date
Resources for the project are intact (financial, personnel, sponsor engagement/interest)			
Original rationale for project is still valid, and project continues to have achievable, ambitious goals			
Project reviews are implemented on a regular basis			
Everyone required shows up at project reviews and meetings			
There are few or no complaints about the project			
The project manager rarely asks the project sponsor for permission, direction, or support			
There is little or no complaint or confusion over conflicts between team members' "day jobs" and the demands of the project			
Project requirements are met despite concerns raised by the company's "everyday" hierarchy			
Project manager is leading the project team well—sustaining team members' enthusiasm and dedication and resolving conflicts quickly			
There is little or no attrition from the team and few or no replacement team members			
Other indicator:			
Other indicator:			

advance. The culture change project that could fall flat can be a rousing success when employees across the company see their advocates influence the final design. The vague belief that the crisis management project is effective can be replaced with a well-documented understanding of how well the crisis is being managed and, if it is falling short of expectations, whether contingent actions are needed.

Alarm bells only make a difference if you respond to their clamor. The point person for the Maine Medicaid project said he was afraid to ask for more resources at the outset of the project because the state was already under financial pressure. What, though, is the point of having all your ducks in a row before a project begins if you are not going to pay any attention once the initiative is moving at full bore? Managing the project once it's in motion is what we will tackle in the next chapter.

How Do We Run a Great Project?

Deriving Outstanding Value from Your Consultant

In This Chapter

Your project is up and running, and your expensive consultant is supposed to be delivering phenomenally valuable results. Is that happening? Much of the answer to that question depends on how well you maintain the project's vitality once it's under way.

Key concepts in Chapter 10 include the following:
- Team strength
- Support and accountabilities
- Managing changes
- Tracking progress
- Health signals

Making It to the Moon

On July 20, 1969, more than a billion people joined in a single, transformative event that has continued to transfix anyone who watches or hears it. After descending the nine-rung ladder, Neil Armstrong in a crackling voice declared, "That's one small step for [a] man; one giant leap for mankind." (See Figure 10-1.) Armstrong's first steps and oft-quoted words are our enduring memory of the Apollo 11 mission to the moon.

Three days earlier, however, in the empty space between the earth and moon, the astronauts performed a three-second burn on the main engine to make a midcourse correction. Three seconds of action on the second of four days of travel made the difference between one of the standout moments in human history and an expensive, possibly fatal disaster.

Closer to the actual moment of landing, the astronauts could see through the capsule's windows that landmarks were passing by ahead of schedule and they would probably land miles past their intended target. To add to their worry, the navigation and guidance computer started blaring cryptic "1202" and "1201" alarms. Engineers on the ground

Figure 10-1 Neil Armstrong Descending the
Ladder and Stepping onto the Moon

Source: NASA

in Houston determined that these issues were not critical and that the descent could continue. The *Eagle* landed safely in a rocky area west of the original landing zone.

Chances are, your project is a bit less complex than sending a man to the moon using 1960s technology. Nevertheless, you will probably have to perform at least one "three-second burn" to ensure your initiative lands in the Sea of Tranquility instead of tumbling into space. As an executive who has hired a consultant and is overseeing an important, corporate initiative, your responsibility is to keep a watchful eye on alarms and warning signals, to ferret out those moments when a midcourse correction is needed, and to differentiate them from the blaring, but benign, alarms.

The Seven Vitamins and Minerals for a Healthy Project

It may seem that correctly hiring a consultant is as laborious as giving birth. As with any other process, the pain involved decreases the more often and consistently you employ best practices; in this case the best practices are constructing the right project, finding the right consultant, and optimally arranging all the pieces before the project starts. Still, if childbearing is the work you have undertaken so far, then child rearing is your next undertaking. To keep your project maturing healthfully until it's all grown up and your results are delivered, you need to monitor its diet of seven essential vitamins and minerals:

1. Team strength
2. Inclusion
3. Support
4. Approach
5. Changes
6. Progress
7. Health signals

To monitor the seven essential vitamins and minerals, you are going to create a master checklist. The checklist will take less than an hour to develop, and it will ensure your project is executed and implemented with excellence. Plan to run through the checklist on your own or with the steering committee roughly 10 times during the life of the project or weekly for very short projects.

This is a bit like a pilot's preflight checklist—very routine and you should be able to get through it in a matter of minutes; however, if an alarm pops up, you will need to address it immediately in order to avert a potential disaster.

1. Team Strength: Is Our Team Still the Right Team, and Is It Functioning Well?

The first essential ingredient in your initiative's health is the project team's health. As with everything you do, people are the key to making a project successful. Therefore, regularly throughout the project you are going to ask a series of questions that monitor team dynamics and composition.

Are Competencies on the Team Still Sufficient, or Do We Need Any New Competencies to Achieve the Desired Outcome?

When you were searching for a consultant, you created a list of key competencies that were needed to achieve your desired outcome. Similarly, before the project started, you created a list of competencies needed on your side of the table so that you could staff it appropriately. You may also have noted some areas where the project team was weak. Take all those competencies and add them to this section in your master checklist. Consider these questions:

- Has the consulting firm lived up to its billing? Is it demonstrating that it brought the expertise it promised? If not, you need to sit down with the lead consultant immediately and address the issue.

- Are the internal team members exhibiting necessary competencies? Is everyone who was assigned to the team engaged and contributing? One company's enormous SAP implementation project was led by an up-and-comer as part of the company's formal leadership development program. After eight months, the program rotated him to a different assignment, and overnight he was off the team.

- Have the needs of the project changed in a way that requires new or different competencies? Whether or not the scope of the project has changed, the requirements to achieve your goals may be emerging differently than you had originally envisaged.

For instance, one company looking into the hazardous waste market realized six weeks into the project that it needed an expert in airborne particulates.

If deficiencies in the team's competency level appear, don't let them fester and don't hope they will improve on their own. Immediately talk with the consultant if a problem exists on her side of the equation, and if internal talent is underperforming or lacking, there may be a way the consultant can help you plug the holes. If you have to negotiate with other departments or with your boss for additional resources, you can count on that taking longer than you would like, in which case the earlier you start those discussions, the earlier you can acquire the talent you need for the project.

Is the Team Acting Cohesively?

A top-notch team, pushing a project forward, displays unmistakable characteristics that you and everyone on the project team must model. Include the following team traits on your checklist:

- **Trust.** Do the members of the team generally trust each other, and do they trust the project leader? Don't confuse trust with agreement. People can disagree and still trust each other. Trust is built on candor, honesty, a willingness to admit mistakes, reliability, actions that are consistent with beliefs, and beliefs that are consistent with core values.

- **Common goal.** Are members of the team working toward a common goal, or have separate agendas crept into the mix? Do team members still agree on what success looks like? Some team members may start to subordinate the project's goals as the needs of their department, functional area, or division shift. You must address these changes in priority as soon as they arise, or they may lead to conflict, poor results, or an abandoned project.

- **Decision making.** Is the team using the right decision-making approach at the right time? The FARCI framework in Chapter 9 was established to facilitate this. What decisions has the team had to make, and has it used the appropriate style for those decisions? A midsize trucking company tried to finesse a battle between departments by assigning coleaders to each of the project's subteams. Rather than strengthening decision making, the coleaders abdicated their responsibilities and pointed fingers at each other.

It's commonplace for a strong, opinionated project leader to progressively make more autocratic decisions. Conversely, insecure or inexperienced project leaders often open every little decision up to a democratic process when a quick, autocratic decision is needed. Your role is to notice movement away from the ideal and guide decision making back to its optimal course.

· **Communication.** Are participants actively communicating their opinions on what is needed for the project to succeed? Do team members grasp each other's expectations and concerns? More projects fail due to poor communication than to almost any other reason. This is arguably too big an issue to be handled by a few subitems on a checklist; however, all the other checks and balances will help you triangulate on communication issues. Your challenge here will be getting factual information rather than checking a few boxes and hastening to the next task.

Each time you run through your master checklist, conduct a few five-minute interviews with team members. Your questions to them are:

1. What is necessary at this point to ensure the project succeeds?

2. What specifically are you expecting from _____? (Fill in the blank with the name of one or two other members of the team.)

3. What commitments must you fulfill to meet the expectations of _____? (Fill in the blank with the name of one or two other members of the team.)

Look for congruence among your interviewees' answers, and if you notice significant discrepancies, address them promptly. The idea is to surface issues early, so that they can be dispatched before they balloon into project-killing tangles.

Are the Members of the Team, Individually and as a Team, Being Held Accountable?

Invariably mistakes will be made along the way, either by the team as a whole or by members of the team. How you handle those mistakes will influence the team's ongoing progress. Hold your project team accountable by:

- **Not blaming.** The goal is to figure out what has gone wrong and how to fix it rather than to point fingers and assign blame.

- **Ascertaining what led up to the error.** What was the situation, and is it something that could be recognized and avoided in the future?

- **Reinforcing positives.** What did the team or team members do right? Point out those positive attributes. Affirmation and reinforcement are often as important as correcting errors.

- **Identifying corrections.** What did not work, and how does the team or an individual team member correct the errors?

- **Taking responsibility generously.** The reason blame enters the equation is that people don't want to take responsibility, which means they don't want to contribute the resources or perceived loss of ego needed to amend the problem. Your solution is to have everyone who *could* have been involved in the error join in taking responsibility. Standing arm-in-arm and jointly addressing problems creates an appreciable sense of team strength and community. In other words, act like a team and take the lumps together.

- **Focusing on next steps.** When working through problems, 90 percent of your focus ought to be on what to do next. Specifically, what will the team or team members do to get past the mistake, continue with positive momentum, and put the project on an even better trajectory?

2. Inclusion: Are We Still Including the Right People?

The second essential ingredient to your initiative's health is also related to people and follows up on the buy-in work you performed prior to the project's start. For example, a national supplier of office products hired a consultant to help the company streamline its supply chain. The executive who hired the consultant was focusing on his own division when he brought the consultant on board. However, a few weeks into the project, the group president, an executive with much broader responsibility, saw that the project would affect multiple divisions and insisted that the project team expand to include vice presidents from other divisions.

The following questions are ones you should ask during your regular check-in on the project.

Is the Project Affecting the Work, Responsibility, Job Scope, Power, Status, or Pride of Anyone You Had Not Anticipated Prior to Kickoff?

Perhaps the scope or direction of the project has changed enough that a different department is being affected. Or as often happens, someone you overlooked at first is resistant to change. A tool-and-die manufacturer's process improvement project suddenly stalled when the vice president of R&D realized the initiative would reveal major problems in another initiative he had spent two years implementing. Rather than risk losing face, he stubbornly resisted the process improvement. An ounce of prevention here will prevent pounds of pain later on.

Given Changes in the Project, Are There Other People Whose Knowledge Is Directly Relevant to Decisions That Are Being Enacted?

If the project has not changed, then this won't apply; however, if the project has wandered from its original approach, then perhaps there are others within the company whose expertise could be a boon.

Have the Stakeholders Changed?

Similarly, if the project's approach or scope has changed, you may need to update the FARCI matrix to include a new set of stakeholders. Are more divisions affected than you originally realized? More departments or functions? Every business is a complex web of interconnected activities; however, we tend to think narrowly about the effects of our actions and projects. The operations group at a uniform manufacturer undertook a project to improve its manufacturing efficiencies and, as a result, started producing fewer but larger batches of each uniform. Unfortunately, the two-day impact on the availability of different uniforms, which seemed like a minor side effect, severely compromised the sales group's story to customers. As you continue down the path of your project, be on the lookout for ripples disturbing unexpected shores.

Is Anyone Diverting Resources, Disseminating Misleading Information, or Injecting Negative Energy?

In other words, is anyone sabotaging the project? It's helpful to include a devil's advocate on the team who sparks healthy debate, as long as the person goes along with the project team's decision once the debate is concluded. Unrestrained negativity, however, will suck the power out of a project and siphon off the dedication necessary to produce an impressive success.

Negative energy can come from your side of the table or the consultant's side, and it's not always malicious. An executive who promised resources may have decided that priorities have changed for her and that she actually needs those resources more urgently elsewhere. You need to identify these types of issues early and address them head-on as quickly as possible. Get the saboteur back on board the boat, rowing in the same direction, or replace her.

3. Support: Are We Living Up to Our Accountabilities?

Before you started the initiative, the executive sponsor agreed to stand behind the project, and your company agreed to dedicate a certain level of personnel, time, and capital resources. If you are using best-practice contracts, you may have built in compensation events that will increase the cost of your project should you fail to live up to your promises (see Chapter 7). Therefore, the third essential ingredient you need to track is very simple: are you still living up to your side of the agreement? Nothing is as frustrating for consultants as a client who handcuffs them and prevents them from delivering superior results.

Is the Executive Sponsor Supporting the Project Team When Conflict Arises with Departments, Functional Areas, Business Units, or Other Stakeholders?

One of the world's largest candy manufacturers brought in a consultant to help coordinate a worldwide upgrade of its computers—no mean feat when you have over 50,000 employees scattered across the globe. Unfortunately, the project was underfunded from the start; and when it became clear that the project was falling farther and farther behind, the executive sponsor did not make the case to his peers for additional funding. Without support from the top, the project unraveled, and today the

IT department is still struggling with a panoply of operating systems and hardware across the company.

Are the People Dedicated to the Project Still Giving as Much Time and Energy as Needed?

One reason you strive to deliver rapid results is that energy dissipates exponentially over time on many projects. New priorities arise, new fires flare up, and new ideas (which are more provocative than old ideas) attract talent like moths to a flame. If dedicated resources are dwindling, you need to inform the stakeholders of the consequences and up the zeal on the project. Beware of a project that seeps focus like a slowly leaking tire, or before you know it, you'll be stranded by the side of the road with a flat and no one interested in helping you back into the fast lane.

Are We Responding to the Consultant on a Timely Basis and Providing the Information We Promised?

This is one of the biggest reasons projects fail to meet their deadlines. Consultants working under a properly constructed contract will endeavor to complete your project with excellence in the shortest time frame possible. When the timetable slips on a project, often the cause is the client's slow delivery of information, failure to give timely feedback, or simple neglect while other priorities are handled. One reason the risk-handling structures outlined in Chapter 7 work well is that they hold your side of the team accountable. If you notice the project is slipping, find out whether your team is holding up progress and what you can do to facilitate rapid action.

Are We Fulfilling Our Promises of Space, Equipment, or Other Capital Resources?

This checkpoint is very straightforward: if we promised the consultant a workspace in four offices around the globe, remote access to a critical database, or equipment on demand, are we delivering on those promises? The consultant on a cost-savings project at a grain milling plant requested that his client install a networked laptop at the station where grain was loaded into rail cars. Weeks into the project, the laptop was stuck in requisitions, while hundreds of thousands of dollars in cost-savings opportunities slipped by. Although the consulting firm could (and did eventually) purchase the laptop itself, it could not get the device networked into the corporate systems without the proper paperwork in place. You can prevent this type of blunder by jumping on capital requirements early and taking shortages seriously.

Are We Attending Meetings That Are Necessary for the Project to Progress?

Attendance at meetings is a great leading indicator of a project's health, and I recommend you track this as part of the overall health section of your project dashboard. Calendar conflicts are inevitable, particularly on a complex project with team members from many departments or geographies. Nevertheless, if the same personnel are consistently absent from key meetings, you need to have a one-on-one talk with the truants and gauge their dedication to the project. If you find commitment lacking, get a sense for whether their priorities have changed, they have lost enthusiasm for the project, they no longer believe the project will work, they don't think they are needed, or they are now opposed to the project; or, perhaps have they not been showing up because they simply haven't been held accountable. As the project leader or executive sponsor, you are responsible for keeping the team's motivation strong. Increasing absences at project meetings are an excellent early warning signal of a project headed south.

Are We Communicating as Transparently and Fully as We Promised at the Outset of the Initiative?

You have obligations to internal stakeholders as well as to the consultant on a project. When you set up the project, you developed a matrix that indicated who would be informed of certain decisions; and if the project's impact on your organization is widespread, you set up a communication plan. Are you following those guidelines? Are you continuing to keep all departments and functions in the loop? It's not unusual for a project team to become lax in this area, particularly if one division, function, geographic area, or individual is challenging. The team may decide it's easier to forge ahead without following the communication protocols you established at the outset.

4. Approach: Is Our Approach Working Well?

The fourth essential ingredient is the health of the approach you are using in your project. Are you using best practices and adjusting where necessary to achieve your desired outcomes? Some executives become "approach police," loudly decrying every deviation from the original plan; however, victory is defined as taking the enemy camp, not as following your attack plan to the letter. Even for an implementation project for which you have a well-vetted plan and are paying an "outsource professional" to execute your plan with excellence and precision, your plan should come under regular scrutiny to confirm it will lead to your desired destination.

Does the Approach Appear to Be Taking Us Toward Our Desired Outcomes, or Should We Adjust the Way We Are Approaching the Initiative?

A fast-food chain that wanted to determine how often it should be sending out coupons hired a consultant who touted a best-practice approach to promotion optimization. After a few weeks of analysis, the consultant realized that the client had so thoroughly trained its customers to use coupons that the important question was not how often to send them out, but what the best value and combination of coupons would be. That exercise called for an entirely different approach.

Are the Team Members Locked into the Project Plan, or Are They Keeping Their Eyes on the Desired Outcome and Adjusting as Needed?

As I have mentioned, few battles are won by sticking to a plan that is buckling under its exigencies. In my experience, engineers and professional project managers excel at keeping internal team members and consultants on the straight and narrow with detailed reports and frequent team conference calls; however, these advantages sometimes make a project unnecessarily rigid.

For instance, the project plan for a pharmaceutical company seeking to improve its communications with physicians called for the consultant to conduct a series of 25 one-on-one interviews with urologists. During the first five interviews, the consultant found the responses to be remarkably consistent; and after no helpful new information emerged from five additional interviews, the consultant suggested the project forgo the remaining 15 interviews and take advantage of the time savings to advance the remainder of the plan. The project manager at the pharmaceutical firm refused to make this change because it was contrary to the agreed-to approach; and to her great consternation, the consultant was not willing to refund a portion of his fees in return for conducting fewer interviews. She could not lift her gaze from the plan level to the desired outcomes, and as a result, an opportunity to make rapid progress and build positive momentum slipped by.

Has the Consultant or Team Concluded What the Problem Is or What the Solution Should Be Before All the Relevant Information and Knowledge Have Been Accounted For?

People often jump to conclusions, and consultants have a strong inclination to leap early. In many cases you'll be better off with a working solution now than a slightly better solution later; nevertheless, don't let the project team make decisions before it really knows what is going on. The CEO of a multinational electronics company hired a consultant to determine why one product team was floundering. The hired gun started firing off recommendations within days of interviewing the U.S. employees, before hearing the first word from their colleagues around the world. How sound do you think those recommendations were? Not very, and the CEO admonished the consultant to do his job more thoroughly before prescribing solutions.

If the Consulting Firm or Project Team Has Surmised the Problem or Solution, Is It Now Close Minded?

The follow-on to a rush to judgment is often a full-on martial defense—as if the recommendation is the team's baby cub that must be guarded with life and limb against all threats. In 2000, the internal consulting team at a well-known private equity firm was asked to develop a digital strategy for the group's many print media holdings. At the time, the advent of online magazines and news sites was decimating the media companies' subscription revenue. Since the dot-com bubble had burst mid-2000, the internal consultant insisted the owners drop their focus on a digital strategy and switch, instead, to cost cutting. The consultants' advice was a snap judgment based on the hysteria surrounding dot-bombs. Yet, despite plenty of evidence that the bursting bubble was separate from fundamental trends in consumer behavior, the consulting team clung to its recommendation with pit-bull determination. It adamantly pushed its cost-savings agenda while ridiculing others' efforts to defend against emerging digital competitors.

If We Are Employing a C2B2A Approach, Are the Iterations Happening as Frequently as We Anticipated?

The iterative approach explained in Chapter 5 calls for multiple rounds of solutions and improvements as you wind your way closer and closer to your desired objective. If your project utilizes a feedback loop, you should regularly evaluate whether the loop is active and is functioning effectively. Is the team regularly getting customer feedback? Are the team members listening to customer criticism and incorporating it, or are they becoming defensive and shying away from input sessions?

Is the Project Creating Quick Wins?

Include work streams in your project approach that are intended to produce early, measurable results. Quick wins cement the team's purpose, support, and dedication. They build momentum that can carry the project through doubts and doldrums, and they secure resources that may have been in question early on. If the quick wins you had hoped for are not materializing, dig into the approach to deduce what is causing the shortcomings. Is the approach no longer valid? Are the short-term misses indicative of a deeper problem?

A research company's project to integrate its computer systems across divisions was supposed to quickly generate comprehensive reports of accounts receivables and accounts payables. When the report was delayed week after week and arrived with numerous errors, the executive sponsor could tell that the project was deeply flawed, and she was able to respond with corrective action.

5. Changes: Are We Managing Changes Appropriately?

Virtually all projects shift and adjust along the way. The approach, the players, the stakeholders, the expected outcomes, and many other aspects can deviate from the original mission. As Helmuth von Moltke sagely noted, "No battle plan survives contact with the enemy," and similarly, few project plans survive contact with the real world. Therefore, the fifth essential ingredient is how well you are managing those changes in your project plan.

Are Changes Happening Within the Framework We Put in Place?

In other words, are the appropriate people making the decisions to change, and are relevant people included in those decisions? If the scope of the project needs to be expanded or redirected, has that been handled properly?

Are We Communicating Those Changes Using a Powerful, Experiential Approach?

In Chapter 11, the CUBES approach is covered in depth as a framework for cementing behavior changes. Ask the five questions below, based on the CUBES approach, to evaluate how well you are communicating changes for the project's desired outcome, success hurdles, team composition, timing, and so forth:

1. Are we communicating changes in concrete, specific terms?

2. Are we communicating how the changes affect stakeholders in the project?

3. Are we communicating sufficient information candidly enough and consistently enough that recipients believe us?

4. Are we communicating the context necessary for stakeholders to know what we're talking about?

5. With all the above points in mind, are we keeping the communications simple?

6. Progress: Are We Moving the Ball Forward?

The point of the project is to solve issues or achieve aspirations; therefore, the sixth essential ingredient is progress toward the desired outcome. This ingredient intentionally overlaps with the question of whether your approach is working well. Since the purpose of your project is to reach a desired outcome, not to engage in interesting activities that keep consultants gainfully employed, fixating on progress is a worthwhile behavior. Fortunately, you set yourself up to monitor progress easily when you developed your project dashboards in Chapter 9.

Are We Meeting the Major Milestones We Specified on Our Progress Dashboard?

Your dashboard should contain clear, midproject milestones that indicate activities have been completed. While results, not activities, are the focus of a consulting project, if you have chosen the right approach, the activities are a decent bellwether of forward movement.

Are the Indicators of Success We Set Up in Our Progress Dashboard Indicating Movement in the Right Direction?

A supplier to the banking industry hired a consultant to lead a two-year-long partnering effort with one of its largest customers. After almost a full year of activity, none of the promised efficiencies had yet emerged because, as it turned out, setting up the governance and structure for the partnership took far longer than anyone had anticipated. While activity was definitely taking place, the indicators of success were still dawdling at the zero mark. If the executive sponsor had looked solely at the milestones—which had been updated along the way to reflect the correct time required for establishing the partnership infrastructure—she would have concluded that the project was proceeding smoothly, albeit slowly. However, since she also kept a tight watch on the success indicators, she knew the early fruits from the project looked unimpressive and she proactively held top-to-top management meetings to forestall her customer's concerns. By looking at success indicators and taking appropriate action, a critical effort that could have sunk under customer dissatisfaction was kept afloat until its successful conclusion.

Are We Documenting Key Decisions Along the Way?

Some decisions are part of the project plan, and other decisions may concern project scope, resources, timing, expectations, and so forth. Whatever the decision type, best practice is to document the elements of the decision. Typically this will include:

- Why a decision was necessary, along with any necessary background information. This can be brief.
- The choices that were considered.
- The rationale for the decision.
- The implications of the decision.

Memorializing each decision does not have to be a burdensome, administrative task. A quick e-mail or memo to all the relevant team members is often sufficient. For larger, more important decisions, you may want to document them in a periodic report to the project sponsors or stakeholders.

Are We Noting Any Persistent Bottlenecks in the Project So That We Can Address Them and Keep the Initiative Moving Forward Quickly?

Anything can go wrong in a project, from exogenous events that require a fundamental shift in direction to an important team member leaving the company—and just about everything in between. As you saw in Chapter 6, there are at least a dozen common, malefic factors that can plague a consulting initiative. When the same problem crops up multiple times, however, you have a special situation that demands pointed attention. Perhaps the approvals process consistently slows down when it hits the legal department's desk, or each round of software testing is delayed because the data coming out of the inventory system have errors. You or your team needs to flag any repeat problems, quickly diagnose the root cause, and determine which actions, if any, you can take to prevent another incident.

Is the Consultant Providing Real Value?

During your periodic review, consider whether the consultant's work is accretive to the efforts you would be doing without him. A Danish company commissioned a marketing consultancy to help design a strategy for growth. The consulting team conducted broad-based interviews and then reported back the ideas it found throughout the company. For their fee of $250,000, the paid advisors had regurgitated information the client already knew. This was hardly the makings of a successful project, and the client should have mandated a meeting of the minds after the very first disappointing result. Is your consultant bringing new ideas to the table? Is she pushing back on your ideas? If not, either tell the consultant to turn up the heat or eliminate her from the mix.

Are the Project Team and Consultant Staying on Task?

In the previous example, in which the consultants were providing very little incremental value, the executive sponsor sat down with the managing director of the consulting firm to express his displeasure. To his surprise, the leader of the consulting firm came armed with a long list of tasks the CMO had asked the firm to do, all of which were tangential to the project and all of which took time and energy away from the task at hand. This does not excuse the consultants, whose responsibility was to elevate issues that were preventing them from helping their client achieve the desired outcome. The example does show, however, how easy it is for teams to become distracted.

7. Health Signals: Are There Torpedoes in the Water?

The seventh essential ingredient is paying attention to the warning signs that a project is going to crumble. One key to making sure you have a better track record with consultants is stopping looming failures and turning them around or canceling them. When you assemble your own, customized master checklist for your project, you can eliminate duplicates or highlight areas of particular importance. The Early Warning Project Health Checklist, which was introduced in Chapter 9, is reprised in Table 10-1.

Summary

Whether your project is a rousing success or it collapses into a career-limiting pile of kindling depends on how well you manage and maintain it as it progresses. Every project hits bumps in the road. Will they stop your project short or be a minor inconvenience? Will you recognize if your initiative's wheels are about to fall off? You will if you constantly monitor the seven vitamins and minerals outlined in this chapter.

The consultant whose value is questionable can be dismissed or redirected within weeks rather than after the project is completed. The department head whose recalcitrance will render all your hard work useless can be identified and brought into the fold before it's too late. The internecine arguments that threaten to tear the project team apart can be halted while they are unfriendly disagreements and before they devolve into project-limiting brawls. The consultant who would point at you for not providing the resources necessary to deliver great results will have nowhere to point because, in fact, you will have lived up to your promises.

After years of preparation and four excitement-filled days of space travel, Neil Armstrong hand-piloted the lunar module of Apollo 11 to

Table 10-1

Section C. Early Warning Project Health Checklist	Date	Date	Date
Resources for the project are intact (financial, personnel, sponsor engagement/interest)			
Original rationale for project is still valid, and project continues to have achievable, ambitious goals			
Project reviews are implemented on a regular basis			
Everyone required shows up at project reviews and meetings			
There are few or no complaints about the project			
The project manager rarely asks the project sponsor for permission, direction, or support			
There is little or no complaint or confusion over conflicts between team members' "day jobs" and the demands of the project			
Project requirements are met despite concerns raised by the company's "everyday" hierarchy			
Project manager is leading the project team well—sustaining team members' enthusiasm and dedication and resolving conflicts quickly			
There is little or no attrition from the team and few or no replacement team members			
Other indicator:			
Other indicator:			

its safe landing with only 20 seconds of fuel to spare. No doubt you will deliver your results with much less drama. While footprints on the moon may stay fixed and undisturbed for millennia, the fruit of your efforts could be much more fleeting. How to make the impact of your project persist is the subject of the next chapter.

How Do We Lock in Value?

Making Change Stick After the Consultant Leaves

In This Chapter

By some estimates, more than 70 percent of corporate training has no effect, and clients and consultants alike bemoan expensive deliverables that gather dust on the shelf. Since the end result of many consulting projects is a change in behaviors, sustaining the new behaviors long term often creates a tremendous boost in value. This chapter covers the obstacles to making behavior change stick and gives specific strategies for overcoming them.

Key concepts in Chapter 11 include the following:
- Why sustaining behavior change is difficult
- Repetition and emotional impact
- The CUBES framework
- Appropriate time for change

Recidivism at Aroflote

When Robert Reynolds stepped into the role of senior vice president, global marketing and sales, for Aroflote Navigational Systems in April 2010, the company rested comfortably on the 70 percent market share it had commanded for over 20 years. Reynolds had risen to his new title through a series of positions that leveraged either his skills as an excellent financial analyst or his quiet, unassuming leadership style. The senior vice president job would perfectly utilize his strengths on both fronts since it required a deft touch with budgets, sales incentives, and highly tenured personnel.

In May 2010, customers started complaining about seams separating on Aroflote's flagship device, and dissatisfaction intensified until, at the beginning of July, Aroflote issued a recall and halted shipments. Reynolds and his team tap-danced through six months of product shortages and back orders before the source of the problem was identified and corrected. The negative impact on revenue was immediate; however, the more insidious, lasting damage was to Aroflote's reputation. Aroflote's marketing, customer service, and sales teams were wholly unprepared for customers who viewed them with distrust and skepticism.

In February 2011, Reynolds hired Agen Consulting to help turn around Aroflote's slumping sales via a costly project promisingly titled "The Aroflote Way." Processes and personnel in marketing, customer service, and sales would be transformed into a new way of doing business: a customer-centric, consultative approach quite different from the "take us or leave us" attitude Aroflote had developed during its decades atop the industry.

Fast-forward to February 2012 and to Frank Penn, the enterprising, new senior vice president stepping into the shoes left vacant when Reynolds was fired six months previously. After only a few weeks, Penn found none of his personnel were using a customer-centric, consultative approach, and market share was continuing to tumble. Penn decided a phone call to Agen Consulting was in order. Agen's response startled and disappointed Penn.

After Reynolds was fired, we were shut out. We tried unsuccessfully for months to contact the CEO in order to keep adoption of the Aroflote Way progressing, and advised him that if he didn't communicate properly to the troops, all the work we had done would be compromised.

We actually have videos of your personnel demonstrating the new habits we taught them, so we know they did learn consultative selling. We appreciate you calling, and we'd love to help; however, it's not a surprise to us that your people reverted to their old ways, and at this point we would have to start over with a new project.

Aroflote makes a good case study because the need for change and the difficulty in maintaining it were as obvious as the Eiffel Tower. Consulting projects are all about creating change—whether it is correcting an issue that is dragging down performance or identifying a way to raise the bar, something has to change, and just as importantly, those changes must be sustained if you are to realize the value promised by the project.

This chapter is not an exploration of how to achieve change. There are hundreds of tractates on that topic, and many of the requirements for change are baked into Chapter 10—for instance, appropriate involvement and the C2B2A method. Instead, this chapter is about one specific problem that seems to plague many consulting engagements: fleeting value.

Why Focus on Behavior Change?

The output of the vast majority of projects involves changing behaviors or the prospect of such changes. In other words, the new design, or skills, or processes, or strategy, that you and your consultant have labored to produce will only achieve your expectations if the people in your organization make it work consistently and as you intended.

There are exceptions, of course. A website redesign may involve nothing new at all for you or your employees. On the other hand, if the new website incorporates a blog or active social networking, then to capture that value, you have to successfully adopt some new behaviors. A handful of the projects used as examples in Chapter 3 are reprised in Table 11-1, showing how most of them incorporate behavior change or the prospect of behavior change.

Should We Have Expected Behavior Change?

If you were counting on a consulting project to alter work habits within your organization and employees appear to have quickly returned to their accustomed ways of doing business, start by examining your own expectations.

Table 11-1

Example Project	Associated Behavior Changes
Where and how should we expand our technology	After we choose a market, we will then have to develop a market attack plan and implement that plan. If we want to replicate the process of choosing, we also need to learn and adopt that process
Figure out a way to fit more cars into our rail yard	New processes will need to be learned and implemented. New roles and responsibilities among departments will have to be understood
Help develop a new pen computer for our customer	No immediate behavior change required
Coach my VP to be a better leader	VP needs to develop his own people better, exhibit less volatility, and become more of a team player
Improve our buying group	The buying group will need to follow new processes or learn new skills

Did We Pursue the Right Project?

One reason the first section of this book pushed you to dig into the value and type of project before bringing a consultant on board is that companies often pursue projects that can't achieve their goals. For example, training projects often fail because motivation, not a lack of skills, was causing subpar results. After the training project concludes, the executive sponsor is dismayed to find no meaningful shift in behavior or results; but you can't train your way out of organizational conflict or poorly designed jobs.

Similarly, an executive expecting leaps in employee productivity after a massive IT infrastructure project will be sorely disappointed if, as is often the case, it turns out that policies and processes, not infrastructure, have produced the bottleneck.

Was Behavior Change Part of the Project?

Recall from Chapter 3 that your project should be designed to deliver either a recommended decision, a recommended plan for implementing that decision, or the implementation of a plan. Of those three valuable project outcomes, only one *immediately* creates behavior change: implementation. In other words, many projects are not designed to create on-the-ground differences in what happens at your company. Nor should they be. Initiatives that yield a decision give you strategic direction; however, until you actively pursue that strategy, it won't affect employees' activity. For instance, the client whose aim was to improve his buying group's performance started, appropriately, with a project designed to determine where he should focus first. He could have leapt headlong into an implementation project; but as you just read, tackling the wrong project is one of the major reasons many expenditures on consultants are ineffective. While decision-oriented projects are well worth undertaking, if you hire a consultant to help you determine strategy, don't expect her to create lasting change by the time she walks out the door. Her recommended decision promises only the prospect for change and the responsibility for actualizing the new direction rests on you.

Similarly, projects designed to deliver a detailed implementation plan do not, on their own merit, include implementation. The client who wanted his salespeople to articulate the company's core message more consistently was initially looking for a trainer; however, after reflecting further, he realized his first order of business was a establishing a blueprint for sales force development. The preliminary results of his project were a detailed plan to improve his team's performance; yet until he put that plan into action, he couldn't expect any change at all. In other words, the lasting value from his initiative accrued after the formal plan-development project ended.

Was There a Solid Change-Management Plan?

If you hired a consultant to develop a solution and you don't have a solid change-management plan to follow during implementation, then you are setting yourself up for disappointing results. As mentioned earlier, a full exploration of change management is outside the scope of this book. To learn more about this discipline, I recommend reading the work of John Kotter and of Richard Axelrod. In addition, one of my favorite processes for working through change is based on the work of Robert Mager and Peter Pipe, whose *Analyzing Performance Problems* is never far from my reach.

Why Is Behavior Change from Projects Difficult to Sustain?

Conventional wisdom has held that to alter employees' conduct, you need to point people in a new direction, give them an incentive to act according to your wishes, or both. The truth is much more interesting. Recent research into the brain and human behavior has yielded fascinating results that you can directly leverage to make your projects more valuable over the long term.

The degree to which people adopt or modify a behavior is based on the emotional impact and frequency of their experiences. Behaviors are, almost literally, burned into your brain as the layout of your synapses physically reorganize to reflect your experience. Think back to the first time your schoolteacher rewarded you with a public accolade. (If you can't remember it, imagine it.) Maybe you had volunteered the right answer or helped another student or simply sat quietly. Whatever you did provoked your teacher's positive attention, and you likely walked on cloud nine for the rest of the day. Do you think you repeated the activity that engendered praise? You bet you did! You may still be doing it today—volunteering answers or helping others or sitting quietly—because of the strong emotions your brain links to that behavior.

Some events carry such a powerful emotional impact that they strongly embed behavior after only a few repetitions. How often do you have to experience burning pain before you stop putting your hand on a hot stove? Usually, once is enough. Other behaviors are embedded through ongoing repetition. For instance, let's say you are a fresh-faced college graduate embarking on your first job in a manufacturing plant. During the first week, your manager points to items piling up at several stations and remarks, "That's a sign of inefficiency. Any time you see inventory, look for a way to streamline the process." After a week spent looking for surplus components, your effort to cut waste is not yet a deeply embedded disposition and you could abandon it quite easily. After a year of noticing inventory pile-ups and responding each time with efficiency suggestions, the habit would be more challenging to break. With two decades under your belt of routinely pointing out

Figure 11-1 Stickiness of Workplace Behaviors

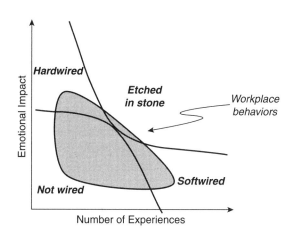

excess stock to the workers at each station, you could try to concentrate instead on the maintenance of the workstations or the quality of output, but the old, familiar inclination to suggest inventory reduction measures would reassert itself after a couple of weeks or months.

Combining emotional impact with repetition yields the map in Figure 11-1, depicting which behaviors are easily altered and which are more difficult to modify. The gray oval estimates the universe of typical employee activities.

Not Wired

When a behavior has not been practiced and there is very little emotional impact, there is no "wiring" keeping it in place. For instance, a new employee walking a document through your legal sign-off system for the first time would present little resistance to a change in the system, even if the new approach was disadvantageous for her.

Softwired

When a behavior has been practiced often and there is low emotional impact, it is softwired. You are fighting a habit, and, therefore, sustaining a change will require you to continually reinforce the new activities or processes until the new routine becomes a habit. This will be the case even if the new system holds obvious advantages over the one it is replacing.

When an international steel manufacturer tried to encourage its business unit managers to collaborate on corporate innovation, it found that the managers would work together quite productively for a few weeks and then drift back into their own silos until the next time they were reminded of the need for cross-divisional solutions. The managers worked on their own priorities because that's what they had done for many years, not because emotionally weighty events taught them that engaging with other divisions was a dangerous activity. Without constant reinforcement, even the managers who bought into the advantages of cross-divisional collaboration would gradually revert to their narrow, business unit focus.

Hardwired

When a behavior is based on high emotional impact, after only a few instances there is, almost literally, hardwiring in the form of firmly ensconced neural pathways rooting that behavior in place. Your path to stickiness here will have to address the emotional component. There is no other way to change hardwiring, and putting reminders and incentive systems in place will not work in the long term without emotional reinforcement.

For example, longtime employees at an East Coast chemical company were notoriously reluctant to champion innovation projects. Even attractive financial rewards and public recognition granted to employees who suggested improvements failed to spur original thinking, at least in public. A series of one-on-one interviews revealed the pervasive belief that, historically, employees were fired if they championed an innovative idea that failed. Every employee knew of one or two colleagues who befell this fate. The beheading of one or two risk-taking colleagues is enough to teach most personnel not to stick their heads out, even for an enticing reward.

Etched in Stone

Finally, there are behaviors with high emotional impact that have been practiced habitually over years. These behaviors are the hardest to change, and often it is easier to rethink your expectations of the personnel involved. Interestingly, when "business casual" attire became more commonplace a decade ago, many bankers and lawyers fought vociferously against the sartorial change in their offices. Their power ties and flashy cufflinks were an ingrained, emotionally charged part of their identity.

The good news is that most business behavior is not rooted in deep emotions, which means that most of the time you will not encounter stiff resistance to whatever reforms you are asking your organization to adopt, so long as the employees see the shifts as being in their own best interests. That said, be on the alert for strong emotional ties with the current approach. If your consultant's recommendation involves modifying the status quo, it is incumbent upon you to uncover the viscerally driven objections and overcome them on the emotional battlefield.

How Do We Build a Frame for Change That Locks in Value? The CUBES Framework

You can apply your understanding of behavioral backsliding to bolster the long-term value of your initiatives by properly structuring the project outputs and, importantly, the organization's postproject actions. The implementation phase of your work is where you will most commonly encounter fear, resistance, cognitive limitations, miscommunication, disagreements, and other typically human traits at play. During and subsequent to implementation, the softwiring or hardwiring kicks in; the more firmly the old behaviors are entrenched, the more challenging it becomes to sustain your consultant's solutions and enjoy the intended, long-term benefits. The CUBES approach below was developed to help address the emotional side of the equation during implementation.

CUBES stands for *concrete, useful, believable, envisionable,* and *simple.* If you employ all five elements of the framework, you will stand in good stead to enjoy successful implementation and lasting value. When current behavior is not wired, you can be lax with this approach; however, as softwiring and hardwiring enter the mix, your diligence in putting every element in place becomes more critical.

Concrete—What Do You Mean By That?

Never let a consultant walk out the door without clearly explaining precisely what you or your organization is supposed to do. Too many clients are cowed by the complex theoretical answers their consultants provide and, for the sake of their ego, fail to ask the consultant, "What does that mean in terms of what we will be doing differently on a person-by-person, day-to-day basis?" If the project is intended to deliver a decision, then insist upon a specific, identifiable, and easy-to-grasp recommendation. You need to know exactly where you are headed when you start to create the implementation plan.

For example, the client who hired a consultant to recommend how to improve his buying group's performance would have seen little long-term change if he had allowed the consultant to simply recommend that they adopt "enterprise purchasing," even if that was exactly what was needed. Enterprise purchasing is too theoretical. The client needed to know that the legal group would have to learn risk allocation concepts, the operations managers would have to learn a new parts-substitution process, and so forth.

Useful—What's in It for Them?

In general, personnel will only follow new strategies, adopt new processes, and implement new skills if they see clearly what's in it for them. If the utility of whatever you are suggesting, at a personal, individual basis, is not patently evident, you will get complacency or even push-back. Not everybody benefits from change, and it is naive to expect those whose livelihoods, egos, or comfort is deleteriously affected to take on the alterations you suggest and stick with them. Either you will have to convince them that the project will, in fact, be useful for them, or you will have to find a way to work around them and acquire the benefits based on the efforts of other people.

High-level, strategic projects are prone to being perceived as irrelevant by employees, which is one reason new strategies don't stick and the organization doesn't "get it." When you and the consultant determine that global expansion is the linchpin in your five-year growth plan, personnel in the domestic workforce may not see the usefulness of that at all. Do you think they are going to jump into every facet of planning and implementing the global plan? Probably not, unless you show them how the new strategy is a big win for them.

What constitutes a big win? Anything that will make the employees feel like they are being more successful. That does not mean, by the way, anything that pads their wallets, though pecuniary rewards don't hurt. If your project will give them more autonomy, improve their working relationships, help them grow personally or professionally, or tie them to a bigger purpose they believe in, you can make it useful to them.

As part of your implementation plan, ensure you are addressing the usefulness for all the employees (and nonemployees) who will be touched by the changes, or else you may not see those improvements adopted long term.

Believable—Why Should They Trust You?

The sister to usefulness is believability. Without it you have merely convinced yourself that your project is good for everyone involved. Unfortunately, this is an area where many breakdowns occur. Executives assume that because they are convinced of the utility of the changes, everyone else in the organization will be convinced too, or the top brass believe that they can simply mandate acceptance. Both assumptions are big mistakes.

Long-term benefit requires wholehearted support from the people affected by your project. That means not only must they see the promise of usefulness, but they must believe your promises will come true. Interestingly, the latest research into human behavior shows that belief must occur at an emotional level as well as a cognitive one. In other words, you cannot simply reason your way into belief through sound logic and compelling arguments.

Aroflote's marketing and sales personnel accepted at an intellectual level that customer-centric thinking and consultative selling could help them reverse their precipitous sales decline. Emotionally, however, they just didn't buy it. For as long as most of them had been employed, customers had reacted positively to the Aroflote name, and very little planning or customer-oriented thinking had been necessary. Since the shift in customer sentiment had nothing to do with marketing or sales, the personnel in those groups didn't believe refinements on their part were truly necessary. As a result, when Robert Reynolds was fired and Agen Consulting disappeared, they reverted to their tried-and-true activities.

To effect long-term change, Aroflote would have needed the rest of Agen's plan to be deployed, a big part of which involved numerous role plays and quick, early wins. These would have allowed the marketing, sales, and customer service groups to experience the benefits of the new processes at a gut level. Quick wins are vitally important in any project where the value to you depends on behavioral change.

If you control the whole process—for instance, if you are transforming the operations system in one of your plants, per the consultant's recommendation—then allowing your personnel to participate in a success may be fairly easy. If you don't control everything, however, as was the case with Aroflote, then you should resort to simulations. You set up as realistic a scenario as possible, and then you walk your employees through it, live, until they experience the success of the new approach firsthand.

These simulations are best done firsthand, as role plays. However, it is also effective to have your employees watch someone, who represents them, go through the process live or as a role play. A third way to perform a simulation is to bring in a real-life example from outside your company (or outside the group undergoing a makeover) and have your personnel follow along as the outsider recounts her experience in detail. The key, though, is to walk through it live and re-create the experience emotionally, not just intellectually.

While Aroflote is a good example, the process I outlined works for any type of behavior change. I experienced the power of this concept firsthand in my own business, part of which involves mentoring consultants to create more valuable projects with their own clients. After years of instructing consultants on the "Why bother?" conversation you read about in Chapter 1, I finally led the discussion with one consultant's client while the consultant listened in. The difference in the consultant's performance from that day forward was like night and day, leaps and bounds beyond the improvement my other mentees made. Why? She experienced the new way of talking with clients live and in person. She also felt, at a visceral level, the benefit of the process while it happened.

When you engage your employees in simulations to encourage belief, you will also gain advance notice of objections and resistance to your desired changes. If, during role plays, Aroflote's marketing people consistently balked at incorporating customer feedback into their instruction booklets, then management could have asked why and developed adjustments before trotting the new processes out to a live customer. Similarly, through this approach you will gain an early sense of where you need to manage your personnel's expectations. Your consultant's recommendations will include upsides and downsides and will often require hard work on your company's part. You need to prepare the members of your team for whatever slog awaits them in order to cement their belief in the usefulness you are promising.

Envisionable—Can They See the Story?

One of the most useful, enduring lessons I learned while working under some consulting maestros early in my career was to always design project deliverables around the question "What's your story?" If my story wasn't crystal clear and easily repeatable, then it was not ready for prime time. Without the story, the clients might not be able to envision the solution I was recommending, and as a result, they wouldn't understand it well and might adopt it poorly (or not at all). My mentors taught me to weave research findings, conclusions, and recommendations together into a tale the client could picture, or envision, easily.

Here's an illustration: For many years we conducted time-diary studies with our clients' sales forces in order to understand how they were actually using their time and, thereby, reveal opportunities to increase productivity. Initially our reports consisted of a series of charts and graphs indicating that the administrative burden on the sales force was too high (which is always the case). Clients would nod their heads, and they would make an effort to lessen the administrative overhead for a few months. It rarely continued for long because those bar charts had the emotional impact of a block of cheese.

Then we started telling stories of "a day in the life of Joe," a typical salesperson developed from the aggregated data. Joe would start his day off at 7 a.m. handling e-mail that came in overnight and submitting his call plan, a process that could take 90 minutes. Then Joe would drive half an hour to his first appointment, where he would sit for 45 minutes in the waiting room before stepping in to see the buyer. And the story of Joe's day would continue, replete with his successes and frustrations, until 7 p.m., when he finally closed his office for the night. (See Figure 11-2.) The story varied considerably from client to client, but the one thing that remained the same was that the executives could now clearly envision, with emotional context, what was going on in the field.

Understanding improved dramatically, as did long-term adoption of the measures we would put in place to remove administrative burden. Adding a few extra reporting requirements on the call plan didn't seem like a big deal to an executive sitting at headquarters; however, when she could see Joe in her mind's eye spending 15 minutes more in his office wading through administrative work rather than getting on the phone with customers, it became intolerable.

Figure 11-2   Stories Versus Statistics

"From 2:00 to 4:15 p.m., Joe fills in the daily
inventory reports, taking a 15-minute
break to handle a customer phone call."

Before consultants start to present their solution, ask them to begin by briefly foreshadowing the story they want to tell. Likewise, every time you ask your employees to adopt a new way of doing business, present it as a narrative they will be able to easily envision.

Simple—Is Our Change Plan Manageable?

Complexity is the enemy of accuracy, reliability, understanding, and action. We all know the admonition "keep it simple, stupid," and we have all experienced great ideas that have been crushed under the weight of their own complexity. Too many new ideas, too many new requirements, and even too many choices will confuse and overwhelm personnel, with unfortunate results.

If your consultant recommends 17 new positions and a spiderweb of handoffs and process checks for your small department, then the implementation will sputter, and over time the intended benefits will fade away. Your organization will simplify your overly complex schemes for you by leaving out steps, collapsing pieces, or, eventually, abandoning the solution altogether in favor of the old processes that the employees know and understand.

Consultants sometimes resort to complexity because they feel they have to justify their fees. They fear that you will look unfavorably at a simple approach as something you could have done yourself. As a result, the consultants overcomplicate their processes to make themselves look more valuable and less like a commodity—and to discourage you from replicating what they do without paying them for their ideas.

Continuing in this vein, many consultants overcomplicate their recommendations so that their client doesn't respond, "Sheesh, that's just common sense. Why did I pay so much for you to tell me that?" At one client, adding three extra maintenance workers at its Carlisle division to reduce machine downtime looked obvious once the consultant recommended it. When the idea was presented, you could almost see the disappointment at the simplicity and, in retrospect, unmistakable solution. Later, when reflecting on the consultant's value, the client discounted the prior five years during which his company had made do with three fewer maintenance workers; the client forgot that no one was talking about hiring a few more maintenance crew before the project was done. Instances like this rattle consultants, and as a result, they are sometimes loathe to recommend such a simple solution.

When an executive makes the mistake of entering into a VTM contract on a project where there is a lot of leeway (see Chapter 8), the consultant has a powerful incentive to complicate her approach. After all, if the consultant scans the warehouse for five minutes and says, "Just move that box 5 feet to the right," how much will she get paid? Yet sometimes an extremely valuable solution is just that simple.

Another component of simplicity is the number of changes being introduced at one time. A painful multiplier effect starts creeping in when you stack unrelated or loosely connected corrections and modifications and innovations on top of each other. Overwhelm sets in, everything takes longer, and the likelihood that any one improvement will stick falls dramatically.

Are We Allowing Sufficient Time for Change?

Wouldn't it be great if your organization would turn on a dime and then sprint in whatever new direction you point? Executives from every industry bemoan the time it takes to implement improvements. When you have paid thousands or millions of dollars for a consultant to develop a

Figure 11-3 Time Required for Change

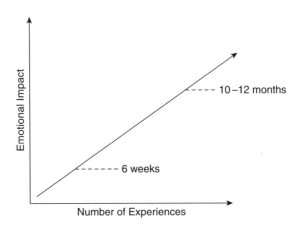

game-changing solution for your company, you want it in place, producing results posthaste.

If your new strategy, or process, or approach does not require a shift in behavior, then fast results may be in the cards. However, when you need the people in your organization to adopt some wholesale shifts in how they go about their jobs, then you have to be ready for a long haul. By and large, consultants who promise you instant results are selling you a bill of goods. Recent research suggests it takes at least 6 to 10 months for the brain to physically remap neural pathways.[1] If you are trying to inculcate a new culture in your department, division, or company, you can count on it taking the better part of a year to stick.

The more wiring that needs to be changed and the harder that wiring, the longer it will take to remap your employees' brains. (See Figure 11-3.) This isn't a matter of motivation, desire, smarts, or adaptability. It's biology you are facing, which is a new consideration for most executives.

The five keys to managing time appropriately so that you will get long-term results are:

1. Start with realistic expectations of the extent and timing of change. If you implement a new order system across the globe, you cannot expect overnight adoption. On the other hand, you could potentially expect 50 percent adoption by the end of 3 weeks and full adoption by the end of 12 weeks.

2. Match the timing of your change plan to the emotional impact and frequency with which the current habits were formed. For a nonwired process, you may only need to guide the behavior for six weeks to make it stick—perhaps 25 to 30 repetitions of a new approach that has low emotional involvement and is used daily, such as filing a report or turning off the office lights before departing for the evening. If you are refashioning a nonwired process that transpires only a few times a year, such as quarterly planning or a periodic maintenance operation, the current approach will have shallow roots, and you may only need two or three repetitions to firmly establish the new procedure.

   When facing a hardwired or etched-in-stone habit, count on the better part of a year with constant reinforcement and guidance to fully ensconce the new behaviors. A salient example for most executives is the e-mail inbox: successfully training employees to review their e-mail only twice per day takes many months of reinforcement because the emotional reward from frequently checking e-mail is high (new information, the opportunity to appear responsive) and the habit has been practiced daily since the 1990s. The lack of ongoing reinforcement over a sufficient time is why people consistently revert to checking their inboxes multiple times per hour, despite all the books and training seminars exhorting them to shake the habit.

3. Match the emotional impact of your change plan to the emotional rooting of the current behavior. The CUBES framework outlined above can serve as your guide for creating experiences that heighten stickiness. Build a story and arrange for quick wins that demonstrate usefulness at a visceral level.

4. Limit the number of transformations you are undertaking at any one time, particularly if they are only loosely related. Changes that look to you like they are closely related, because they are tied to your new strategy, may not look related at all from the perspective of the people being asked to shift their beliefs and actions.

5. Design your projects with a long tail, requiring consultants to check in on regular intervals and refine, adjust, or reinforce their solution as necessary so that it stays in place for the long haul.

Summary

After all the preparation, sweat, expense, and time you put into hiring a consultant and then managing the project, you deserve to enjoy outstanding returns for years to come, not benefits that disappear like steam in a cool breeze. Executive bookcases across the globe are weighed down by consultants' plans that never survived implementation or were set aside and forgotten when organizational resistance proved too stiff. Worse, perhaps, are the binders sitting side by side with nearly identical recommendations, purchased at great expense five years apart.

The "Aroflote Way" initiative fizzled after a few months. Your projects, in contrast, can deliver lasting value when you account for the challenges involved in creating lasting behavior changes. The multimillion-dollar global upgrade to your systems will pay out faster and for longer when your change plan includes compelling demonstrations wrapped in a well-articulated story. The new negotiation approach you want your national accounts team to embrace will meet less resistance and produce wins for many years when you plan on a full year of coaching and reinforcement and when you contract the consultant to fine-tune the approach during the entire adoption cycle.

The final step in your experience with consultants should be basking in the glow of phenomenal returns and success beyond your expectations. Hiring gurus can be a tricky, frustrating, stress-inducing business; however, if you follow the best practices discussed over the past 11 chapters, you will be in great shape to find, hire, and derive outstanding results from outside experts.

Easy Reference Guide

Choosing High-Value Projects

Valuation

Why bother?

> *Bridge to Nowhere.* What is the real, measureable impact on your customers, business, or employees? Five whys. Hard benefits and soft benefits.
>
> How much does the project contribute to the overall goal? Bigger picture form.
>
> Put the project value on the same scale as the cost. *Cost in time versus cost in dollars.*
>
> How often or for how long will the project's impact be enjoyed? *One-time gains, repeating gains, fixing problems, increasing benefits.* Three-year time horizon. Multiplier effect.

Is that all?

> *Naming countries.* Increasing, reducing, improving, and creating.

What if we didn't?

Egocentricity error. *Duct tape wheel.* Nothing is irreplaceable. Rule of thumb: factor down by 35 percent.

Employees versus Consultants

Richard and Lilly versus IBM.

Can We?

Do we have competency? Proven success, required skill sets, talented enough, transferable, or easy-to-learn skills.

Is experience helping or hurting? Familiarity? Know what we don't know? *Johari's window. Dupe and rasha.* Curse of knowledge.

Is perspective helping or hurting? Anyone's turf threatened? Anyone acquiring power or prestige? Extra work? Fearful of outcome? Need to save face?

Do we have capacity? Short term, long term? Recurring? Peak capacity?

Should We?

Can we get sufficient results? *Success, not perfection.* Consultant makes meaningful difference? Familiar results versus raising the bar.

Core to success? Performance improvement? Unique IP?

More efficient inside versus outside? Capacity, temporary capacity, temporary peak capacity.

Employees Versus Consultants

We can/we should: keep inside.
We can/we shouldn't: prioritize.
We can't/we should: learn.
We can't/we shouldn't: partner.

Context Document

Toyota Camry versus helicopter.
Situation. Strategy, concise, catalyst, decision, need.

Objectives. *ERQuip.* Why? What is required? What is our evidence? Is this the best way?

Three outcomes: recommended decision, plan, or implementation. Diagnostic versus execution projects. Advice versus delegation. Precise outcome, overall goal, results versus activities.

Indicators of success. Quantitative or qualitative, one or more per objective, doesn't bias the result, short-term indicators, proxy indicators, leading versus lagging, CRAVE (concrete, reliable, available, valid, engaging).

Perceived risk and concerns. About consultants. About the project.

Value. Conservative and concrete.

Parameters. Time, money, people.

Not an RFP. Don't overdetail. No contract structure or fees.

Finding and Choosing the Right Expert

Finding and Selecting

FoxMeyer Drugs. Swissair.

Diagnostician or implementer? Implementation expertise = diagnostic bias. *Never hire a consultant to make a recommendation who has a vested interest in one possible decision.* Avoid chameleons. What is your specialty? How are your clients better off? Two good consultants better than one mediocre consultant.

Superior expertise versus matching situation: industry, high-level process, targeted process, subject, reason why. *Clothing distributor. Industry is usually least important.*

Triangle of trade-offs: fast, talented, or inexpensive.

Right consultant: experience with your outcome, pushes back, high responsiveness, rapport, project-specific criteria.

Right approach: linear versus C2B2A, optimal detail, realistic assessment of requirements, excellent change plan, appropriate timelines, long tail, backup plans.

Finding: consortiums usually are best. *Sarah searching for Lean expert.* Brokers can work. Clearinghouses, big names, searching yourself, informal networks all have problems. How likely is success? Is ROI still acceptable? Are they the real deal? Ten references.

Big Versus Small

Small: solo, group, boutique. Large: midsize (50+), big, mega.
Small independents are usually the best choice.
Knowledge economy—no economies of scale. Rising entrepreneurialism—working the system versus reshaping the system. *Source
of HBR articles.* Apps phenomenon—anyone anywhere. Access
to the expert. *Butch Harmon.* Your goals versus consultant's
goals—who's the customer?
Go big for cachet; large, complex execution; battalion of doers.
Use consortium to deal with finding, managing, communicating,
problem myopia, problem rigidity, capabilities, practical versus
theoretical, managing risk.

Risk, Fees, and Contracts

Reducing Risk

Limestone theme park and SSC.
Risk-adjusted cost and risk-adjusted value. "If" = risk.
Common risks and effects: project doesn't work, low value, misses
dates, more expensive, painful to manage, becomes irrelevant,
alienates personnel, hurts repute, leaked information, doesn't maximize value, suboptimal consultant or solution, suboptimal project.
Consultant risks: project takes more resources, hurts repute, low
fees, lose employee, ties up resources, poor project, underpriced.
Sources of risk: you, consultant, environment.
Reducing risk: preventive actions, metrics and checkpoints, good
value estimates, correctly scope and resource, correct fee structures, best contracts, don't hire problems, people management,
monitor information sharing, early warning obligation.
Reducing impact: backup plans, parallel projects, internal relations
programs, contractually reallocate risks.

Options and Risk Reallocation

Fort Wayne's snow plowing option.
Variation is secret to valuing and reallocating risk. Ask for information or information net. Reducing risk, increasing likelihood of
success creates more value than reducing fees.

Project Tuning Keys: Scope—three variations. Fee structure and incentives. *Dismiss fairness issues.* Access to consultant, access to future projects, cancelability duration, payment terms, flexibility, intrusiveness, publicity, skill transference, timing, timing flexibility.

Ten steps: Context Document, levels of success, valuation for each level, Contract Tuning Keys, preferred consultant (stop here for small initiatives), Consultant Tuning Keys, strategic bundles, revised estimates (*Dear Joe letter. Fees and estimates of success*), evaluate and tweak, choose and move.

Fees and Contracts

Pop Magard's overbudget, late-to-arrive success.

How Much to Pay

No more than 15 percent of risk-adjusted value. Focus on results more than fees. *A 4 percent increase in likelihood of success offsets 50 percent increase in fees.*

Cost of employees versus consultants: fully loaded costs, RoLC (U.S. average 6 to 1), risk adjustment, other uses of funds? Shorter project is worth more.

Basis for Payment

Find the right knot. Avoid VTM projects: moral hazard, activity versus solution, cost versus value, burden of due diligence, increased risk, adversarial relationship.

Project leeway, boundedness (*100-yard dash versus scavenger hunt*).

High leeway–bounded: value-based fees; high leeway–unbounded: stipend; low leeway–bounded: fixed time and materials; low leeway–unbounded: piece rate.

Skin in the game: lower short-term risk, higher complexity, measurement difficulties, disagreements, increases cost, increases long-term risk. No more than 10–50 percent at risk; stipulate controls; valid, leading indicators, indisputable metrics, performance hurdles.

Timing of Payment

Up front, phases, deliverables (focus on deliverables versus outcomes, increases costs), calendar (*employees versus consultants*). Use escrows.

Successful Implementation

Preparing for Projects

Maine's fiasco.

Sufficient buy-in. Unwavering support from the top. Right level of inclusion—decision-making style (Autocratic, Evaluative, Participative, Democratic, Consensus). Include the right people. Communicate the right information (worry = ambiguity plus indecision; trust mitigates worry). Fair and appropriate.

Prepared for risks.

Right resources at the ready. Right competencies: technical, fiefdom, leadership, communication. Plan scarce resources.

Guidance mechanisms. Involvement in decisions: FARCI—final approves, approves recommends, consulted, informed. Progress dashboard: milestones, indicators of success, project health indicators.

Running Projects

Minor corrections on the way to the moon.

Seven vitamins and minerals master checklist. Ten times during project.

Team strength. Sufficient competencies, acting cohesively, accountability.

Inclusion. Is project affecting anyone unanticipated? Others' knowledge needed? Have stakeholders changed? Anyone sabotaging?

Support. Executive sponsor giving support, dedicated resources, consultant is responsive, meeting our obligations, attending meetings, communicating as promised.

Approach. Making progress toward desired outcome, adjusted as needed, not jumping to conclusions, open-minded, C2B2A iterations, quick wins.

Managing changes. Within FARCI framework, CUBES communication.

Progress. Meeting milestones, movement on indicators of success, documenting key decisions, noting persistent bottlenecks, consultant providing value, team staying on task.

Health signals. Ten-point early warning checklist.

Locking in Value

Recidivism at Aroflote.

Focus on behavior change. Right project, behavior change expected, solid change-management plan.

Sustaining behavior change: emotional impact and frequency. Not wired, softwired, hardwired, etched in stone.

CUBES framework: Concrete, useful, believable, envisionable, simple.

Allow sufficient time. Six to ten months for changes in the brain. Realistic expectations. Match change-plan timing to wiring—hardwired can take a year.

Notes

INTRODUCTION

1. CHAOS Summary 2009 report from The Standish Group.
2 Source: 2007 U.S. Economic Census.

CHAPTER 1

1. The examples used throughout the book are factual except for the identifying details of companies and executives, which have been changed to respect confidentiality.

CHAPTER 5

1. April 2010 through March 2011.

CHAPTER 6

1. "Magnablend Proceeding with Plans; Community Bands Together," Ellis County, Texas, Right to Know, http://ellisrtk.com/index.php/magnablend-fire-2011/community-action/212-magnablend-continues.
2. While risk professionals distinguish between untoward events and the results of those events (cause versus effect), for the purposes of this discussion, anything different from what you planned or expected is lumped under the term *risk*.

CHAPTER 7

1. Dom Nicastro, "Weather Brings Thoughts of Surplus Snow Budgets on North Shore," http://www.wickedlocal.com/gloucester/news/x842385915/Weather-brings-thoughts-of-surplus-snow-budgets-on-North-Shore.

2. PowerPoint presentation, "Weather Risk Management," http://www.casact.org/about/ECCppts/WeatherRisk.ppt.

3. An exception to this is the 100 percent money-back satisfaction guarantee. This is a way in which the consultants can give the appearance of agreeing to such a contract. With money-back guarantees, either the consultants are counting on the fact that you won't take them up on the guarantee, or they are building an adjustment into their price—which I cover in Chapter 8. The few consultants who do agree to this 100 percent risk scenario, like Marshall Goldsmith, are often very good and charge commensurately high fees.

Chapter 9

1. Alan Holmes, "Maine's Medicaid Mistakes," *CIO*, April 15, 2006, http://www.cio.com/article/20133/Maine_s_Medicaid_Mistakes?

Chapter 11

1. Norman Doidge, *The Brain That Changes Itself: Stories of Personal Triumph from the Frontiers of Brain Science,* New York: Penguin, 2007.

Index

A

Access, Contract Tuning Keys,
147, 153
Accountability
support in running projects, 218,
224–226
team strength, 221–222
Actions
by cohesive team, 220–221
preventive, 130–138
standard for, risk allocation and
reduction, 133
Activities *vs.* objectives, preparing
for projects, 53
Adversarial relationships, VTM
contracts, 175
Alienation of employees by project, as
risk, 125, 131, 134, 137–138
All-Hands Process Review, 141
Analyzing Performance Problems
(Mager and Pipe), 240
Approaches
to finding the right consulting firm,
84–94
to running projects, 218, 226–229
Approval, FARCI approach, 208–209
Armstrong, Neil, 217
Assessment of requirements, right
approach, 82

B

Available, CRAVE checklist, 57–58
Axelrod, Richard, 239

Backup plans, 83, 139–140
Behavior change, to lock in value,
237–243
change management plan,
239–240
expectations of, 237–240
implementation, 239
reason to focus on, 237
sustained, 240–243
Behavior stickiness, 241–242, 251
Believable, CUBES framework,
245–246
Bias, 55–56, 71–72
Bigger Picture context and form,
10–13, 22
Bottlenecks to progress, 232
Brokers, 89–90, 93, 110
Buy-in, project readiness, 195–203
communication, 201–202
decision-making styles, 198–199
executive support, 196–197
level of ambiguity, 201
level of inclusion, 197–201
project perceived as fair and
appropriate, 202–203

project readiness, 204–205
right people, 200–201

C

C2B2A project approach, 81–82, 229
Calendar-based payment, 189
"Can we?" employees *vs.* consultants, 29, 34, 36, 40–43
Cancelability as Contract Tuning Keys variation, 147, 154
Cap fee, 169, 171, 174
Capability
  competency questions, 29–34
  size of consulting firms, 113
Capacity
  employees *vs.* consultants, 35–36
  size of consulting firm, 108
Cash flow issues, fee structure risk, 151
Catalyst, in situation statement, 48
Change
  approach to, 229–230
  change management plan, 239–240
  right approach to plan for, 83
Checklists
  consultant evaluation, 84
  consultant risks, 127
  CRAVE, 57–58
  early warning on project health, 213
  risk allocation and reduction, 131
  "should we?" employees *vs.* consultants, 39
Checkpoints as preventive actions, 132–134
Choice (*See* Consultants, finding and selecting; High-value projects, choosing)
Clear Thoughts (Latham), 202
Clearinghouses to find consultants, 88–89, 93
Client
  key consulting person lost to, 128
  as source of risk, 123–126
  (*See also* High-value projects, choosing)
Cohesive team actions, 220–221
"Commercial menu" contracts, 161

Common goal for cohesive team actions, 220
Common risks and effects, 123–129, 131
Communication
  buy-in, project readiness, 201–202
  cohesive team actions, 221
  CUBES approach, 230
  inclusion of right people, 225–226
  project resource readiness, 205–206
  skills and size of consulting firms, 111–112
Competencies
  capability questions, 29–31, 34
  project resource readiness, 204–206
  team strength, 219–220
Competitive advantage, 38, 43, 125, 131, 137
Complexity
  fee structure risk, 151–152
  skin-in-the-game contracts, 183
Conciseness, in situation statement, 48
Concrete
  CRAVE, 57–58
  CUBES, 243–244
  as value section property, 60
Confidentiality agreements, 137–138
Conservatism, value section, 60
Consortium model, 90–93
ConsultantChoice™ software, 83
Consultants
  avoid problem consultants, 136
  vs. employees, 25–44
  evaluation checklist, 84
  identify Contract Tuning Keys, 160–161
  identify preferred consultant, 159
  progress review, 232–233
  project risks, 126–130
  references, 94
  reputation damage, 128
  risks, 126–130
  working through challenges, 109–115

Consultants, finding and selecting, 69–95
  overview, 69, 94–95
  approaches to finding the right consulting firm, 84–94
  best not chosen, as risk, 125–126, 131, 139
  brokers, 89–90, 93, 110
  characteristics of right approach, 81–84
  characteristics of right consultant, 78–81, 84
  clearinghouses, 88–89, 93
  consortium model, 90–93
  consultant evaluation checklist, 84
  consulting disasters, 70
  contract negotiation, 144–166
  diagnostician *vs.* implementer, 71–73
  do-it-yourself search for independent consultant, 86–87, 93
  Easy Reference Guide, 255–256
  expertise *vs.* matching situation, 74–77
  fees and contracts, 167–190
  finding and selecting, 69–95
  informal consulting network, 87–88, 93
  large, brand-name firms, 84–85, 93, 107–108
  likelihood of success, 92, 94
  references for individual consultant, 94
  return on investment (ROI), 94
  risk allocation and reduction, 119–143
  size of consulting firms, 96–118
  Swissair, 70
  triangle of trade-offs, 77–78, 206–207
  (*See also* High-value projects, choosing; Implementation)
Consulted, FARCI approach, 208–209
Consulting firms, size of, 96–118
  overview, 96, 115
  access to the experts, 103–105

alignment of goals, 105–107
  apps phenomenon, 103
  consortium model, 110–115
  consultant challenges, 109–115
  Easy Reference Guide, 255
  entrepreneurialism, 101–102
  knowledge economy, 100–101
  large, brand-name firms, 84–85, 93, 107–108
  large consultants, 98–99, 107–108
  small, independent consultants, 98–109
Consulting projects (*See* Projects; *specific topics*)
Context Document, 45–66
  overview, 46–47
  elements to exclude, 64–65
  risk reallocation, 158
  section 1: situation, 47–49
  section 2: objectives, 49–53
  section 3: indicators of success, 53–58
  section 4: perceived risks and concerns, 59–60
  section 5: value, 60–62
  section 6: parameters, 62–64
  uses, 65–66
Contract negotiation, 144–166
  access to consultant, 147, 153
  access to future projects, 147, 153
  cancelability, 147, 154
  Contract Tuning Keys, 147–157
  duration, 147, 154
  early warning obligation, 137–138
  fee structure, 147–153
  flexibility, 147, 155, 157
  incentives, 147–153
  intrusiveness, 147, 155–156
  payment terms, 147, 154–155
  preventive actions in, 136–138
  publicity, 147, 156
  risk reallocation, 141–142, 161–162
  scope, 147–149
  skills transference, 147, 156–157
  timing, 147, 157

Contract structure, 172–187
  achievement boundary, 176–177
  basic fee structures, 177–182
  bounded projects, 176–177
  equity-equivalent contracts, 185–186
  fixed time and materials (FTM)
    contracts, 177, 179–181, 187
  leeway on projects, 175–176
  piece rate contracts, 177,
    181–182, 187
  skin-in-the-game contracts, 182–185
  stipend contracts, 177–179, 187
  value-based fees contracts,
    177–178, 187
  variable time and materials (VTM)
    contracts, 172–175
Contract Tuning Keys, 147–157, 159
Cost
  estimating value of project, 10–13
  project exceeds budget, as risk, 123,
    131–132, 134–135, 138, 140
  of risk, 145–146
  skin-in-the-game contracts, 183–184
  (See also Contract negotiation; Fees
    and fee structure)
CRAVE checklist, 57–58
Creating, as driver of value, 19, 21
Criticality, core vs. noncore activities,
    37–38
CUBES framework, 130, 230, 243–249
Curse of knowledge, objectives, 49–50

D
Decisions and decision making
  cohesive team actions, 220–221
  in situation statement, 49
  styles for project readiness, 198–199
Deliverables, diagnostician vs.
    implementer, 73
Deliverables-based payment, 188–189
Diagnostician, 71–73
Disagreement, skin-in-the-game
    contracts, 183
Documentation of progress, 231–232
Do-it-yourself search for independent
    consultant, 86–87, 93
Drivers of value, 19–21

Due diligence and VTM contracts,
    173–174
Duration
  Contract Tuning Keys variation,
    147, 154
  of impact, estimating value of
    project, 14–17

E
Early warning
  as contract obligation, 137–138
  guidance mechanisms, project
    preparation, 212–214, 233–234
Easy Reference Guide, 253–259
Efficiency, employees vs. consultants,
    38–39
Egocentricity error, "what if we
    didn't?," 21–23
Emotions and change, 241–242, 251
Employee alienation, as project risk,
    125, 131, 134, 137–138
Employees vs. consultants, 25–44
  overview, 25, 43–44
  "can we?," 29, 34, 36, 40–43
  capability questions, 29–34
  capacity questions, 35–36
  competitive advantage, 38, 43
  criticality, core vs. noncore activities,
    37–38
  Easy Reference Guide, 254
  efficiency and ROI, 38–39
  fee structure, 170–172
  intellectual property, 38
  keep inside, 40, 42
  learn from consultant, 40–42
  outside help decision rational, 27–28
  partner with consultant, 40–41, 43
  prioritize (inside), 40–43
  "should we?," 29, 36–43
  sufficiency, 36–37
Endres, Bob, 148, 161
Engaging, CRAVE checklist, 57–58
Enterprise resource planning (ERP)
    project, 168, 213–214
Environment as source of risk, 130
Envisionable, CUBES framework,
    247–248

Escrow-based payments, 189–190
Estimating value of project, 3–24
    accurate estimating as preventive
        action, 133–134
    overview, 3, 24
    Bigger Picture context and form,
        10–13, 22
    contribution, 10–13
    drivers of value, 19–21
    duration of impact, 14–17
    Easy Reference Guide, 253–254
    frequency and multiplier effect,
        17–18
    scale, 13
    valuation improvements, 18–24
    "why bother?," 4–8
"Etched in stone" workplace behavior,
    241–243, 251
Evaluation of risk reallocation,
    164–165
Executive support, 196–197,
    224–225
Expectations of behavior change,
    237–240
Experience and expertise
    capability questions, 31–32, 34
    diagnostic bias, 72
    finding and selecting the right
        consultant, 74–77
    of right consultant, 78–79
    triangle of trade-offs, 77–78,
        206–207

F
Facebook, 148–152, 158–162
Fairness issues, fee structure risk, 152
FARCI approach, 208–209, 223
Fees and fee structure, 167–190
    overview, 167, 190
    basic fee structures, 177–182
    calendar-based payment, 189
    cap fees at percent of risk-adjusted
        project value, 169, 171
    Contract Tuning Keys variation,
        147–153
    deliverables-based payment,
        188–189

Easy Reference Guide, 257–258
employees vs. consultants,
    170–172
escrow-based payments, 189–190
fee variability risks, 128–129
fixed time and materials (FTM)
    contracts, 177, 179–181, 187
flat vs. penalty-reward, 150–152
focus on consultant results,
    169–170
how much to pay, 169–172
phase-based payment, 187–188
piece rate contracts, 177,
    181–182, 187
risks, 128–129
stipend contracts, 177–179, 187
structure developed correctly,
    135–136
timing of payment, 186–190
triangle of trade-offs, 77–78,
    206–207
up-front payment, 186–187
value-based fees contracts,
    177–178, 187
Final approval, FARCI approach,
    208–209
Finding a consultant (See Consultants,
    finding and selecting)
Fixed time and materials (FTM)
    contracts, 177, 179–181, 187
Flat fees, 150–152
Flexibility, Contract Tuning Keys, 147,
    155, 157
Focus of VTM contracts, 173
Focus on consultant results, fees,
    169–170
Fort Wayne snow plowing, 145
FoxMeyer Drugs, 70
French, Robin, 79
Frequency and multiplier effect,
    17–18

G
Goals, 220, 227–228
Guidance mechanisms, project
    preparation, 207–213, 223,
    233–234

H

Heath, Chip and Dan, 49
High-level process expertise of
    consultant, 75
High-value projects, choosing
  Context Document, 45–68
  contract negotiation, 144–166
  Easy Reference Guide, 253–254
  employees *vs.* consultants, 25–44
  estimating value of project, 3–24
  preparing for projects, 45–68
How much to pay, fee structure,
    169–172

I

IBM, 26–27, 44
Implementation
  behavior change, to lock in
      value, 239
  change and locking in value,
      235–252
  Easy Reference Guide, 258–259
  outcomes that add value, 51
  preparing for projects, 193–215
  project does not deliver value, 129
  running projects, 216–234
Implementer, 71–73
Improving as driver of value, 19–20
Incentive plans, 150–151
Incentives, Contract Tuning Keys,
    147–153
Increasing as driver of value, 19–20
Indicators of success
  Context Document, 53–58
  guidance mechanisms, project
      preparation, 209–212
  preparing for projects, 53–58
  as preventive actions, 132–134
  progress, 231
  risk allocation and reduction [c6],
      132–133
  skin-in-the-game contracts, 184–185
Industry expertise of consultant, 75
Informal consulting network, 87–88, 93
Informed, FARCI approach, 208–209
In-house talent (*See* Employees)
Institution of Civil Engineers, 160

Intellectual property, employees *vs.*
    consultants, 38
Internal relations programs, 141
Intrusiveness, Contract Tuning Keys,
    147, 155–156
Irrelevant, project becomes, as risk,
    123, 131–132
"Is that all?" underestimation error,
    18–21
Iterative project approach, 81–82, 229

J

*Journal of Personality and Social
    Psychology*, 21
Jumping to conclusions, approach, 228

K

Key information to competitor, as risk,
    125, 131, 137
Kotter, John, 239

L

Lagging indicators of success,
    56–57
Large, brand-name firms, 84–85,
    93, 107–108
Latham, Ann, 202
Leadership, project resource
    readiness, 205
Leading indicators of success, 56–57
Learning, employees *vs.* consultants,
    40–42
Level of ambiguity, project
    readiness, 201
Level of detail, right approach, 82
Level of impact, 126
Level of inclusion, project readiness,
    197–201
Levels of success and risk, 158
Likelihood
  defined, 126
  risk and preventive actions,
      130–138
  of success, 92, 94
Limestone theme park, Bedford,
    IN, 120
Linear project approach, 81–82

Locking in value, 235–252
  overview, 235, 252
  behavior change, 237–243
  CUBES framework, 243–249
  Easy Reference Guide, 259
  sufficient time, 249–251
  sustained behavior change, 240–243
  timing, 250–251
Long tail
  of right approach, 83
  time required for change, 251–252
Longevity of firm, 109
Long-term capacity, 35–36

M
Made to Stick (Chip and Dan Heath), 49
Mager, Robert, 240
Maine Medicaid, 194–195
Management
  executive support, 196–197, 224–225
  skin-in-the-game contracts, 183
Measurements (*See* Indicators of
    success)
Meetings, 226
Milestones, 210–213, 230–231
Million Dollar Consulting (Weiss), 36
Money as parameter, 64
Moral hazard of VTM contracts,
    172–173
Multiplier effect, 17–18

N
Naming countries metaphor,
    underestimation error, 18–21
Need, in situation statement, 49
Negative energy, 224
Network, informal, 87–88, 93

O
Objectives
  Context Document, 49–53
  establishing indicators of success, 54
  preparing for projects, 49–53
Outcomes that add value, 51
Outside help decisions, employees *vs.*
    consultants, 27–28
Overall goal, objectives section, 52

P
Parallel projects, 140–141
Parameters, Context Document, 62–64
Partner with consultant, 40–41, 43
Payment terms, Contract Tuning Keys,
    147, 154–155
  (*See also* Fees and fee structure)
Penalty-reward fees, 150–152
People, as parameter, 63–64
Perceived risks, Context Document,
    59–60
Perspective, capability questions, 32–34
Phase-based payment, 187–188
Piece rate contracts, 177, 181–182, 187
Pipe, Peter, 240
Precise outcome statements, objectives
    section, 52
Preparing for projects, 45–68
  overview, 45, 66, 193, 213–215
  activities *vs.* objectives, 53
  Context Document, 45–66
  CRAVE checklist, 57–58
  Easy Reference Guide, 254–255, 258
  guidance mechanisms, 207–213
  indicators of success, 53–58
  objectives, 49–53
  outcomes that add value, 51
  parameters, 62–64
  perceived risk and concerns, 59–60
  resource readiness, 204–207
  risk preparation, 203–204
  situation, 47–49
  sufficient buy-in, 195–203
  value, 60–62
Preventive actions, 130–138
Prioritize, 40–43, 147, 156–157
"Problem myopia," 112–113
Process rigidity, 112–113
Professional management, consulting
    firms, 111
Project flow, 72, 81
Project management
  consulting firm size, 107–108
  excessive, as risk, 123, 131, 136
Projects
  buy-in, 207–213
  disasters, 70

failure, as risk, 123, 131–132,
134–135, 138–140
perceived as fair and appropriate,
202–203
preparing for, 207–213
soft benefits, 21
Project-specific criteria, consultant,
80–81
Proxy indicators of success, 56
Publicity, Contract Tuning Keys,
147, 156

Q
Qualitative indicators of success, 54
Quantitative indicators of success, 54
Quick wins, approach, 229

R
Rapport, right consultant, 80
"Reason why" expertise of
consultant, 75
Recommendations
decision/plan that adds value,
51, 239
FARCI approach, 208–209
Reducing as driver of value, 19–20
References for individual consultant, 94
Reliable, CRAVE checklist, 57–58
Reputation damage by project, as risk,
125, 128, 131, 134–135, 140
Resources
better uses elsewhere, as risk, 126,
131, 139
correct allocation for project,
134–135
inclusion of right people, 225–226
key resources could be used
elsewhere, 129
project requires more, as consultant
risk, 126, 128
Responsibility, team, 221–222
Responsiveness of right consultant, 80
Results, objectives section, 52–53
Return on investment (ROI), 38–39, 94
Ridge, Garry, 43
Right people, 200–201
Right project, 238

Risk and risk reduction, 119–143
All-Hands Process Review, 141
overview, 119, 121, 142–143
backup plans, 139–140
cap fees at percent of risk-adjusted
project value, 169, 171
client risks, 123–126
consultant risks, 126–130
contractually reallocate risks,
141–142
Easy Reference Guide, 256–257
fee structure, 128–129
impact reduction, 138–142
perceived risks in Context Document,
59–60
preventive action, 130–138
reallocation of risk, 146–166
risk-adjusted cost and risk-adjusted
value, 121–123
run parallel projects, 140–141
skin-in-the-game contracts, 182–184
sources of risk, 129–130
use metrics and checkpoints,
132–133
VTM contracts, 174
Risk management, consulting firm size,
114–115
Risk reallocation, 146–166
overview, 144, 165–166
Context Document use, 158
Contract Tuning Keys, 147–157,
159–161
create contract bundles, 161–162
evaluation and tweaking, 164–165
identify preferred consultant, 159
levels of success and risk, 158
moving forward, 165
solicit revised estimates, 162–164
ten steps to reallocation, 158–165
valuation revision, 158–159
variation, 146–166
Risk-adjusted cost and risk-adjusted
value, 121–123
Ross, Michael, 21
Running projects, 216–234
overview, 216, 233–234
approach, 218, 226–229

Running projects, (*cont'd.*)
  change management, 218, 229–230
  Easy Reference Guide, 258–259
  health signals, 218, 233
  inclusion of right people, 218,
    222–224
  moon landing, 217–218
  progress, 218, 230–233
  seven vitamins and minerals,
    218–234
  support, 218, 224–226
  team strength, 218–222
Rush to judgment, 228

S
Sabotaging the project, 224
Scale, value of project, 13
Scarce resources, 206–207
Scope
  Contract Tuning Keys, 147–149
  correct, 134–135
  does not maximize value, as risk,
    125, 131, 139
Selecting a consultant (*See* Consultants,
    finding and selecting)
Shared information, monitoring,
  137–138
Short-term capacity, 35–36
Short-term indicators of success, 56
"Should we?" employees *vs.*
  consultants, 29, 36–43
Sicoly, Fiore, 21
Simple, CUBES framework, 248–249
Situation
  Context Document, 47–49
  expertise *vs.* matching situation,
    74–77
Size of firm (*See* Consulting firms, size of)
Skills transference, Contract Tuning
  Keys, 147, 156–157
Soliciting revised estimates, 162–164
Sources of risk, 129–130
Specialty, diagnostician *vs.*
  implementer, 73
Speed, triangle of trade-offs, 77–78,
  206–207
Stakeholders, 218, 222–224

Stickiness of workplace behavior,
  241–242, 251
Stipend contracts, 177–179, 187
Strategy, in situation statement, 48
Subject expertise of consultant, 75
Sufficiency, employees *vs.* consultants,
  36–37
Sufficient time, 249–251
Superconducting Super Collider
  (SSC), 120
Sustained behavior change,
  to lock in value, 240–243
Swissair, 70

T
Talent
  in-house (*See* Employees)
  size of consulting firms, 109
  triangle of trade-offs, 77–78,
    206–207
Targeted process expertise of
  consultant, 75
Team approach, 227–228, 232–233
Technical competencies, 204–205
Theory *vs.* practicality, size of
  consulting firms, 113–114
Third-party experts (*See* Consultants)
Time
  deadlines as risk, 123, 131–132,
    134–135, 138, 140
  inclusion of right people, 225
  as parameter, 63
  variable time and materials (VTM)
    contracts, 172–175
Timelines of right approach, 83
Timing
  Contract Tuning Keys variation,
    147, 157
  of payment, 186–190
Toyota Camry hybrid, 46
Transformations, time required
  for, 251
Triangle of trade-offs, fee structure,
  77–78, 206–207
Trust in teams, 220
Tweaking risk reallocation,
  164–165

U

Underestimation error, "is that all?," 18–21

Up-front payments, 186–187

Useful, CUBES framework, 244–245

V

Valid, CRAVE checklist, 57–58

Valuation
estimating value of project, 3–24
improvements to, 18–24
revision and risk reallocation, 158–159

Value
Context Document, 60–62
locking in value, 235–252
outcomes that add value, 51
preparing for projects, 60–62
progress review, 232

project does not deliver as expected, 123, 131–132, 134–135, 138–140 (*See also* High-value projects, choosing)

Value-based fees contracts, 177–178, 187

Variation, risk reallocation, 146–166

W

WD-40, 43–44

Weiss, Alan, 36

"What if we didn't?" egocentricity error, 21–23

"What's the risk?" valuation improvements, 23–24

"Why bother?" estimating value of project, 4–8

Willingness to push back, 79–80

Wiring behavior, 241–242, 251

Workplace behavior stickiness, 241–242, 251

About the Author

 David A. Fields is the founder and managing director of The Ascendant Consortium, a group specializing in accelerating results, lowering risk, and increasing the ROI that companies can achieve from consultants. His clients have included Abbott Laboratories, Coinstar, International Paper, ITT, Kodak, GlaxoSmithKline, Symbol Technologies, Domino's Pizza, and scores of other successful organizations.

Lauded as an innovative and provocative thinker, and recognized in *AdvertisingAge* magazine's "Marketing Top 100," David writes a monthly column for *Industry Week,* and his commentary and strategic insights have appeared in *USA Today, CNN Money, Investor's Business Daily, The Philadelphia Inquirer, Advertising Age, Business Week, SmartMoney*, and dozens of other publications.

David holds an MS and BS, both from Carnegie Mellon University, and lives in Connecticut. Learn more about the author at http://ascendantconsortium.com and http://DavidAFields.com.

Motivational Speaking

Bring David A. Fields to your next meeting or conference and increase your Return on Expertise.

Companies and associations around the globe hire David to deliver dynamite keynotes and intensive workshops inspiring their organizations to derive more value from inside and outside experts. For more information or to contact David directly, visit http://DavidAFields.com/speaker or e-mail david@DavidAFields.com.

Mentoring for Consultants

Become the Type of Consultant Smart Executives Find and Want to Hire

David has coached and mentored hundreds of consultants around the world who wanted to improve their practice, create more value, and attract more clients. Learn more about David's outstanding mentor programs and read testimonials at http://DavidAFields.com/consultants or contact David directly at david@DavidAFields.com.

Free Resources for Executives

You deserve a successful result when you invest your money and time in an outside expert. You're entitled to a high ROI, the highest likelihood of success, and the lowest risk of failure. Author David A. Fields has produced FREE resources to help you get just that. These resources will help you apply the practical tips in *The Executive's Guide to Consultants* to your business.

Visit **www.DavidAFields.com/Resources**

to download these FREE resources:

Selecting the Right Consultant

Want an easy way to compare consultants and choose the best one? ConsultantChoice™ is an easy-to-use software tool tailor-made to make your decisions easier, faster, and better.

Free Checklists and Templates

You don't have to cobble together your own checklists with the book's great tips. Download a full packet with all the tips, templates, and checklists you need to find, hire, and get great results from your next consulting project.

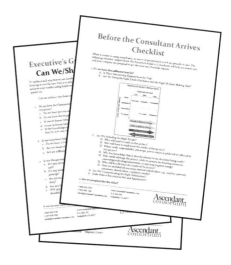

Better Results for Executives

Find the Right Consultant
Finding breakthrough thinking, best-in-class processes, and flawless execution is easier said than done. There are almost 500,000 consulting firms in the United States that want to provide their expert advice to you. The Ascendant Consortium is a world-class solution for finding excellent, prequalified, powerful consultants.
Learn more at http://DavidAFields.com/RightTeam.

Command Higher Return on Expertise
Is it possible to double or even triple the risk-adjusted value of a project, as described in *The Executive's Guide to Consultants*? Absolutely! We see it every day with a vast variety of projects for clients in every industry. You can expect a better outcome, with more valuable results and lower risk.
Learn more at http://DavidAFields.com/HighValue.

Negotiate a Better Contract with Consultants
Guaranteed results, budget protection, unlimited access, rapid response. Those benefits and more can be hardwired into your contracts with consultants. The techniques explained in the book are the tip of the iceberg when it comes to negotiating the best engagement agreements. We can help you develop a contract that inspires your consultant to deliver results beyond your expectations.
Learn more at http://DavidAFields.com/Contracts.

Executive and Team Training
Want to be able to apply the ideas in the book every day across your entire company? David A. Fields offers one-hour, half-day, one-day, and three-day workshops that will equip your company with the skills to get great results every time you turn to an outside expert.
Learn more at http://DavidAFields.com/Training.

Contact David A. Fields to learn more:

david@DavidAFields.com

203-438-7236